ON THE CHRISTIAN FAITH

The Library of Liberal Arts
OSKAR PIEST, FOUNDER

The Library of Liberal Arts

ON THE
CHRISTIAN FAITH

Selections from the Institutes,
Commentaries, and Tracts

JOHN CALVIN

Edited, with an Introduction, by
JOHN T. McNEILL
Professor Emeritus of Church History
Union Theological Seminary

The Library of Liberal Arts
published by

THE **BOBBS-MERRILL** COMPANY, INC.
A SUBSIDIARY OF HOWARD W. SAMS & CO., INC.
Publishers • INDIANAPOLIS • NEW YORK

John Calvin: 1509-1564

. . . .

COPYRIGHT © 1957

THE LIBERAL ARTS PRESS, INC.

Printed in the United States of America

Library of Congress Catalog Card Number: 58-7660

Fourth Printing

CONTENTS
·················

KEY TO ABBREVIATIONS   vi

EDITOR'S INTRODUCTION   vii

SELECTED BIBLIOGRAPHY   xxxi

NOTE ON THE TEXT   xxxiv

ON THE CHRISTIAN FAITH

From the Institutes

Book I. On the Knowledge of God the
Creator   3

Book II. On the Knowledge of God the
Redeemer in Christ Which Was Revealed
First to the Fathers Under the Law and
Since to Us in the Gospel   42

Book III. On the Manner of Receiving the
Grace of Christ, the Benefits Which We
Derive from It, and the Effects Which
Follow It   63

Book IV. On the External Means or Aids by
Which God Calls Us into Communion with
Christ and Retains Us in It   98

From the Commentaries

   On Genesis   129

   On Isaiah   151

   On the Psalms   155

   On John   176

   On Romans   182

From the Tracts

   The Reply to Sadolet   193

   BIOGRAPHICAL INDEX   213

KEY TO ABBREVIATIONS

CO   *Joannis Calvini Opera quae supersunt omnia.* Ed. by G. Baum, E. Cunitz, E. Reuss, and continuators. 59 vols. Brunswick and Berlin, 1863–1900. (*Corpus Reformatorum* series.)

ANF   *The Ante-Nicene Fathers.* Ed. by A. Roberts and J. Donaldson. 10 vols. (American reprint of the Edinburgh edition.) New York, 1908–1910; Grand Rapids, 1951–1956.

Migne, *PG*   J. P. Migne, *Patrologiae cursus completus, Series Graeca.* 161 vols. Paris, 1859–1866.

Migne, *PL*   J. P. Migne, *Patrologiae cursus completus, Series Latina.* 218 vols. Paris, 1844–1855.

NPNF   *The Nicene and Post-Nicene Fathers.* Ed. by P. Schaff. 14 vols. New York, 1887–1894.

EDITOR'S INTRODUCTION

I

This book of selections from the writings of John Calvin is designed to illustrate the character of his theology. As a young student at Paris, Calvin came under some of the ablest teachers of his time, and, possessing great natural gifts, his mind matured early. He was fourteen when in 1523 he left his home city, Noyon, to attend the university of Paris. He long afterwards took occasion to "testify to posterity" that he owed to his first Latin teacher at the university, Maturin Cordier, that introduction to learning which made possible all that he had meanwhile accomplished. The period of Cordier's instruction was a few months only, but in old age the gifted teacher joined his eminent pupil in Geneva, there to spend his last years. John Major, Scottish philosopher, theologian, and historian, an elderly scholar of great distinction, most probably had Calvin for a time among his numerous pupils; and others of his Paris professors were scholars renowned in the schools of Europe. Later at Orléans and Bourges he had as his instructors men of unsurpassed reputation in legal science. When the French king, Francis I, appointed the "Royal Readers" (or "Lecturers"), Calvin turned to the intense study of Greek and Hebrew under their expert instruction. In all these varied studies, however, he acquired only a very limited acquaintance with theology. Thousands of theologians have been the readers and disciples of this man who never had a formal theological training.

His first substantial published work, *Commentary on Lucius Anneas Seneca's Two Books on Clemency* (1532), marked him as a humanist interested in enlightened and benevolent government who wrote exceptionally good Latin. Luther had then been for fifteen years in active leadership of the Reformation, and Zwingli had ended his career as the reformer of

German Switzerland. Calvin must have had some acquaintance with the work of these reformers, but he seemed to have chosen rather to follow the example of Erasmus. Yet two years later we find him beginning to write in a very different strain. Thenceforth his life, in study, writing and action, was to be wholly given to the cultivation of an evangelical and scriptural Christianity and the reformation of the Church. We cannot date this redirection of Calvin's life with certainty, but the evidence seems to point to April, 1534. There is some evidence that it came as the culmination of an inward struggle, and he indicates that it was delayed by his stubborn attachment to the practices of the unreformed Church. He himself regarded the change as wrought by the intervention of God. He states this simply and without elaboration: "God by a sudden conversion subdued my heart to teachableness." [1] To learn what God would teach, he now turned with zeal to the study of the Bible. Many inquirers pursued him with their questionings, and the effort to explain to them what he found in the Scriptures and to persuade them of its truth quickly transformed the brilliant young scholar into a theologian.

Some months earlier, Calvin had been obliged to take flight from Paris as a result of an utterance of Nicholas Cop, son of the king's physician, then recently chosen rector of the university, who had been for a decade in the circle of Calvin's friends. Through Cop and others, Calvin was in touch with a group of scholars, some years older than himself, who were looking toward the reform of the French Church in a spirit of biblical humanism. These men had been inspired by the now very aged Jacques Lefèvre of Etaples. Lefèvre had been driven from Paris before Calvin's time there through the hostility of the theological faculty (the Sorbonne) and had finally

[1] From the Preface to the *Commentary on the Psalms* (1558). Calvin's words are: "animum meum . . . subita conversione ad docilitatem subegit" (*CO*, XXXI, 21). For a variant translation see the English edition by James Anderson, *Commentary on the Book of Psalms* (Grand Rapids, 1949), I, xl. An account of Calvin's conversion is to be found in John T. McNeill, *The History and Character of Calvinism* (New York, 1954), pp. 107-118.

been compelled to retire to Nérac, where he had the political protection of Marguerite d'Angoulême, the king's sister. This gifted princess was a well-known writer and had shown herself favorable to the cause of Lefèvre and his followers. Her own book, *The Mirror of a Sinful Soul*, had been condemned as heretical by the Sorbonne. As rector, Cop at once undertook the defense of Marguerite in the university. He and his friends probably had high hopes of turning the tide in favor of reform in the nation. In his rectorial address, November 1, 1533, he boldly voiced the new ideas. The effect was completely disappointing, however, and he soon found himself a fugitive from France, while Calvin, accused of "familiarity with the rector," made a hasty flight from his Paris lodging, leaving his possessions to the police. Calvin may have been consulted by Cop in the preparation of the address, but there is no proof that he was Cop's ghost writer.

Calvin had been intended by his father for the priesthood, and though later his father induced him to study law, he still held benefices that had been assigned to him in childhood in the church at Noyon and might have been expected to take ordination at about the age of twenty-five. He was to reach that age July 10, 1534. The previous months were spent chiefly at Angoulême in the paternal home of another friend where he had access to a large library. But early in April, 1534, Calvin journeyed from this retreat to Nérac to visit Lefèvre, the defeated patriarch of the biblical humanists who had hoped for reform without disruption of the Church. We have no specific report of the conversation between these men, who were representatives of two different approaches to reform. We are told by Theodore Beza that Lefèvre "was delighted with young Calvin" and predicted for him a great service to "the kingdom of heaven in France." [2] Others report that in his last years Lefèvre was saddened by the sufferings of those who had felt his influence and remorseful over his own timid-

[2] From Beza's *Vita Calvini* (*CO*, XXI, 123); in English, *The Life of John Calvin by Theodore Beza*, tr. by Henry Beveridge (Philadelphia, 1909), p. 12.

ity. However that may be, it seems not unlikely that the interview helped to convince Calvin of the futility of seeking a scriptural reform unless its proponents were prepared to go beyond the position of Lefèvre and his disciples and detach themselves from the papal obedience. At once thereafter he proceeded to Noyon and resigned his benefices.

Those who voiced Protestant opinions in France were subject to persecution, and their peril now increased. When irresponsible radicals among them circulated placards crudely attacking the Mass, there followed a widespread heresy hunt that brought many to prison and some to death at the stake. About the beginning of the year 1535, Calvin reluctantly left France—carrying with him, we may suppose, some notes he had made for a book—and took lodging in Catherine Klein's student boarding house in Basel. It was this city of scholarship and freedom that Erasmus had chosen for his final retreat. In his last months in France Calvin had been pursued by inquirers in religion so that he had no opportunity for continuous study. In Basel he went under an assumed name, his disguise being penetrated only by a few scholars. As he read and wrote, he was disturbed by news of increasing persecution in France. This is reflected in the book on which he was laboring. It was completed in manuscript in August, 1535, and published in March, 1536, under the title *Institutio Christianae Religionis*. The main part of the title of this first Latin edition may be translated *Institute* [3] *of the Christian Religion, containing almost the whole sum of piety and whatever it is necessary to know in the doctrine of salvation.*

The word *institutio* had been used by Erasmus and many others in Latin titles in the sense of "instruction." As the title of a compendium we might render it "textbook" or "handbook," and Calvin's *Institutio* was designed as a manual for religious inquirers as well as a manifesto or confession giving expression to the new scriptural doctrines then gaining adherents. The second phrase of the title, *totam pietatis summam,*

---

[3] *Institutio* was rendered "Institution" in the English translation until 1813, when the plural "Institutes" was employed by John Allen.

may have recalled to early readers a title familiar to them, the *Summa theologiae* of Thomas Aquinas, and may even have suggested comparison with that medieval masterpiece. Calvin had left Basel before the book appeared, and it is not certain that he was responsible for every word of the title. But there is some reason to regard it as a book of piety or religion rather than a treatise of theology as that word had been commonly used. Calvin was acquainted with the closely woven syllogistic argumentation of the scholastic writers, but he thought their method futile and outdated, and ill adapted to produce the religious commitment or "piety" that he would have his readers share with him. Dean Henri Strohl of Strasbourg remarks that Calvin's was not a deductive mind.[4] He has passages of keen reasoning, but he often addresses himself much less to our rational judgment than to our emotion, conscience, and will. He seeks indeed the intellectual assent of the reader, but he habitually presses on to effect his moral persuasion and enlist him in a plan of life that will effectively testify to the doctrines affirmed. He is deeply convinced and will not have us forget that every man has to do with God all his days.[5] For him this is our chief concern in all life's events and decisions. Religion is not a matter of detached opinion or of acquiescence in traditional authority, but of the existential appropriation of divine truth.

The genius of Calvin lay less in the originality than in the almost unmatched readiness of his mind. Men who knew him were astonished by his memory for personal as well as literary details. His mental range was wide, but all that he had read seemed instantly available for use in argument. With seeming effortlessness he brings us a passage from a Church Father or a classical essayist or poet, or an issue raised by some scholastic or contemporary writer, or a bit of remote historical data, to be smoothly integrated with the matter of his flowing discourse. Most of our great writers have possessed this gift in

---

[4] Henri Strohl, *La Pensée de la Réforme* (Neuchâtel and Paris, 1951), p. 123.

[5] *Inst.* III. 7. 2.

some degree, but few have shown the copiousness and, so to speak, the indexed orderliness of Calvin's mental store. In particular, the entire content of Holy Scripture is at his command. Whatever respect he pays nonbiblical writers, they have value for him only insofar as they shed light upon the teachings of the Bible, which for him form the sole criterion of religious truth. He very rarely speaks of "theology" and seems not to think of himself as a theologian except in the sense that he is an interpreter of the Word of God as it is found in Scripture. He appeals the more convincingly to the authority of Scripture from the fact that he knows it through and through and can cite its passages as one who has reflected upon their meaning.

Luther had affirmed the unique authority of the Bible as God's Word, and Melanchthon had written a sketch of Christian doctrine (*Loci communes*, 1521) on this principle—a book admired by Calvin and later published in Geneva in a French translation with a preface by him. There was already in French a vigorously written concise primer of evangelical doctrine by William Farel (*Summary and Brief Declaration*, 1524, revised 1534) in which a good many points of emphasis in Calvin's teaching were anticipated. Huldreich Zwingli, too, had written with a similar use of Scripture his *Commentary on True and False Religion* (1525) and his *Exposition of the Faith* (1531). But it was left for Calvin to present the one comprehensive and systematic organization of Christian doctrine on a scriptural basis that has become a classic.

This can hardly be said to have been achieved in the first edition of the *Institutes;* it was, rather, an impressive essay toward such a definitive treatise. The first four of its six chapters followed the familiar order of medieval handbooks for laymen: the law, the Creed, the Lord's Prayer, the sacraments. Of course, Calvin's expositions of these were far from medieval. Of the sacraments he recognized only two as authorized in Scripture, and he employed a chapter to show why the five other rites approved as sacraments by the Roman Church ought to be rejected as unscriptural. His last chapter was a lively discussion of Christian liberty. The book challenged attention, and a second edition was soon called for. By the time it was ready, Calvin's first period in Geneva (1536-38) had ended, and he was conducting the French refugee church in Strasbourg.

The second edition (1539) was in seventeen chapters and was more than two and one-half times the size of the first. Some of the added chapters dealt with topics that came to have prominence in historic Calvinism, such as the knowledge of God, predestination, civil government, and the Christian life. In 1541 Calvin translated this Latin text into French, thereby making one of the most important contributions to the rise of French prose. In that year he returned to Geneva, where he was to labor until his death in 1564. Amid his tasks of church organization, commentaries, tracts, sermons, and letters flowed from his pen; but the *Institutes* continued to expand in new editions. The edition of 1559,[6] the last Latin edition for which he himself took responsibility, is almost five times the size of the first edition. It is a splendid folio, the work of the scholarly French printer Robert Estienne (Stephanus), who had transferred his business from Paris to Geneva.

The work was now divided into four "books" treating respectively the knowledge of God the Creator, the knowledge of God the Redeemer, the receiving of the grace of Christ, and the Holy Catholic Church. There are in the four books eighty chapters in all, each of these subdivided into numbered sections for convenient reference. A comparison of the editions shows that Calvin repeatedly interchanged parts of the work with a view to improving the sequence of topics. "I was never satisfied," he wrote in the preface to the final edition, "until it was arranged in the order in which it is now published."

But with all the changes made in the structure of the *Institutes*, very few sentences of the 1536 text, or of any intervening edition, are omitted in that of 1559. If sentences are changed, it is for clarification and not to mark a change of opinion. Unlike most theologians, Calvin in a quarter of a

[6] A copy is in the Folger Shakespeare Library, Washington, D. C.

century did not revise his position with regard to any doctrine of substance or retract anything he had written. What was added was consistent with what had been stated before and seemed a natural continuation of it. "In the doctrine which he taught at the beginning," wrote Beza, his associate and successor, "he remained firm to the end." [7] Indeed, not only in his study but also in his administrative tasks and public controversies, his judgments were promptly made and tenaciously defended. Few men have ever approached so closely to complete consistency. With some men, consistency is achieved as a painful pose, but Calvin's mind naturally worked in that fashion, and he could not have done otherwise. This was in fact an asset to his cause and a factor of stability amid the revolutionary currents of his age. But it is not surprising that many of his readers have been repelled by the unqualified certainty, finality, and lack of elasticity in the pattern of his thought. At the same time it must be said that he is sometimes content to leave us with an unresolved antithesis or to indicate a realm of mystery beyond rational exploration.

II

It is natural that our selections to illustrate Calvin's theology should be derived largely from the *Institutes*, the chief compendium of his doctrines. His occasional treatises also constitute an extensive body of work. These contain a variety of material, such as replies to the writings of opponents, documents of church order and worship, and treatises on special topics in theology. They contain much that is rather too special for an introductory book of sample material.[8] In 1539 Calvin wrote, at the request of the magistrates of Geneva though he himself was then in Strasbourg, a reply to an appeal

---

[7] Beza, *op. cit.* (*CO,* XXI, 170; Beveridge tr., p. 112).

[8] A selection from this material has recently appeared in a fresh translation: *Calvin: Theological Treatises,* translated with introductions and notes by J. K. S. Reid ("The Library of Christian Classics," Vol. XXII; Philadelphia: The Westminster Press, 1954).

made by Cardinal James Sadoleto to the Genevese urging their return to the Roman obedience. Calvin in the course of his vigorous reply defends those who have felt bound in conscience to become Protestants. Some parts of this tract are included here for the light they indirectly shed upon the course of his own religious development and the formation of his doctrinal convictions.

No part of Calvin's voluminous writings is more marked by discernment and felicity of expression than his commentaries on books of the Bible. These are so extensive that the English translation of them fills forty-five volumes of substantial size. He began with Romans (1539), followed this with the other letters of St. Paul and the remaining New Testament epistles, and then turned to Isaiah (1551) and other Old Testament books. His work on *The Harmony of the Three (Synoptic) Gospels* was not published until 1563, the year before his death, which saw also the completion of three other commentaries. He was struggling through Ezekiel when the approach of death halted him at the twentieth chapter. His commentaries on Romans, Isaiah, John, Genesis, and the Psalms (cited in the order in which he wrote them) are usually regarded as somewhat richer in content than the others; but all his interpretations of the New Testament books are of high quality and are still challenging reading. His *Sermons on Job* is a book of discourses longer than the *Institutes* that has largely the character of a commentary.

A few extracts from this biblical library of Calvin's commentaries are here presented. They are on passages relatively familiar to readers of the Bible and offer typical examples of Calvin's way of expounding it. There is a fluent and casual quality in the commentaries that we do not find in the *Institutes*, partly no doubt the result of the fact that they were drawn largely from shorthand notes of his lectures. It will not escape the reader that he employs a keen historical imagination to recreate the scenes recorded in Scripture, and endeavors to explain and judge the motives of persons who participate in them. Thus in his descriptions of the sacrifice of Abraham and of the marriage in Cana he enlists our interest by a skillful use of conjectural detail. But invariably doctrinal and moral ideas are wrought into the treatment in such a way as to exhibit the unity of Scripture and the common witness of both Testaments to Christ. His verse-by-verse method does not lend itself to elaborate argumentation, but gives him opportunity for many a flash of insight and many a thrust at a theological foe.

III

The powerful influence which Calvin exercised upon his own and later generations would have been much reduced if he had not possessed a remarkable style. In his case "style" may be a misleading word, unless it is at once understood that with Calvin "the style is the man"—that it is nothing extraneous, but his peculiarly appropriate way of communicating his thoughts and feelings. He constantly exhibited quite exceptional powers of communication by means both of tongue and of pen. His friend Beza remarks on this quality:

> For, by the hard studies of his youth and by a certain acuteness of judgment confirmed by practice in dictating, he was never at a loss for an appropriate and weighty expression, and wrote very much as he spoke.[9]

He writes with energy and driving force, with more of persuasive rhetoric than of close logic. He rarely makes use of a formally complete syllogism, but where the thought has a syllogistic quality he may employ the enthymeme, or reduced syllogism, in which one premise is unstated and left to the reader to supply.[10] This is a kind of logical shorthand which reduces the sense of the importance of logic. He is more likely to enlarge on the use of adjectives and adverbs, which he uses freely to impress his opinions upon the mind; and he

---

[9] Beza, *loc. cit.*

[10] See Quirinus Breen, "John Calvin and the Rhetorical Tradition," *Church History*, XXVI (1957), 3-31.

commands a wide vocabulary of approval and condemnation. The reader is not allowed to escape from any serious point of doctrine into a realm of neutrality or indecision. In order to forestall our adverse vote, Calvin tries to deal with all actual and conceivable opposing arguments, and often with the motives of those who may favor them. He is an advocate in court, with adequate oratorical resources, making a case for God and His Word. And the jury he addresses is not composed of experts only, but of everyone who will read.

Calvin possessed an unusual familiarity with Cicero, and this fact doubtless affected his syntax and vocabulary, but it may not have been of interest to him that some of his sentences have a Ciceronian ring. He was, however, well aware of the importance of rhetorical effects, while he sought these without resorting to unnatural devices. Clarity, simplicity, and brevity were the ruling principles of his discourse, whether in Latin or in French. His French has been praised as highly as his Latin, and since, when he wrote his French version of the *Institutes*, no substantial works of argument existed in that language, he had in this no model. From his instruction by Cordier when a young student he had known and exploited the possibilities for persuasion of language skillfully used, and this had become hardly less a part of the man than his anchorage in scriptural religion. He did not cease to be a man of letters when he became a dedicated reformer. As a writer he was versatile as well as eloquent. However immovable his convictions, he could adapt his expression to his readers and hearers. The vocabulary of his sermons is much simpler than that of his treatises, and the sprightly variety of his commentaries is in contrast with the sustained urgency of the *Institutes*. He wrote or dictated his compositions rapidly and easily, not delayed by the halting meticulousness of the self-conscious stylist. Though he gave little immediate attention to his rhetoric, he was a true rhetorician in the sense that a style of rare effectiveness had been "built in" with his education while he was still in his teens.

IV

Calvin's own experience of conversion, together with his study of the sacred writings, gave him a vivid sense of the immediacy of God's dealing with men. His point of departure, like that of Augustine, is "God and the soul," or, rather, as he purposely turns the expression, "God and ourselves." It is only by means of the Scriptures that the right relation of man to God can be discerned. It is in the knowledge of God that the perfection of a happy life consists; [11] but true knowledge of him is impossible without "piety" (*pietas*), in which reverence is joined with love. He sometimes speaks of his teaching as "the Christian philosophy" (an expression much used by Erasmus), but he is not a philosophical theologian. He does not feel any necessity of proving that God exists, since he is convinced, in agreement with Cicero,[12] that all men have some sense of deity. Nor does he allow himself to speculate on "what God is in himself": he would only know and teach "what he is like in relation to us." [13]

He holds it to be of the utmost urgency to learn this, since through the tragic legacy of Adam's sin we are in dire need of the salvation of God. Calvin has before his view the grandeur and misery of man. All that the eye can see in the created universe mirrors in overwhelming splendor the divine majesty and perfections. The marvelous powers of the human mind, of memory, imagination, and invention, give proof of man's divine origin and endowment. Yet sin has left us so blind and inattentive that we fail to consider these marks of God's handiwork, either in the outer world or within ourselves. Since we are incapable of reading the revelation of God in his works, he has mercifully chosen to reveal himself in his Word as it is found in Scripture.

[11] *Inst.* I. 5. 1.
[12] Cicero, *De natura deorum*. Of pagan works, this dialogue of Cicero is the one most frequently cited in the *Institutes*.
[13] *Inst.* I. 10. 2. Cf. I. 2. 2.

Calvin's view of the authority of Scripture is not so much at variance with traditional teaching as is sometimes assumed. That God is the author of Scripture was a scholastic commonplace. What is distinctive is his unqualified affirmation that the Scripture authority is exclusive, the Bible alone the source and norm of Christian doctrine, and the fact that he erects his whole structure of theology upon this foundation. This does not mean that everything in the development of doctrine, worship, and church government from the first century to his own is canceled or condemned. But all is tested by the rule of Scripture. On this principle a Church council that forbade the use of images in churches is commended, while one of a later age that approved it is censured. And while (with Augustine) Calvin feels the inconvenience of the vocabulary used by the orthodox in the Arian controversy of the fourth century, he applauds their efforts to defend trinitarian doctrine "as taught in the Scripture." He has very great respect for the Church Fathers and for the earlier councils, but does not hesitate to disapprove the utterances of either where they seem to depart from the doctrines of the gospel. It is remarkable, indeed, how much he finds to approve in the development of the Church prior to the eighth century, when, in his view, the age of papal domination really began. Of the Fathers, Augustine is far more frequently cited than any other, and in nearly all instances with approval. But he also likes to quote in the interests of reform such monitors as St. Gregory the Great and St. Bernard. His references to the earlier scholastics, including Thomas Aquinas, are critical but not severely hostile. His more sweeping censures are reserved for the champions of the late medieval theology and Church, and especially the leaders of the Sorbonne in his own century—who had aroused his ire by their approval of the harshest persecutions, in which his own friends suffered.

Calvin did not anticipate later defenses of the authority of the Bible in terms of verbal inerrancy. He never treated with systematic exactness the relation of the Word of God to the words of Scripture. He is very sure of the fact that the Bible is inspired; but in his commentaries he habitually regards the writers of Bible books as authors with minds of their own. While he studies with care and skill the words of each passage, he is primarily concerned not with the words themselves but with the doctrines to be derived from them. He adopts a "natural and obvious" interpretation of Scripture and avoids allegorical expositions,[14] yet he recognizes that some passages are themselves written allegorically or otherwise figuratively and has only scorn for the "syllable-chasers" who force such passages to say doctrinally what they do not say literally.[15] He brings to bear upon the text his philological and grammatical knowledge, and does not hesitate to correct both Luke and Paul where, following the Septuagint, they adopted defective Greek renderings of the Hebrew text. The apostles, he notes, were pretty free (*liberiores*) in quoting the words of Scripture. Since they were satisfied to express the matter, they did not make the words a point of conscience.[16] Yet he can speak of the apostolic writers as "authentic amanuenses of the Holy Spirit," and he is zealous to assert the unimpaired authority and reliability of the holy book. It is safe to say that for Calvin the Bible was in its teaching infallible throughout; but he is obliged to admit that its words are not free from all defects.

Recent studies of Calvin's theology have laid emphasis upon the central place of Christ in all his thinking. The real theme of Scripture is Christ the Saviour, by whose grace man, alienated by sin, may be reconciled to God. Christ is in the Old Testament in partial anticipation, and the gospel is "the clear manifestation of the mystery of Christ." [17] If Christ's splendor had not shone, God would have remained remote and hidden. Calvin frequently alludes to the progressive nature of the Scripture revelation from the "feeble spark"

14 *Commentary on Galatians* 4. 22-26.

15 *Inst.* IV. 17. 23.

16 *Commentary on Romans* 3. 4. On Hebrews 11. 21 he has a similar remark.

17 *Inst.* II. 9. 2.

that Adam saw until Christ the Sun of Righteousness illumined the whole world.[18] Moses and the prophets, in showing ways of reconciliation between God and man, were offering a foretaste of the grace of Christ.

It has sometimes been erroneously assumed that Calvin's theology is essentially that of the Old Testament. A count of the passages he cites in the *Institutes* indicates a preponderance of almost three to one in favor of the New Testament. What is more to the point, a thoughtful examination of his treatment of many key passages of the Old Testament shows that he habitually represents its teaching as in harmony with the gospel and as bearing witness to Christ. This it does not only directly but also by what is called typology. Events and ordinances in the Old Testament are taken as "types" that foreshadow the full and clear revelation that is to come with Christ. Thus the ancient sacrifices have significance as pointing onward to the sacrifice of Christ, and the land of Canaan is a "type" of the blessed life to come.

Man, the alienated sinner, is pardoned and justified when he is given faith in Christ. The faith which is associated with justification is secretly imparted by the Holy Spirit, and it contains an element of knowledge which is supplied from the Scripture. The truth of Scripture is attested to us not by rational proofs but by "the inner witness of the Spirit." This is no very exact conception, but Calvin did his utmost to guard it against any wayward or merely individualistic use. In humble faith and obedience the justified sinner enters on a course of growth in holiness. This "regeneration" or sanctification is a lifelong process. In this earthly life perfection is never attained; we are but pilgrims toward an afterlife of bliss in unimpaired communion with God.

Calvin's treatment of the Christian life in its social relationships receives the space of five short chapters in the *Institutes*,[19] but the topic is never far from his sermons and commentaries. His notion of the Christian is not of one who seeks salvation

18 *Inst.* II. 10. 20.
19 *Inst.* III. 6-10.

in detachment from the common concerns of men. Whatever his status or calling, he serves his God by serving his fellows and contributing to the social good. The whole range of his economic, family, and political relationships offers a sphere of opportunity for self-denying service rendered in gratitude and obedience to God. He may expect no earthly reward for this. With great frequency, especially in the commentaries and in the *Sermons on Job*, Calvin points to the miseries and losses with which the children of God are afflicted in this life. This body of material is sufficient to refute completely the view some have advanced that he held prosperity the evidence of election. The Christian bears his afflictions in patient hope and in lively anticipation of the life to come—*meditatio futurae vitae*.[20]

But not all men share in the salvation of God. It is a gift which he bestows on some and withholds from others by his inscrutable will, without regard to any man's worthiness. Calvin is far from original in this. He stands at the culmination of a resurgence of Augustinian theology that had been represented by such men as Thomas Bradwardine (d. 1349) and Gregory of Rimini (d. 1358), as well as by Wyclif, Huss, and Luther. His doctrine of predestination goes somewhat beyond that of Augustine but, essentially, hardly beyond that of Gregory of Rimini, except in the fact that it is supported with a greater array of Scripture texts. Calvin's observation of life as well as his searching of Scripture led him to conceive of the destiny of each man as determined by a divine decree by which, before time began, each was appointed to salvation or damnation. No theologian speaks more feelingly than Calvin of God's fatherly love; but he is so captured by the thought of the divine majesty and sovereign sway over all things that he sees God's will active in all that takes place. All teachers recognized as orthodox had held that the nonelect would be lost eternally; and Calvin cannot conceive of their

---

[20] *Inst.* III. 9. In II. 10. 11-17 he treats at length the sufferings of the patriarchs, arguing that the promises of God to them were to be fulfilled in the future life.

perdition without an explicit act of God's will. With skill and insistence he defends this double predestination, vigorously meeting the charge that it makes God unjust or unloving or the author of sin, and differentiating his position from that of Stoic fatalism. But he earnestly warns against incautious discussion of the doctrine, the mystery of which he does not claim to comprehend. The status of each with regard to election is known to God alone; we dare not judge of our neighbor's destined state. Using the language of Augustine, Calvin urges us to "desire the salvation of all." Amid life's trials assurance of God's love may sometimes desert the elect, but they can never be rejected, and in general they are upheld by the confidence that God is their sufficient protector.

Calvin's rigorous doctrine of predestination and reprobation has offended numerous readers and caused much controversy. He himself speaks of the "dread decree" of reprobation, and this aspect of the doctrine has proved unacceptable to many devout as well as indifferent persons. But he felt compelled so to interpret the testimony of Scripture. He was impressed, too, by the undeniable fact that masses of mankind had no opportunity to know the gospel, and by the incorrigible wickedness of some men who seemed beyond redemption in their enmity toward God. Calvin's hell is the unspeakable anguish, not of literal fire, but of eternal alienation from God.

Some pages of the material selected offer illustration of Calvin's doctrine of the Holy Catholic Church, a subject to which he gave much penetrating thought. He saw the Reformation as the recovery of the true Church which had been obscured from sight in the previous age. With Luther he regards the words "communion of saints" in the Apostles' Creed as a description of the preceding phrase, "Holy Catholic Church." The Catholic Church is then not to be identified with a visible organization, but consists of all, in all times and places, who are within the number of the elect and the communion of Christ. Its membership is known to God only. The visible Church of professed Christians imperfectly represents it. Calvin sees the task of reform as that of so cleansing and reviving the visible Church as to bring it into accord with the true Church, which is spiritual and invisible to men. The visible Church will then become, so far as possible, also one, holy, and catholic or universal (that is, without limits of place or race or time). Calvin is thus to be regarded as one of the most "ecumenical" thinkers of his century.[21] The doctrine owes something to Augustine's conception of the City of God, but it is built up mainly by the author's fresh grasp of the Church of the New Testament and the early centuries, which he sees in fundamental contrast with the pre-Reformation Church of Western Europe.

The pattern of the ministry reflects some elements of certain (more or less experimental) practices then recently introduced in the Reformed Churches of Zurich, Basel, and Strasbourg; but it is in large degree independently shaped on the basis of New Testament evidence. The presbyters, who are ministers of the Word and sacraments, are of the same order as bishops. Calvin was not totally opposed, as some have thought, to episcopacy, but he assailed the medieval episcopate as tyrannical and pastorally incompetent. Under his influence the Reformed Churches,[22] with the exception of that of Hungary, discarded the episcopate and were governed by associated presbyters. They were thus "presbyterian" in polity, whether so-called or not.

The minister, according to Calvin, is a man set apart, by the inner call of the Holy Spirit and the outward call and ordination of the Church, to functions of great importance. These are chiefly preaching, teaching, administering the sacraments, and, along with nonpreaching elders, exercising discipline. The marks by which a branch of the true visible Church is known are: the Word rightly preached, the sacra-

[21] His efforts and writings especially bearing on this are described in Ruth Rouse and S. C. Neill (eds.), *A History of the Ecumenical Movement, 1517-1948* (London and Philadelphia, 1954), pp. 48-54.

[22] The term "Reformed" is applied to that branch of the Reformation which is not Lutheran, and also in distinction from the "left wing" or radical groups, and commonly also from Anglicanism.

ments rightly administered, and sound discipline by which these are maintained. Calvin's painstaking exposition of the two scriptural sacraments constitutes an impressive element in his writings. That he has more to say about the sacraments than about preaching is not surprising in view of the controversies of his time. He gives them high importance, yet holds them not effective in themselves except as signs representing the grace of Christ proclaimed in the Word. They are to be celebrated in the words of Scripture, and accompanied by preaching.

Infant baptism, by which the children of believers are initiated into the Church, is defended by him at length. He regards it as having replaced circumcision, formerly a valid sacrament, and finds the practice of it implied in the New Testament. He assails the Anabaptists, who deny the rite to the "little ones" whom Christ invited and embraced. He refuses to condemn the doctrine of baptismal regeneration, but emphasizes the spiritual effect of baptism in the experience of the growing child whose knowledge that the Church has received him for training is a "powerful stimulus" to the Christian life.

At a time when the celebration of the Eucharist had been much neglected, Calvin was one of the few to advocate "frequent communion." Ideally he would have it each time the Church assembled; [23] but in Geneva he could not induce the magistrates to allow its celebration even every Sunday. He did succeed in making the Lord's Supper a sacrament of great solemnity. It was mainly to protect it from the participation of scandalous offenders that his system of discipline was established. This provided for "fraternal correction" by the elders, and in grave cases required the exclusion of the offender from communion. The harsher penalties employed in Geneva were by action of the civil power. The Church of Geneva was in large degree organized according to the principles laid down in Book IV of the *Institutes*.

For Calvin the sacrament of the Supper provides "a true and

[23] *Inst.* IV. 17. 44.

substantial communication of the body and blood of the Lord"—not only a "real presence" but a true impartation of Christ's body. The manner in which this is understood to take place, however, is spiritual. The body, he insists, is not, as some Lutherans were arguing, enclosed within the bread. At the ascension, Christ's body was translated to heaven, where it abides. At the sacrament the Holy Spirit mysteriously unites us with Christ in heaven, so that we truly receive all that the sacramental elements represent. United with Christ, we are also united with our fellow communicants, so that we cannot fail to love and care for them. "We cannot love Christ without loving Him in our brethren." [24] The social implications of this doctrine are far-reaching.

V

What is central and fundamental in the whole structure of Calvin's theology? To this question the experts offer somewhat divergent answers. A generation ago it was usual to explain his system on the basis of his doctrine of the inviolable sovereignty of God, with its concomitants of predestination and providence. Certainly these doctrines could hardly have been stated more emphatically than he has stated them. Yet in the *Institutes* predestination is treated within the framework of the doctrine of salvation, and the treatment is punctuated with exultant references to the undeserved and wondrous mercy of God to his chosen ones. It is preceded by discussions of regeneration and justification, in which the saving work of Christ is made available to those in whom the Holy Spirit arouses faith. By sin against a sovereign, holy, and gracious God, man lost his paradise; by a divinely imparted faith the elect are permitted to regain it. It is to this theme of salvation, with all its implications for life in this world and hope for the world to come, that Calvin's attention is ultimately directed. We noted that in his discussion of the knowledge of God he declines to speculate on the being of

[24] *Inst.* IV. 17. 38.

God and concerns himself throughout with the way in which
God manifests himself to us men, who stand in dire need of
salvation. This is the very subject matter of Holy Scripture.
The purpose of the *Institutes*, Calvin tells us, was "to prepare
candidates in sacred theology for the reading of the divine
word." [25]

The Scripture is Calvin's sole written authority and his
major source of material. His faith comprehends both Testaments and holds them in harmony. The Old Testament is, in
its intimations of reconciliation between God and man, an
anticipation of the gospel. The three Persons of the Trinity
are for him (to use the language of a seventeenth-century
Calvinist statement) "equal in power and glory." God the
Creator is never dissociated from God the Redeemer, and the
role of the Holy Spirit is magnified in both creation and redemption, as well as in the inspiration and interpretation of
Scripture.

Calvin's theology forms a substantially coherent system, and
in this reflects an orderly mind. But he is not so much concerned to give to his system a faultless structure as to present
in its wholeness the teaching of the Scripture itself, bringing
into relief its great messages to man. Guided by its inspired
writers, he would have his readers awed by the majesty of God,
shamed by the sin of man, astonished and deeply thankful
for the divine mercy which no man can deserve. Strangely, it
might seem, this theology that makes so much of the initiative
of God and denies all merit to man's works is linked with an
ethical doctrine of active and enterprising service to the
Church and the human community. But wherever Calvin
calls our attention to this sphere of duty, the motives on
which the Christian's service rests come to expression in clear
and sufficient terms—gratitude for the undeserved gift of
grace and love for our fellow men, who, however unworthy,
yet bear upon them the image of God. No one has written a

25 From the Epistle to the Reader in the 1539 edition. In Peter Barth
and Wilhelm Niesel (eds.), *Calvini Opera selecta*, III (Munich, 1928),
xiv, 6.

theological system that is not open to challenge and objection, and to this fallibility of theologians Calvin is no exception. But one at least of the charges leveled against him, that of a de-energizing fatalism, is without foundation. In his writings we are not in an atmosphere of fate, but in the company of the living God. Life consists of *negotium cum Deo,* a series of transactions with God; and the life of faith is not a resigned quiescence, but is distinguished by an energizing gratitude that bears fruit in vigorous action.

VI

A word may be added on Calvin's place in the theological and ecclesiastical world of his age. Amid much controversy, the sixteenth century witnessed a genuine revival of Christianity. This assumed a variety of forms and permanently changed the ecclesiastical organization of Europe. The Reformation in Germany gave rise to historic Lutheranism, established in a large number of German principalities and in the Scandinavian lands. The comparable but distinct movement led by Zwingli in German Switzerland became closely linked with the forces called forth by Calvin and as a result a series of "Reformed" churches emerged. In Continental states, with certain exceptions, these churches were often harassed and sometimes severely persecuted by hostile governments. In these circumstances, for the most part, they clung tenaciously to Calvin's teachings. The Scottish reformer, Knox, was to a large degree a disciple of Calvin, and the Kirk of Scotland became steeped in Calvin's thought. In England, too, his influence was very great. During the reign of Elizabeth I (1558-1603) his Latin works were read by Anglican and Puritan students and scholars, and English translations of many of his writings were in circulation. His correspondence with archbishops Cranmer and Parker was friendly. For most Puritans of the whole period before Jonathan Edwards, Calvin was an almost indisputable authority.

In 1549 Calvin signed with Zwingli's successor, Bullinger,

a basis of agreement on the principal points of divergence that had arisen between the German and French Reformed churches of Switzerland. He desired and sought a similar agreement with the Lutherans. He repeatedly expressed the highest admiration for Luther, and he willingly subscribed to the Augsburg Confession in the form in which it was in use between 1540 and 1560. His differences from Luther were limited, but chiefly in a vital area of theology—the doctrine of the Lord's Supper. These differences were magnified in controversy after Luther's death (1546), and at the death of Calvin's friend Melanchthon (1560) the possibility of a fruitful co-operation between Lutheran and Reformed became remote. Yet Calvin clung to the hope of full mutual recognition and communion between these major branches of Protestantism. His aim was in fact the unity of all evangelical churches.

Since he rested authority in the Scripture as interpreted by the Holy Spirit, he was in unabated contention against the principles of Roman Catholicism on the one hand and of Anabaptism on the other. His objection to the former (apart from prevalent abuses) lay in the fact that the Roman theology allowed tradition and hierarchical direction to share authority with Scripture. In the case of the latter the error was the recognition, as having valid authority, of revelations or promptings of the Spirit uttered without reference to the Scripture. For Calvin Scripture and the Holy Spirit were inseparable. Thus wherever the authority of Scripture was impaired or abandoned on claims either of historic tradition or of new revelation, Calvin drew the line of fellowship. But within this frontier he was an ardent and consistent advocate of ecumenical principles. He was prepared to unite with men with whom he could not as yet in all things agree, and he repeatedly made specific proposals for conferences to promote the harmony and unity that he associated with the true Catholic Church of the Apostles' Creed.

This brief review of the chief elements of Calvin's theology is designed for readers to whom the field is a new one, as an aid in approaching the selections that follow. Theology, since it has to do with cherished beliefs and practices, has always been a realm of sharp controversy, and was never more so than during the time of Calvin. Some portions of his writings are marred by needless vehemence and vituperation. In spite of this blemish, which he shares with his friends and opponents, Calvin has been read with lively interest by persons of various religious persuasions whose minds are awakened to the importance of the Christian heritage. While relatively few today would profess themselves without reservation his disciples, his writings are perhaps more closely studied in our century than ever before. He has a place not only in the history of theology but in the history of thought and expression in Western Europe, and his impact on life and religion has been world-wide and incalculable. This little book is no substitute for the *Institutes* and the vast corpus of his other writings, but it may help young readers to gain some initial conception of the reformer's mind, and to evaluate with informed judgment the opinions on Calvin expressed in works of history. In addition, these fragments of his teaching present a challenge and a stimulus to anyone who wishes to face for himself the ultimate issues of life.

JOHN T. McNEILL

SELECTED BIBLIOGRAPHY

Calvin's Works

Joannis Calvini opera quae supersunt omnia. 59 vols. Brunswick, 1863-1900.

Joannis Calvini opera selecta. 5 vols. Edited by Peter Barth and Wilhelm Niesel. Munich, 1926-36.

Calvin's Commentaries. 45 vols. Edinburgh, 1844-55; Grand Rapids, 1947-48.

A Compend of the Institutes of the Christian Religion by John Calvin. Edited by Hugh Thompson Kerr, Jr. Philadelphia, 1939.

Institutes of the Christian Religion. Translated from the Latin, and collated with the author's last edition in French, by John Allen. 3 vols. London 1813. Seventh American edition, revised and corrected, with an introduction by Benjamin B. Warfield. 2 vols. Philadelphia, 1945.

Institutes of the Christian Religion. A new translation by Henry Beveridge. 3 vols. Edinburgh, 1845. 2 vols. London and Grand Rapids, 1953.

Instruction in Faith. Translated by Paul T. Fuhrmann. Philadelphia, 1949.

Tracts. Translated by Henry Beveridge. 3 vols. Edinburgh, 1844-51.

Theological Treatises. Translated by J. K. S. Reid. London and Philadelphia, 1954.

Collateral Reading

Breen, Quirinus. *John Calvin, A Study in French Humanism.* Grand Rapids, 1932.

Clavier, Henri. *Etudes sur le Calvinisme.* Paris, 1936.

Dakin, Arthur. *Calvinism.* London, 1941.

Doumergue, Emile. *Jean Calvin, les hommes et les choses de son temps.* 7 vols. Lausanne, 1899-1927.

Dowey, Edward A., Jr. *The Knowledge of God in Calvin's Theology.* New York, 1952.

Fröhlich, Karlfried. *Gottesreich, Welt und Kirche bei Calvin.* Munich, 1930.

Fuhrmann, Paul T. *God-Centered Religion.* Grand Rapids, 1942.

Gloede, Günter. *Theologia naturalis bei Calvin.* Gutersloh, 1934.

Harbison, E. Harris. *The Christian Scholar in the Age of the Reformation.* New York, 1956.

Harkness, Georgia. *John Calvin, the Man and His Ethics.* New York, 1931.

Hunt, R. N. Carew. *Calvin.* London, 1933.

Hunter, A. Mitchell. *The Teaching of Calvin.* 2nd ed. London, 1950.

Lecerf, A. *Etudes calvinistes, recueilles et introidites par André Schlemmer.* Neuchâtel, 1949.

Mackinnon, James. *Calvin and the Reformation.* London, 1936.

McNeill, John T. *The History and Character of Calvinism.* New York, 1954.

―――― (ed.). *John Calvin on God and Political Duty.* New York, 1956.

――――. "Thirty Years of Calvin Study," *Church History,* XVII (1948), 207-240.

Niesel, Wilhelm. *The Theology of Calvin.* Translated by Harold Knight. London and Philadelphia, 1956.

Parker, T. H. L. *The Doctrine of the Knowledge of God; a Study in the Theology of John Calvin.* Edinburgh, 1952.

――――. *The Oracles of God; an Introduction to the Preaching of John Calvin.* London, 1947.

――――. *Portrait of Calvin.* Philadelphia, 1955.

Strohl, Henri. *La pensée de la Réforme.* Neuchâtel and Paris, 1951.

Stuermann, Walter Earl. *A Critical Study of Calvin's Concept of Faith.* Tulsa, 1952.

Torrance, Thomas F. *Calvin's Doctrine of Man.* London, 1949.

Walker, Williston. *John Calvin, Organizer of Reformed Protestantism, 1509-1564.* New York, 1931.

Warfield, Benjamin B. *Studies in Calvin and Calvinism.* New York, 1931.

Wencelius, Léon. *L'Esthétique de Calvin.* Paris, 1937.

Wendel, François. *Calvin: sources et évolution de sa pensée religieuse.* Paris, 1950.

Wernle, Paul. *Der evangelische Glaube nach den Hauptschriften der Reformatoren,* Volume III: *Calvin.* Tübingen, 1909.

Whale, John S. *The Protestant Tradition; an Essay in Interpretation.* Cambridge, 1955.

NOTE ON THE TEXT

The selections from Calvin's *Institutes* presented in this volume are taken from the seventh American edition of the John Allen translation, published by the Presbyterian Board of Christian Education, Philadelphia. Calvin's titles of the four books of the *Institutes* have been retained; his chapter titles, however, have been omitted, and in their place the present editor has substituted his own section headings and summaries of omitted material so that the whole reads as a continuous argument. He has also added a number of footnotes of his own, which are bracketed.

The selections from the *Commentaries* are from translations by various authors originally published in Edinburgh, 1844-55, and currently republished by the William B. Eerdmans Company, Grand Rapids, Michigan. In both the *Institutes* and *Commentaries*, punctuation and spelling have been modified to conform to preferred current usage.

"The Reply to Sadolet," from the *Tracts*, is reprinted from *Calvin: Theological Treatises*, translated by J. K. S. Reid (Volume XXII in "The Library of Christian Classics") by permission of the publisher, Westminster Press, Philadelphia.

O.P.

FROM THE INSTITUTES

FROM THE INSTITUTES

BOOK I

ON THE KNOWLEDGE OF GOD THE CREATOR

1. 1. *Knowledge of God and of ourselves inseparable*

True and substantial wisdom consists principally of two parts: the knowledge of God and the knowledge of ourselves. But while these two branches of knowledge are so intimately connected, which of them precedes and produces the other is not easy to discover. For, in the first place, no man can take a survey of himself but he must immediately turn to the contemplation of God, in whom he "lives and moves," [1] since it is evident that the talents which we possess are not from ourselves and that our very existence is nothing but a subsistence in God alone. These bounties, distilling to us by drops from heaven, form, as it were, so many streams conducting us to the fountainhead. Our poverty conduces to a clearer display of the infinite fullness of God. Especially, the miserable ruin into which we have been plunged by the defection of the first man compels us to raise our eyes toward heaven, not only as hungry and famished to seek thence a supply for our wants, but, aroused with fear, to learn humility. For, since man is subject to a world of miseries and has been spoiled of his divine array, this melancholy exposure discovers an immense mass of deformity; everyone, therefore, must be so impressed with a consciousness of his own infelicity as to arrive at some knowledge of God. Thus a sense of our ignorance, vanity, poverty, infirmity, depravity, and corruption leads us to perceive and acknowledge that in the Lord alone are to be found true wisdom, solid strength, perfect goodness, and unspotted

[1] Acts 17. 2.

3

righteousness; and so by our imperfections we are excited to a consideration of the perfections of God. Nor can we really aspire toward him till we have begun to be displeased with ourselves. For who would not gladly rest satisfied with himself? Where is the man not actually absorbed in self-complacency while he remains unacquainted with his true situation, or content with his own endowments and ignorant or forgetful of his own misery? The knowledge of ourselves, therefore, is not only an incitement to seek after God, but likewise a considerable assistance toward finding him.

1. 2. *Man's unworthiness in the light of God's perfection*

On the other hand, it is plain that no man can arrive at the true knowledge of himself without having first contemplated the divine character and then descended to the consideration of his own. For—such is the native pride of us all—we invariably esteem ourselves righteous, innocent, wise, and holy till we are convinced by clear proofs of our unrighteousness, turpitude, folly, and impurity. But we are never thus convinced while we confine our attention to ourselves and regard not the Lord, who is the only standard by which this judgment ought to be formed. Because, from our natural proneness to hypocrisy, any vain appearance of righteousness abundantly contents us instead of the reality; and, everything within and around us being exceedingly defiled, we are delighted with what is least so, as extremely pure, while we confine our reflections within the limits of human corruption. So the eye, accustomed to see nothing but black, judges that to be very white which is but whitish or perhaps brown. Indeed, the senses of our bodies may assist us in discovering how grossly we err in estimating the powers of the soul. For if at noonday we look either on the ground or at any surrounding objects, we conclude our vision to be very strong and piercing; but when we raise our eyes and steadily look at the sun, they are at once dazzled and confounded with such a blaze of brightness, and we are constrained to confess that our sight, so piercing in viewing terrestrial things, when directed to the sun is dimness itself. Thus also it happens in the consideration of our spiritual endowments. For as long as our views are bounded by the earth, perfectly content with our own righteousness, wisdom, and strength, we fondly flatter ourselves and fancy we are little less than demigods. But if we once elevate our thoughts to God and consider his nature and the consummate perfection of his righteousness, wisdom, and strength, to which we ought to be conformed—what before charmed us in ourselves under the false pretext of righteousness will soon be loathed as the greatest iniquity; what strangely deceived us under the title of wisdom will be despised as extreme folly; and what wore the appearance of strength will be proved to be most wretched impotence. So very remote from the divine purity is what seems in us the highest perfection.

1. 3. *Consternation of the saintliest men in God's presence*

Hence that horror and amazement with which the Scripture always represents the saints to have been impressed and disturbed on every discovery of the presence of God. For when we see those who before his appearance stood secure and firm so astonished and affrighted at the manifestation of his glory as to faint and almost expire through fear, we must infer that man is never sufficiently affected with a knowledge of his own meanness till he has compared himself with the divine majesty. Of this consternation we have frequent examples in the Judges and Prophets, so that it was a common expression among the Lord's people: "We shall die, because we have seen God." [1] Therefore the history of Job, to humble men with a consciousness of their pollution, impotence, and folly, derives its principal argument from a description of the divine purity, power, and wisdom. And not without reason. For we see how Abraham, the nearer he approached to behold the glory of the Lord, the more fully acknowledged himself

[1] Judg. 13. 22.

to be but "dust and ashes"; [2] and how Elias could not bear his approach without covering his face, his appearance is so formidable.[3] And what can man do, all vile and corrupt, when fear constrains even the cherubim themselves to veil their faces? This is what the prophet Isaiah speaks of: "The moon shall be confounded, and the sun ashamed, when the Lord of hosts shall reign" [4]—that is, when he shall make a fuller and nearer exhibition of his splendor, it shall eclipse the splendor of the brightest object besides. But though the knowledge of God and the knowledge of ourselves be intimately connected, the proper order of instruction requires us first to treat of the former and then to proceed to the discussion of the latter.

2. 1. *The piety requisite for the knowledge of God*

By the knowledge of God, I intend not merely a notion that there is such a being, but also an acquaintance with whatever we ought to know concerning him conducing to his glory and our benefit. For we cannot with propriety say there is any knowledge of God where there is no religion or piety. I have no reference here to that species of knowledge by which men, lost and condemned in themselves, apprehend God the Redeemer in Christ the Mediator; but only to that first and simple knowledge to which the genuine order of nature would lead us if Adam had retained his innocence. For though in the present ruined state of human nature no man will ever perceive God to be a father or the author of salvation or in any respect propitious but as pacified by the mediation of Christ, yet it is one thing to understand that God our Maker supports us by his power, governs us by his providence, nourishes us by his goodness, and follows us with blessings of every kind, and another to embrace the grace of reconciliation proposed to us in Christ. Therefore, since God is first

[2] Gen. 18. 27.
[3] I Kings 19. 13.
[4] Isa. 6. 2; 24. 23.

manifested, both in the structure of the world and in the general tenor of Scripture, simply as the Creator, and afterward reveals himself in the person of Christ as a Redeemer, hence arises a twofold knowledge of him, of which the former is first to be considered and the other will follow in its proper place. For though our mind cannot conceive of God without ascribing some worship to him, it will not be sufficient merely to apprehend that he is the only proper object of universal worship and adoration unless we are also persuaded that he is the fountain of all good and seek for none but in him. This I maintain not only because he sustains the universe, as he once made it, by his infinite power, governs it by his wisdom, preserves it by his goodness, and especially reigns over the human race in righteousness and judgment, exercising a merciful forbearance and defending them by his protection; but because there cannot be found the least particle of wisdom, light, righteousness, power, rectitude, or sincere truth which does not proceed from him and claim him for its author. We should, therefore, learn to expect and supplicate all these things from him and thankfully to acknowledge what he gives us. For this sense of the divine perfections is calculated to teach us piety, which produces religion. By piety I mean a reverence and love of God arising from a knowledge of his benefits. For, till men are sensible that they owe everything to God, that they are supported by his paternal care, that he is the author of all the blessings they enjoy, and that nothing should be sought independently of him, they will never voluntarily submit to his authority; they will never truly and cordially devote themselves to his service unless they rely upon him alone for true felicity.

2. 2. *Curious speculation excluded. God is known to the reverent and obedient*

Cold and frivolous, then, are the speculations of those who employ themselves in disquisitions on the essence of God when it would be more interesting to us to become acquainted with his character and to know what is agreeable to his nature. For what end is answered by professing, with Epicurus, that there is a God who, discarding all concern about the world, indulges himself in perpetual inactivity? What benefit arises from the knowledge of a God with whom we have no concern? Our knowledge of God should rather tend, first, to teach us fear and reverence, and, secondly, to instruct us to implore all good at his hand and to render him the praise of all that we receive. For how can you entertain a thought of God without immediately reflecting that, being a creature of his formation, you must, by right of creation, be subject to his authority, that you are indebted to him for your life, and that all your actions should be done with reference to him? If this be true, it certainly follows that your life is miserably corrupt unless it be regulated by a desire to obey him, since his will ought to be the rule of our conduct. Nor can you have a clear view of him without discovering him to be the fountain and origin of all good. This would produce a desire of union to him, and confidence in him, if the human mind were not seduced by its own depravity from the right path of investigation. For even at the first, the pious mind dreams not of any imaginary deity, but contemplates only the one true God; and, concerning him, indulges not the fictions of fancy, but, content with believing him to be such as he reveals himself, uses the most diligent and unremitting caution lest it should fall into error by a rash and presumptuous transgression of his will. He who thus knows him, sensible that all things are subject to his control, confides in him as his guardian and protector, and unreservedly commits himself to his care. Assured that he is the author of all blessings, in distress or want he immediately flies to his protection and expects his aid. Persuaded of his goodness and mercy, he relies on him with unlimited confidence, nor doubts of finding in his clemency a remedy provided for all his evils. Knowing him to be his Lord and Father, he concludes that he ought to mark his government in all things, revere his majesty, endeavor to promote his glory, and obey his commands. Perceiving him to be a just judge, armed with severity for the punishment of crimes, he keeps his tribunal always in view and is restrained by fear from provoking his wrath. Yet he is not so terrified at the apprehension of his justice as to wish to evade it, even if escape were possible, but loves him as much in punishing the wicked as in blessing the pious, because he believes it as necessary to his glory to punish the impious and abandoned as to reward the righteous with eternal life. Besides, he restrains himself from sin, not merely from a dread of vengeance, but because he loves and reveres God as his Father, honors and worships him as his Lord, and, even if there were no hell, would shudder at the thought of offending him. See, then, the nature of pure and genuine religion. It consists in faith united with a serious fear of God, comprehending a voluntary reverence and producing legitimate worship agreeable to the injunctions of the law. And this requires to be the more carefully remarked, because men in general render to God a formal worship but very few truly reverence him; while great ostentation in ceremonies is universally displayed, but sincerity of heart is rarely to be found.

3. 1. *The sense of deity found in all men*

We lay it down as a position not to be controverted that the human mind, even by natural instinct, possesses some sense of a deity. For that no man might shelter himself under the pretext of ignorance, God has given to all some apprehension of his existence,[1] the memory of which he frequently and insensibly renews; so that, as men universally know that there is a God and that he is their Maker, they must be condemned by their own testimony for not having worshiped him and consecrated their lives to his service. If we seek for ignorance of a deity, it is nowhere more likely to be found than among tribes the most stupid and furthest from civilization. But, as the celebrated Cicero observes, there is no nation so barbarous, no race so savage, as not to be firmly persuaded of the being of a

---

[1] Rom. 1. 20.

God.[2] Even those who in other respects appear to differ but little from brutes always retain some sense of religion, so fully are the minds of men possessed with this common principle, which is closely interwoven with their original composition. Now since there has never been a country or family, from the beginning of the world, totally destitute of religion, it is a tacit confession that some sense of the divinity is inscribed on every heart. Of this opinion idolatry itself furnishes ample proof. For we know how reluctantly man would degrade himself to exalt other creatures above him. His preference of worshiping a piece of wood or stone to being thought to have no god evinces the impression of a deity on the human mind to be very strong, the obliteration of which is more difficult than a total change of the natural disposition; and this is certainly changed whenever man leaves his natural pride and voluntarily descends to such meannesses under the notion of worshiping God.

In the two sections of chapter 3 omitted here Calvin argues that religion is not an invention of designing men, that the idea of a deity is native and indelible, and that the worship of God is what distinguishes men from the brutes.

4. 1. *This knowledge overcome by superstition*

While experience testifies that the seeds of religion are sown by God in every heart, we scarcely find one man in a hundred who cherishes what he has received, and not one in whom they grow to maturity, much less bear fruit in due season. Some perhaps grow vain in their own superstitions, while others revolt from God with intentional wickedness; but all degenerate from the true knowledge of him. The fact is that no genuine piety remains in the world. But in saying that some fall into superstition through error, I would not insinuate that their ignorance excuses them from guilt; because their blindness is

---

[2] Cicero, *De natura deorum* I; Lactantius, *Divinae institutiones* III. 10.

always connected with pride, vanity, and contumacy. Pride and vanity are discovered when miserable men, in seeking after God, rise not, as they ought, above their own level, but judge of him according to their carnal stupidity and leave the proper path of investigation in pursuit of speculations as vain as they are curious. Their conceptions of him are formed, not according to the representations he gives of himself, but by the inventions of their own presumptuous imaginations. This gulf being opened, whatever course they take they must be rushing forward to destruction. None of their subsequent attempts at the worship or service of God can be considered as rendered to him, because they worship not him but a figment of their own brains in his stead. This depravity Paul expressly remarks: "Professing themselves to be wise, they become fools." [1] He had before said, "They became vain in their imaginations." [2] But lest any should exculpate them, he adds that they were deservedly blinded because, not content within the bounds of sobriety, but arrogating to themselves more than was right, they willfully darkened and even infatuated themselves with pride, vanity, and perverseness. Whence it follows that their folly is inexcusable which originates, not only in a vain curiosity, but in false confidence and an immoderate desire to exceed the limits of human knowledge.

In the remaining sections of this chapter Calvin stresses man's willful resistance to this ineradicable sense of God, which turns to superstition and hypocrisy.

5. 1. *God's glory shines in the works of creation*

As the perfection of a happy life consists in the knowledge of God, that no man might be precluded from attaining felicity God has not only sown in the minds of men the seed of religion, already mentioned, but has manifested himself in the formation of every part of the world, and daily presents him-

1 Rom. 1. 22.
2 Rom. 1. 21.

self to public view in such a manner that they cannot open their eyes without being constrained to behold him. His essence, indeed, is incomprehensible, so that his majesty is not to be perceived by the human senses; but on all his works he has inscribed his glory in characters so clear, unequivocal, and striking that the most illiterate and stupid cannot exculpate themselves by the plea of ignorance. The Psalmist, therefore, with great propriety exclaims, "He covereth himself with light as with a garment," [1] as if he had said that his first appearance in visible apparel was at the creation of the world, when he displayed those glories which are still conspicuous on every side. In the same place, the Psalmist compares the expanded heavens to a royal pavilion; he says that "he layeth the beams of his chambers in the waters; maketh the clouds his chariot; walketh upon the wings of the wind"; and maketh the winds and the lightnings his swift messengers. And because the glory of his power and wisdom is more refulgently displayed above, heaven is generally called his palace. And in the first place, whithersoever you turn your eyes, there is not an atom of the world in which you cannot behold some brilliant sparks at least of his glory. But you cannot at one view take a survey of this most ample and beautiful machine in all its vast extent without being completely overwhelmed with its infinite splendor. Wherefore the author of the Epistle to the Hebrews elegantly represents the worlds as the manifestations of invisible things,[2] for the exact symmetry of the universe is a mirror in which we may contemplate the otherwise invisible God. For which reason the Psalmist attributes to the celestial bodies a language universally known,[3] for they afford a testimony of the Deity too evident to escape the observation of the most ignorant people in the world. But the Apostle more distinctly asserts this manifestation to men of what was useful to be known concerning God: "for the invisible things of him from the creation of the world are clearly seen, being understood by

1 Ps. 104. 2.
2 Heb. 11. 3.
3 Ps. 19. 1, 3.

the things that are made even his eternal power and god-head." [4]

5. 2. *The wondrous workmanship of God*

Of his wonderful wisdom, both heaven and earth contain innumerable proofs; not only those more abstruse things, which are the subjects of astronomy, medicine, and the whole science of physics, but those things which force themselves on the view of the most illiterate of mankind so that they cannot open their eyes without being constrained to witness them. Adepts, indeed, in those liberal arts, or persons just initiated into them, are thereby enabled to proceed much further in investigating the secrets of divine wisdom. Yet ignorance of those sciences prevents no man from such a survey of the workmanship of God as is more than sufficient to excite his admiration of the divine architect. In disquisitions concerning the motions of the stars, in fixing their situations, measuring their distances, and distinguishing their peculiar properties, there is need of skill, exactness, and industry; and the provi-dence of God being more clearly revealed by these discoveries, the mind ought to rise to a sublimer elevation for the contem-plation of his glory. But since the meanest and most illiterate of mankind, who are furnished with no other assistance than their own eyes, cannot be ignorant of the excellence of the divine skill exhibiting itself in that endless yet regular variety of the innumerable celestial host, it is evident that the Lord abundantly manifests his wisdom to every individual on earth. Thus it belongs to a man of pre-eminent ingenuity to examine, with the critical exactness of Galen, the connection, the sym-metry, the beauty, and the use of the various parts of the hu-man body. But the composition of the human body is uni-versally acknowledged to be so ingenious as to render its Maker the object of deserved admiration.

[4] Rom. 1. 20.

5. 3. *Intimations of God in human life*

And therefore some of the philosophers [1] of antiquity have justly called man a microcosm, or world in miniature, because he is an eminent specimen of the power, goodness, and wisdom of God, and contains in him wonders enough to occupy the attention of our minds, if we are not indisposed to such a study. For this reason, Paul, having remarked that the blind "might feel after God and find him," immediately adds that "he is not far from every one of us," [2] because every man has undoubtedly an inward perception of the celestial goodness by which he is quickened. But if, to attain some ideas of God, it be not necessary for us to go beyond ourselves, what an unpardonable indolence is it in those who will not descend into themselves that they may find him! For the same reason, David, having briefly celebrated the wonderful name and honor of God, which are universally conspicuous, immediately exclaims, "What is man, that thou art mindful of him?" Again, "Out of the mouths of babes and sucklings thou hast ordained strength." [3] Thus declaring not only that the human race is a clear mirror of the works of God, but that even infants at the breast have tongues so eloquent for the publication of his glory that there is no necessity for other orators; whence he does not hesitate to produce them as fully capable of confuting the madness of those whose diabolical pride would wish to extinguish the name of God. Hence also what Paul quotes from Aratus, that "we are the offspring of God," [4] since his adorning us with such great excellence has proved

[1] [Macrobius, *Commentarii in somnium Scipionis* II. 12; Boethius, *De definitione*, a work now held to have been written by Caius Marius Victorinus, a contemporary of Augustine (*Dictionnaire de théologie Catholique*, II, 920, using a study by H. Usener, 1877); Aristotle, *Historia animalium* 1.]

[2] Acts 17. 27.

[3] Ps. 8. 2, 4.

[4] Acts 17. 28.

him to be our Father. So from the dictates of common sense and experience, the heathen poets called him the Father of men. Nor will any man freely devote himself to the service of God unless he has been allured to love and reverence him by first experiencing his paternal love.

5. 4. *The ingratitude of men*

But herein appears the vile ingratitude of men—that, while they ought to be proclaiming the praises of God for the wonderful skill displayed in their formation and the inestimable bounties he bestows on them, they are only inflated with the greater pride. They perceive how wonderfully God works within them, and experience teaches them what a variety of blessings they receive from his liberality. They are constrained to know, whether willingly or not, that these are proofs of his divinity, yet they suppress this knowledge in their hearts. Indeed, they need not go out of themselves, provided they do not, by arrogating to themselves what is given from heaven, smother the light which illuminates their minds to a clearer discovery of God. Even in the present day there are many men of monstrous dispositions who do not hesitate to pervert all the seeds of divinity sown in the nature of man in order to bury in oblivion the name of God. How detestable is this frenzy, that man, discovering in his body and soul a hundred vestiges of God, should make this very excellence a pretext for the denial of his being! They will not say that they are distinguished from the brutes by chance; but they ascribe it to nature, which they consider as the author of all things, and remove God out of sight. They perceive most exquisite workmanship in all their members, from the head to the feet. Here also they substitute nature in the place of God. But above all, the rapid motions of the soul, its noble faculties and excellent talents, discover a divinity not easily concealed; unless the Epicureans, like the Cyclops,[1] from this eminence should au-

---

1 [Calvin may have been thinking of the Cyclops Polyphemus, the out-

daciously wage war against God. Do all the treasures of heavenly wisdom concur in the government of a worm five feet in length? And shall the universe be destitute of this privilege? To state that there is in the soul a certain machinery corresponding to every part of the body is so far from obscuring the divine glory that it is rather an illustration of it. Let Epicurus answer: what concourse of atoms in the concoction of food and drink distributes part into excrements and part into blood, and causes the several members to perform their different offices with as much diligence as if so many souls by common consent governed one body?

5. 5. Man's gifts from God not accounted for in the "shadowy deity" of ancient poets

But my present concern is not with that sty of swines; I rather address those who, influenced by preposterous subtleties, would indirectly employ that frigid dogma of Aristotle to destroy the immortality of the soul and deprive God of his rights.[1] For, because the organs of the body are directed by the faculties of the soul, they pretend the soul to be so united to the body as to be incapable of subsisting without it, and by their eulogies of nature do all they can to suppress the name of God. But the powers of the soul are far from being limited to functions subservient to the body. For what concern has the body in measuring the heavens, counting the number of the stars, computing their several magnitudes, and acquiring a knowledge of their respective distances, of the celerity or tardiness of their courses, and of the degrees of their various declinations? I grant, indeed, the usefulness of astronomy, but only remark that in these profound researches relating to the celestial orbs there is no corporeal co-operation but that the

---

rageous one-eyed giant of Greek legend who ate the flesh of the members of Odysseus' crew, or of the Cyclopes who armed Zeus with arrows; but it is possible that his mental reference was to Prometheus—a Titan, not a Cyclops—who revolted against Zeus.]

1 [Aristotle, *De anima* II. 1; Eng. tr. by Richard McKeon in *Basic Works of Aristotle* (New York, 1941), pp. 554 ff.]

soul has its functions distinct from the body. I have proposed one example whence inferences may readily be drawn by the readers. The manifold agility of the soul which enables it to take a survey of heaven and earth, to join the past and the present, to retain the memory of things heard long ago, to conceive of whatever it chooses by the help of imagination—its ingenuity also in the invention of such admirable arts—are certain proofs of the divinity in man. Besides, in sleep it not only turns and moves itself round, but conceives many useful ideas, reasons on various subjects, and even divines future events. What shall we say but that the vestiges of immortality impressed upon man are absolutely indelible? Now what reason can be given why man, who is of divine original, should not acknowledge his Creator? Shall we indeed, by the judgment with which we are endowed, discern right from wrong, and shall there be no judge in heaven? Shall we, even in our sleep, have some remains of intelligence, and shall there be no God to govern the world? Shall we be esteemed the inventors of so many useful arts that God may be defrauded of his praise? Whereas experience abundantly teaches that all we have is variously distributed to us by some superior being. The clamor of some about a secret inspiration animating the whole world is not only weak but altogether profane. They are pleased with the celebrated passage of Virgil:

> Know, first, a spirit, with an active flame,
> Fills, feeds, and animates this mighty frame,
> Runs through the watery worlds, the fields of air,
> The ponderous earth, the depths of heaven; and there
> Glows in the sun and moon, and burns in every star.
> Thus, mingling with the mass, the general soul
> Lives in the parts, and agitates the whole.
> From that celestial energy began
> The low-browed brute, th' imperial race of man,
> The painted birds who wing th' aërial plain,
> And all the mighty monsters of the main;
> Their souls at first from high Olympus came. . . . [2]

[2] *Aeneid* 6. Pitt's translation.

Just as if the world, which is a theater erected for displaying the glory of God, were its own creator! For thus writes the same poet in another place, following the common opinion of the Greeks and Latins:

> Led by such wonders, sages have opined,
> That bees have portions of a heavenly mind;
> That God pervades, and, like one common soul,
> Fills, feeds, and animates the world's great whole;
> That flocks, herds, beasts, and men, from him receive
> Their vital breath; in him all move and live;
> That souls discerpt from him shall never die,
> But back resolved to God and heaven shall fly,
> And live for ever in the starry sky.[3]

See the efficacy of that jejune speculation concerning a universal mind animating and actuating the world in the production and encouragement of piety in the human heart. This more fully appears also from the profane expressions of the filthy Lucretius, which are deductions from the same principle.[4] Its true tendency is to set up a shadowy deity and to banish all ideas of the true God, the proper object of fear and worship. I confess, indeed, that the expression, that nature is God, may be used in a pious sense by a pious mind; but, as it is harsh and inconsistent with strict propriety of speech, nature being rather an order prescribed by God, it is dangerous in matters so momentous and demanding peculiar caution to confound the Deity with the inferior course of his works.

In the remaining sections of chapter 5 we have illustration of God's providence, and Calvin calls useless a knowledge of God that is merely of the brain and not of the heart. Man is seen in a labyrinth of error so that the very sources of true knowledge are corrupted.

[3] *Georgics* 4. Warton's translation.
[4] Lucretius, *De rerum natura* I.

6. 1. *Necessity of a scripture revelation*

Though the light which presents itself to all eyes, both in heaven and in earth, is more than sufficient to deprive the ingratitude of men of every excuse—since God, in order to involve all mankind in the same guilt, sets before them all, without exception, an exhibition of his majesty delineated in the creatures—yet we need another and better assistance properly to direct us to the Creator of the world. Therefore he has not unnecessarily added the light of his word to make himself known unto salvation, and has honored with this privilege those whom he intended to unite in a more close and familiar connection with himself. For, seeing the minds of all men to be agitated with unstable dispositions, when he had chosen the Jews as his peculiar flock he enclosed them as in a fold, that they might not wander after the vanities of other nations. And it is not without cause that he preserves us in the pure knowledge of himself by the same means; for otherwise they who seem comparatively to stand firm would soon fall. For, as persons who are old or whose eyes are by any means become dim, if you show them the most beautiful book, though they perceive something written but can scarcely read two words together, yet, by the assistance of spectacles, will begin to read distinctly—so the Scripture, collecting in our minds the otherwise confused notions of deity, dispels the darkness and gives us a clear view of the true God. This, then, is a singular favor, that in the instruction of the Church God not only uses mute teachers, but even opens his own sacred mouth; not only proclaims that some god ought to be worshiped, but at the same time pronounces himself to be the being to whom this worship is due; and not only teaches the elect to raise their view to a deity, but also exhibits himself as the object of their contemplation. This method he has observed toward his Church from the beginning, beside those common lessons of instruction, to afford them also his word; which furnishes a more correct and certain criterion to distinguish him from all fictitious deities. And it was undoubtedly by this assistance that Adam, Noah, Abraham, and the rest of the patriarchs attained to that familiar knowledge which distinguished them from unbelievers. I speak not yet of the peculiar doctrine of faith which illuminated them into the hope of eternal life. For, to pass from death to life, they must have known God not only as the Creator but also as the Redeemer, as they certainly obtained both from his word. For that species of knowledge which related to him as the creator and governor of the world in order preceded the other. To this was afterward added the other internal knowledge, which alone vivifies dead souls and apprehends God not only as the creator of the world and as the sole author and arbiter of all events, but also as the Redeemer in the person of the Mediator. But, being not yet come to the fall of man and the corruption of nature, I also forbear to treat of the remedy. Let the reader remember, therefore, that I am not yet treating of that covenant by which God adopted the children of Abraham, and of that point of doctrine by which believers have always been particularly separated from the profane nations, since that is founded on Christ; but am only showing how we ought to learn from the Scripture that God, who created the world, may be certainly distinguished from the whole multitude of fictitious deities. The series of subjects will, in due time, lead us to redemption. But, though we shall adduce many testimonies from the New Testament, and some also from the Law and the Prophets in which Christ is expressly mentioned, yet they will all tend to prove that the Scripture discovers God to us as the creator of the world, and declares what sentiments we should form of him, that we may not be seeking after a deity in a labyrinth of uncertainty.

Scripture writers were convinced that their doctrine came from God. Obedience to the Word is necessary for right knowledge of God.

In chapter 7, Calvin asserts that the authority of Scripture does not depend on a declaration of the Church, to which the Word was antecedent. He continues:

7. 3. *Augustine's statement on the authority of the Church and belief in the Gospel explained*

I know, indeed, that they commonly cite the opinion of Augustine, where he says "that he would not believe the gospel unless he were influenced by the authority of the Church." [1] But how falsely and unfairly this is cited in support of such a notion it is easy to discover from the context. He was in that contending with the Manichaeans, who wished to be credited without any controversy when they affirmed the truth to be on their side but never proved it. Now, as they made the authority of the gospel a pretext in order to establish the credit of their Manichaeus, he inquires what they would do if they met with a man who did not believe the gospel, with what kind of persuasion they would convert him to their opinion. He afterward adds, "Indeed, I would not give credit to the gospel," etc., intending that he himself, when an alien from the faith, could not be prevailed on to embrace the gospel as the certain truth of God till he was convinced by the authority of the Church. And is it surprising that anyone yet destitute of the knowledge of Christ should pay a respect to men? Augustine, therefore, does not there maintain that the faith of the pious is founded on the authority of the Church, nor does he mean that the certainty of the gospel depends on it, but simply that unbelievers would have no assurance of the truth of the gospel that would win them to Christ unless they were influenced by the consent of the Church. And a little before, he clearly confirms it in these words: "When I shall have commended my own creed and derided yours, what judgment, think you, ought we to form, what conduct ought we to pursue, but to forsake those who invite us to acknowledge things that are certain and afterward command us to believe things that are uncertain; and to fol-

1 [Augustine, *Contra epistolam Manichei quam vocant fundamenti* 5. Text in Migne, *PL*, XIII, 173-207; Eng. tr. by R. Stothert in *NPNF*, IV, 129-150.]

low those who invite us first to believe what we cannot yet clearly see, that, being strengthened by faith, we may acquire an understanding of what we believe, our mind being now internally strengthened and illuminated, not by men, but by God himself?" These are the express words of Augustine; whence the inference is obvious to everyone that this holy man did not design to suspend our faith in the Scriptures on the arbitrary decision of the Church, but only to show (what we all confess to be true) that they who are yet unilluminated by the Spirit of God are, by a reverence for the Church, brought to such a docility as to submit to learn the faith of Christ from the gospel, and that thus the authority of the Church is an introduction to prepare us for the faith of the gospel. For we see that he will have the certainty of the pious to rest on a very different foundation. Otherwise I do not deny his frequently urging on the Manichaeans the universal consent of the Church with a view to prove the truth of the Scripture, which they rejected. Whence his rebuke of Faustus "for not submitting to the truth of the gospel, so founded, so established, so gloriously celebrated, and delivered through certain successions from the apostolic age." But he nowhere insinuates that the authority which we attribute to the Scripture depends on the definitions or decrees of men: he only produces the universal judgment of the Church, which was very useful to his argument and gave him an advantage over his adversaries. If anyone desire a fuller proof of this, let him read his treatise *Of the Advantage of Believing*, where he will find that he recommends no other facility of believing than such as may afford us an introduction and be a proper beginning of inquiry, as he expresses himself; yet that we should not be satisfied with mere opinion, but rest upon certain and solid truth.

7. 4. *The secret testimony of the Holy Spirit convinces us of the divine authorship of Scripture*

It must be maintained, as I have before asserted, that we are not established in the belief of the doctrine till we are

indubitably persuaded that God is its author. The principal
proof, therefore, of the Scriptures is everywhere derived from
the character of the divine speaker. The prophets and apostles
boast not of their own genius or any of those talents which
conciliate the faith of the hearers; nor do they insist on arguments from reason, but bring forward the sacred name of
God to compel the submission of the whole world. We must
now see how it appears, not from probable supposition, but
from clear demonstration, that this use of the divine name is
neither rash nor fallacious. Now, if we wish to consult the true
interest of our consciences that they may not be unstable and
wavering, the subjects of perpetual doubt, that they may not
hesitate at the smallest scruples, this persuasion must be sought
from a higher source than human reasons or judgments or
conjectures—even from the secret testimony of the Spirit. It
is true that, if we were inclined to argue the point, many
things might be adduced which certainly evince, if there be
any God in heaven, that he is the author of the law and the
prophecies and the gospel. Even though men of learning
and deep judgment rise up in opposition, and exert and display all the powers of their minds in this dispute, yet, unless
they are wholly lost to all sense of shame, this confession will
be extorted from them—that the Scripture exhibits the plainest
evidences that it is God who speaks in it, which manifests its
doctrine to be divine. And we shall soon see that all the books
of the sacred Scripture very far excel all other writings. If we
read it with pure eyes and sound minds, we shall immediately
perceive the majesty of God, which will subdue our audacious
contradictions and compel us to obey him. Yet it is acting a
preposterous part to endeavor to produce sound faith in the
Scripture by disputations. Though, indeed, I am far from excelling in peculiar dexterity or eloquence, yet, if I were to
contend with the most subtle despisers of God, who are ambitious to display their wit and their skill in weakening the
authority of Scripture, I trust I should be able, without difficulty, to silence their obstreperous clamor. And, if it were of
any use to attempt a refutation of their cavils, I would easily

demolish the boasts which they mutter in secret corners. But though anyone vindicates the sacred word of God from the aspersions of men, yet this will not fix in their hearts that assurance which is essential to true piety. Religion appearing, to profane men, to consist wholly in opinion, in order that they may not believe anything on foolish or slight grounds they wish and expect it to be proved by rational arguments that Moses and the prophets spoke by divine inspiration. But I reply that the testimony of the Spirit is superior to all reason. For as God alone is a sufficient witness of himself in his own word, so also the word will never gain credit in the hearts of men till it be confirmed by the internal testimony of the Spirit. It is necessary, therefore, that the same Spirit who spoke by the mouths of the prophets should penetrate into our hearts to convince us that they faithfully delivered the oracles which were divinely entrusted to them. And this connection is very suitably expressed in these words: "My Spirit that is upon thee, and my word which I have put in thy mouth, shall not depart out of thy mouth, nor out of the mouth of thy seed, nor out of the mouth of thy seed's seed, forever." [1] Some good men are troubled that they are not always prepared with clear proof to oppose the impious when they murmur with impunity against the divine word; as though the Spirit were not therefore denominated a "seal" and "an earnest" for the confirmation of the faith of the pious because, till he illuminate their minds, they are perpetually fluctuating amidst a multitude of doubts.

7. 5. *To those inwardly taught by the Spirit, the Scripture is self-authenticating*

Let it be considered, then, as an undeniable truth that they who have been inwardly taught by the Spirit feel an entire acquiescence in the Scripture, and that it is self-authenticated, carrying with it its own evidence, and ought not to be made the subject of demonstration and arguments from reason; but

1 Isa. 59. 21.

it obtains the credit which it deserves with us by the testimony of the Spirit. For though it conciliate our reverence by its internal majesty, it never seriously affects us till it is confirmed by the Spirit in our hearts. Therefore, being illuminated by him, we now believe the divine original of the Scripture not from our own judgment or that of others, but we esteem the certainty that we have received it from God's own mouth by the ministry of men to be superior to that of any human judgment and equal to that of an intuitive perception of God himself in it. We seek not arguments or probabilities to support our judgment, but submit our judgments and understandings as to a thing concerning which it is impossible for us to judge; and that not like some persons who are in the habit of hastily embracing what they do not understand, which displeases them as soon as they examine it, but because we feel the firmest conviction that we hold an invincible truth; nor like those unhappy men who surrender their minds captives to superstitions, but because we perceive in it the undoubted energies of the divine power, by which we are attracted and inflamed to an understanding and voluntary obedience but with a vigor and efficacy superior to the power of any human will or knowledge. With the greatest justice, therefore, God exclaims by Isaiah [1] that the prophets and all the people were his witnesses because, being taught by prophecies, they were certain that God had spoken without the least fallacy of ambiguity. It is such a persuasion, therefore, as requires no reasons; such a knowledge as is supported by the highest reason, in which, indeed, the mind rests with greater security and constancy than in any reasons; it is, finally, such a sentiment as cannot be produced but by a revelation from heaven. I speak of nothing but what every believer experiences in his heart, except that my language falls far short of a just explication of the subject. I pass over many things at present, because this subject will present itself for discussion again in another place. Only let it be known here that that alone is true faith which the Spirit of God seals in our hearts. And

[1] Isa. 43. 10.

with this one reason every reader of modesty and docility will
be satisfied: Isaiah predicts that "all the children" of the ren-
ovated Church "shall be taught of God." [2] Herein God
deigns to confer a singular privilege on his elect, whom he
distinguishes from the rest of mankind. For what is the beginning of true learning but a prompt alacrity to hear the
voice of God? By the mouth of Moses he demands our attention in these terms: "Say not in thine heart, Who shall ascend
into heaven? or, Who shall descend into the deep? The word is
even in thy mouth." [3] If God has determined that this treasury
of wisdom shall be reserved for his children, it is neither surprising nor absurd that we see so much ignorance and stupidity among the vulgar herd of mankind. By this appellation
I designate even those of the greatest talents and highest rank
till they are incorporated into the Church. Moreover, Isaiah,
observing that the prophetical doctrine would be incredible
not only to aliens but also to the Jews who wished to be esteemed members of the family, adds at the same time the
reason: because the arm of the Lord will not be revealed to
all.[4] Whenever, therefore, we are disturbed at the paucity of
believers, let us, on the other hand, remember that none but
those to whom it was given have any apprehension of the
mysteries of God.

*In chapter 8 Calvin presents rational proofs to accredit
the Scripture to natural reason, such as: its effectiveness
despite literary simplicity, its antiquity, candor, miracles,
predictions fulfilled, and the enduring consent of the
Church. In chapter 9 he assails the fanatical exponents
of a new revelation. True, the letter of itself is dead, but,
impressed on our hearts by the Spirit so as to show forth
Christ, it is the word of life.*

2 Isa. 54. 13.
3 Deut. 30; Rom. 10.
4 Isa. 53. 1.

10. 1. *Is God as portrayed in Scripture in accord with God as seen in the universe?*

But since we have shown that the knowledge of God, which is otherwise exhibited without obscurity in the structure of the world and in all the creatures, is yet more familiarly and clearly unfolded in the Word, it will be useful to examine whether the representation which the Lord gives us of himself in the Scripture agrees with the portraiture which he had before been pleased to delineate in his works. This is indeed an extensive subject if we intended to dwell on a particular discussion of it. But I shall content myself with suggesting some hints by which the minds of the pious may learn what ought to be their principal objects of investigation in Scripture concerning God and may be directed to a certain end in that inquiry. I do not yet allude to the peculiar covenant which distinguished the descendants of Abraham from the rest of the nations. For in receiving, by gratuitous adoption, those who were his enemies into the number of his children, God even then manifested himself as a Redeemer; but we are still treating of that knowledge which relates to the creation of the world, without ascending to Christ the Mediator. But though it will be useful soon to cite some passages from the New Testament (since that also demonstrates the power of God in the creation, and his providence in the conservation of the world), yet I wish the reader to be apprised of the point now intended to be discussed, that he may not pass the limits which the subject prescribes. At present, then, let it suffice to understand how God, the former of heaven and earth, governs the world which he has made. Both his paternal goodness and the beneficent inclinations of his will are everywhere celebrated; and examples are given of his severity, which discover him to be the righteous punisher of iniquities, especially where his forbearance produces no salutary effects upon the obstinate.

10. 2. *His attributes, such as clemency, goodness, mercy, justice, judgment, and truth, can be observed in a view of his creatures*

In some places, indeed, we are favored with more explicit descriptions which exhibit to our view an exact representation of his genuine countenance. For Moses, in the description which he gives of it, certainly appears to have intended a brief comprehension of all that it was possible for men to know concerning him: "The Lord, the Lord God, merciful and gracious, long-suffering and abundant in goodness and truth, keeping mercy for thousands, forgiving iniquity and transgression and sin, and that will by no means clear the guilty; visiting the iniquity of the fathers upon the children, and upon the children's children." [1] Where we may observe, first, the assertion of his eternity and self-existence in that magnificent name, which is twice repeated; and secondly, the celebration of his attributes, giving us a description, not of what he is in himself, but of what he is to us, that our knowledge of him may consist rather in a lively perception than in vain and airy speculation. Here we find an enumeration of the same perfections which, as we have remarked, are illustriously displayed both in heaven and on earth: clemency, goodness, mercy, justice, judgment, and truth. For power is comprised in the word *Elohim*, God. The prophets distinguish him by the same epithets when they intend a complete exhibition of his holy name. But, to avoid the necessity of quoting many passages, let us content ourselves at present with referring to one psalm [2] which contains such an accurate summary of all his perfections that nothing seems to be omitted. And yet it contains nothing but what may be known from a contemplation of the creatures. Thus, by the teaching of experience, we perceive God to be just what he declares himself in his word. In Jeremiah, where he announces in what characters he

[1] Exod. 34. 6.
[2] Ps. 145.

will be known by us, he gives a description, not so full but to the same effect: "Let him that glorieth glory in this, that he understandeth and knoweth me, that I am the Lord, which exercise loving-kindness, judgment, and righteousness in the earth." [3] These three things it is certainly of the highest importance for us to know: mercy, in which alone consists all our salvation; judgment, which is executed on the wicked every day and awaits them in a still heavier degree to eternal destruction; righteousness, by which the faithful are preserved and most graciously supported. When you understand these things, the prophecy declares that you have abundant reason for glorying in God. Nor is this representation chargeable with an omission of his truth, or his power, or his holiness, or his goodness. For how could we have that knowledge, which is here required, of his righteousness, mercy, and judgment unless it were supported by his inflexible veracity? And how could we believe that he governed the world in judgment and justice if we were ignorant of his power? And whence proceeds his mercy but from his goodness? If all his ways, then, are mercy, judgment, and righteousness, holiness also must be conspicuously displayed in them. Moreover, the knowledge of God which is afforded us in the Scriptures is designed for the same end as that which we derive from the creatures: it invites us first to the fear of God and then to confidence in him, that we may learn to honor him with perfect innocence of life and sincere obedience to his will, and to place all our dependence on his goodness.

10. 3. *Men are inexcusable in multiplying deities*

But here I intend to comprise a summary of the general doctrine. And first, let the reader observe that the Scripture, in order to direct us to the true God, expressly excludes and rejects all the gods of the heathen; because, in almost all ages, religion has been generally corrupted. It is true, indeed, that the name of one supreme God has been universally known

[3] Jer. 9. 24.

and celebrated. For those who used to worship a multitude of
deities, whenever they spoke according to the genuine sense of
nature, used simply the name of God, in the singular number, as though they were contented with one God. And this
was wisely remarked by Justin Martyr, who for this purpose
wrote a book, *On the Monarchy of God,* in which he demonstrates from numerous testimonies that the unity of God was
a principle universally impressed on the hearts of men. Tertullian also proves the same point from the common phraseology.[1] But since all men, without exception, have by their
own vanity been drawn into erroneous notions, and so their
understandings have become vain, all their natural perception
of the divine unity has only served to render them inexcusable. For even the wisest of them evidently betray the vagrant
uncertainty of their minds when they wish for some god to
assist them, and in their vows call upon unknown and fabu-
lous deities. Besides, in imagining the existence of many natures in God, though they did not entertain such absurd
notions as the ignorant vulgar concerning Jupiter, Mercury,
Venus, Minerva, and the rest, they were themselves by no
means exempt from the delusions of Satan; and, as we have
already remarked, whatever subterfuges their ingenuity has
invented, none of the philosophers can exculpate themselves
from the crime of revolting from God by the corruption of his
truth. For this reason Habakkuk, after condemning all idols,
bids us to seek "the Lord in his holy temple," [2] that the faithful might acknowledge no other God than Jehovah, who had
revealed himself in his word.

*Calvin, in chapter 11, condemns using idols or images
in worship. The cherubim of the Old Testament belong
to a puerile stage of religion. He rejects the saying of
Gregory that images are the books of the illiterate; he*

---

[1] [Justin, *De monarchia*, I. 2, in Migne, *PG*, VI, 314 f.; Tertullian, *De
testimonio animae* II, in Migne, *PL*, I, 684. The latter work is translated
by S. Thelwall in *ANF*, III, 175-179.]

[2] Hab. 2. 20.

approves the condemnation of images in the Council of
Elvira (c. 305); he deplores the later honoring and wor-
shiping of images. Chapter 12 continues this argument.
The one true God is to be worshiped exclusively and
without capricious inventions.

13. 1. *God's immeasurability and spirituality*

What is taught in the Scriptures concerning the immensity
and spirituality of the essence of God should serve not only
to overthrow the foolish notions of the vulgar, but also to refute the subtleties of profane philosophy. One of the ancients,[1]
in his own conception very shrewdly, said that whatever we
see, and whatever we do not see, is God. But he imagined that
the Deity was diffused through every part of the world. But
although God, to keep us within the bounds of sobriety, speaks
but rarely of his essence, yet by those two attributes which I
have mentioned he supersedes all gross imaginations and represses the presumption of the human mind. For surely his
immensity ought to inspire us with awe, that we may not at
tempt to measure him with our senses; and the spirituality of
his nature prohibits us from entertaining any earthly or carnal
speculations concerning him. For the same reason, he represents his residence to be "in heaven"; for though, as he is incomprehensible, he fills the earth also, yet, seeing that our minds,
from their dullness, are continually dwelling on the earth,
in order to shake off our sloth and inactivity he properly
raises us above the world. And here is demolished the error
of the Manichaeans, who, by maintaining the existence of two
original principles, made the devil, as it were, equal to God.
This certainly was both dividing the unity of God and limiting
his immensity. For their daring to abuse certain testimonies
of Scripture betrayed a shameful ignorance, as the error itself
evidenced an execrable madness. The Anthropomorphites also,
who imagined God to be corporeal because the Scripture
frequently ascribes to him a mouth, ears, eyes, hands, and feet,

---

[1] Seneca, *Quaestiones naturales* I.

are easily refuted. For who, even of the meanest capacity, does not understand that God lisps, as it were, with us, just as nurses are accustomed to speak to infants? Wherefore such forms of expression do not clearly explain the nature of God, but accommodate the knowledge of him to our narrow capacity; to accomplish which, the Scripture must necessarily descend far below the height of his majesty.

13. 2. *Unity and Trinity*

But he also designates himself by another peculiar character, by which he may be yet more clearly distinguished; for while he declares himself to be but One, he proposes himself to be distinctly considered in Three Persons, without apprehending which we have only a bare and empty name of God floating in our brains, without any idea of the true God. Now, that no one may vainly dream of three gods, or suppose that the simple essence of God is divided among the Three Persons, we must seek for a short and easy definition which will preserve us from all error. But since some violently object to the word "person" as of human invention, we must first examine the reasonableness of this objection. When the Apostle denominates the Son the express image of the hypostasis of the Father,[1] he undoubtedly ascribes to the Father some subsistence in which he differs from the Son. For to understand this word as synonymous with essence (as some interpreters have done, as though Christ, like wax impressed with a seal, represented in himself the substance of the Father) is not only harsh, but also absurd. For the essence of God being simple and indivisible, he who contains all in himself, not in part or by derivation but in complete perfection, could not, without impropriety and even absurdity, be called the express image of it. But since the Father, although distinguished by his own peculiar property, has expressed himself entirely in his Son, it is with the greatest reason asserted that

---

[1] [Heb. 1. 3. The word "hypostasis" is taken from the Greek text; for ὑποστάσεως the Latin has *persona*.]

he has made his hypostasis conspicuous in him; with which the other appellation, given him in the same passage, of "the brightness of his glory" exactly corresponds. From the words of the Apostle we certainly conclude that there is in the Father a proper hypostasis which is conspicuous in the Son. And thence also we easily infer the hypostasis of the Son, which distinguishes him from the Father. The same reasoning is applicable to the Holy Spirit; for we shall soon prove him also to be God; and yet he must, of necessity, be considered as distinct from the Father. But this is not a distinction of the essence, which it is unlawful to represent as any other than simple and undivided. It follows, therefore, if the testimony of the Apostle be credited, that there are in God three hypostases. And, as the Latins have expressed the same thing by the word "person," it is too fastidious and obstinate to contend about so clear a matter. If we wish to translate word for word, we may call it "subsistence." Many, in the same sense, have called it "substance." Nor has the word "person" been used by the Latins only; but the Greeks also, for the sake of testifying their consent to this doctrine, taught the existence of three πρόσωπα (persons) in God. But both Greeks and Latins, notwithstanding any verbal difference, are in perfect harmony respecting the doctrine itself.

In sections 3-6 the use of nonscriptural words, where needed to convey scriptural doctrines, is defended against the ancient heresies of Sabellius and Arius, and the difference between "essence" and "subsistence" is explained.

13. 7. *The eternal Word in John 1:1*

But before I proceed any further, I must prove the deity of the Son and of the Holy Spirit, after which we shall see how they differ from each other. When the Scripture speaks of "the Word of God," it certainly were very absurd to imagine it to be only a transient and momentary sound, emitted into the air, and coming forth from God himself; of which nature were the oracles given to the fathers and all the prophecies. It is rather to be understood of the eternal wisdom residing in God, whence the oracles and all the prophecies proceeded. For, according to the testimony of Peter,[1] the ancient prophets spoke by the Spirit of Christ no less than the apostles and all the succeeding ministers of the heavenly doctrine. But as Christ had not yet been manifested, we must necessarily understand that the Word was begotten of the Father before the world began. And if the Spirit that inspired the prophets was the Spirit of the Word, we conclude, beyond all doubt, that the Word was truly God. And this is taught by Moses with sufficient perspicuity in the creation of the world, in which he represents the Word as acting such a conspicuous part. For why does he relate that God, in the creation of each of his works, said, "Let this or that be done," but that the unsearchable glory of God may resplendently appear in his image? Captious and loquacious men would readily evade this argument by saying that the Word imports an order or command; but the apostles are better interpreters, who declare that the worlds were created by the Son, and that he "upholds all things by the word of his power." [2] For here we see that the Word intends the nod or mandate of the Son, who is himself the eternal and essential Son of the Father. Nor, to the wise and sober, is there any obscurity in that passage of Solomon where he introduces Wisdom as begotten of the Father before time began and presiding at the creation of the world and over all the works of God.[3] For to pretend that this denotes some temporary expression of the will of God were foolish and frivolous; whereas God then intended to discover his fixed and eternal counsel, and even something more secret. To the same purpose also is that assertion of Christ, "My Father worketh hitherto, and I work." [4] For, by affirming that from the beginning of the world he had continually co-operated with the Father, he makes a more explicit declaration of what had been briefly glanced at by Moses. We con-

---

clude, therefore, that God spoke thus at the creation that the Word might have his part in the work and so that operation be common to both. But John speaks more clearly than all others when he represents the Word, who from the beginning was God with God, as in union with the Father the original cause of all things. For to the Word he both attributes a real and permanent essence and assigns some peculiar property; and plainly shows how God, by speaking, created the world. Therefore, as all divine revelations are justly entitled "the word of God," so we ought chiefly to esteem that substantial Word the source of all revelations, who is liable to no variation, who remains with God perpetually one and the same, and who is God himself.

The remainder of chapter 13 is occupied with the disproof of various heresies on the doctrine of Christ, the relations of the Persons of the Trinity, and the deity of the Holy Spirit.

Chapter 14 enters on the discussion of the doctrine of man (called at the outset of Book I "knowledge of ourselves"). Much of this chapter, however, is given to an exposition of the Scripture references to angels and devils.

14. 20. *Delight in the beauty of God's creatures*

Yet let us not disdain to receive a pious delight from the works of God, which everywhere present themselves to view in this very beautiful theater of the world. For this, as I have elsewhere observed, though not the principal, is yet, in the order of nature, the first lesson of faith: to remember that, whithersoever we turn our eyes, all the things which we behold are the works of God, and at the same time to consider, with pious meditation, for what end God created them. Therefore to apprehend, by a true faith, what it is for our benefit to know concerning God, we must first of all understand the history of the creation of the world as it is briefly related by Moses and afterwards more copiously illustrated by holy men, particularly by Basil and Ambrose. Thence we shall learn that God, by the power of his Word and Spirit, created out of nothing the heaven and the earth; that from them he produced all things, animate and inanimate; distinguished by an admirable gradation the innumerable variety of things; to every species gave its proper nature, assigned its offices, and appointed its places and stations; and since all things are subject to corruption, has nevertheless provided for the preservation of every species till the last day; that he therefore nourishes some by methods concealed from us, from time to time infusing, as it were, new vigor into them; that on some he has conferred the power of propagation, in order that the whole species may not be extinct at their death; that he has thus wonderfully adorned heaven and earth with the utmost possible abundance, variety, and beauty, like a large and splendid mansion, most exquisitely and copiously furnished; lastly, that, by creating man and distinguishing him with such splendid beauty and with such numerous and great privileges, he has exhibited in him a most excellent specimen of all his works. But since it is not my design to treat at large of the creation of the world, let it suffice to have again dropped these few hints by the way. For it is better, as I have just advised the reader, to seek for fuller information on this subject from Moses and others who have faithfully and diligently recorded the history of the world.

Then follow (secs. 21-22) warnings against a failure of gratitude and admiration for the beauty and riches of God's created works provided for us that should prompt us to love and serve him with our whole heart.

15. 1. *Man, the noblest work of God, but how fallen!*

We must now treat of the creation of man, not only because he exhibits the most noble and remarkable specimen of the divine justice, wisdom, and goodness among all the works of God, but because, as we observed in the beginning, we cannot attain to a clear and solid knowledge of God without a mutual acquaintance with ourselves. But though this is twofold—the knowledge of the condition in which we were originally created and of that into which we entered after the fall of Adam (for, indeed, we should derive but little advantage from a knowledge of our creation unless in the lamentable ruin which has befallen us we discovered the corruption and deformity of our nature)—yet we shall content ourselves at present with a description of human nature in its primitive integrity. And, indeed, before we proceed to the miserable condition in which man is now involved, it is necessary to understand the state in which he was first created. For we must beware lest, in precisely pointing out the natural evils of man, we seem to refer them to the author of nature, since impious men suppose that this pretext affords them a sufficient defense—if they can plead that whatever defect or fault they have proceeds in some measure from God; nor do they hesitate, if reproved, to litigate with God himself and transfer to him the crime of which they are justly accused. And those who would be thought to speak with more reverence concerning the Deity, yet readily endeavor to excuse their depravity from nature—not considering that they also, though in a more obscure manner, are guilty of defaming the character of God, to whose dishonor it would redound if nature could be proved to have had any innate depravity at its formation. Since we see the flesh, therefore, eagerly catching at every subterfuge by which it supposes that the blame of its evils may by any means be transferred from itself to any other, we must diligently oppose this perverseness. The calamity of mankind must be treated in such a manner as to preclude all tergiversation and to vindicate the divine justice from every accusation. We shall afterward, in the proper place, see how far men are fallen from that purity which was bestowed upon Adam. And first let it be understood that, by his being made of earth and clay, a restraint was laid upon pride; since nothing is more absurd than for creatures to glory in their excellence who not only inhabit a cottage of clay but who are themselves composed partly of dust and ashes.[1] But as God not only deigned to animate the earthen vessel but chose to make it the residence of an immortal spirit,

[1] Gen. 2. 7; 3. 19, 23.

Adam might justly glory in so great an instance of the liberality of his Maker.

15. 2. *The soul an immortal essence distinct from the body*

That man consists of soul and body ought not to be controverted. By the "soul" I understand an immortal yet created essence, which is the nobler part of him. Sometimes it is called a "spirit," for though, when these names are connected, they have a different signification, yet when "spirit" is used separately, it means the same as "soul"—as when Solomon, speaking of death, says that "then the spirit shall return unto God, who gave it." [1] And Christ commending his spirit to the Father,[2] and Stephen his to Christ,[3] intend no other than that, when the soul is liberated from the prison of the flesh, God is its perpetual keeper. Those who imagine that the soul is called a spirit because it is a breath or faculty divinely infused into the body but destitute of any essence are proved to be in a gross error by the thing itself and by the whole tenor of Scripture. It is true, indeed, that while men are immoderately attached to the earth they become stupid, and, being alienated from the Father of lights, are immersed in darkness, so that they do not consider that they shall survive after death; yet in the meantime, the light is not so entirely extinguished by the darkness but that they are affected with some sense of their immortality. Surely the conscience, which, discerning between good and evil, answers to the judgment of God, is an indubitable proof of an immortal spirit. For how could an affection or emotion, without any essence, penetrate to the tribunal of God and inspire itself with terror on account of its guilt? For the body is not affected by a fear of spiritual punishment: that falls only on the soul; whence it follows that it is possessed of an essence. Now the very knowledge of God sufficiently proves the immortality of the soul which rises above the world, since an evanescent breath or inspiration could not arrive at the

1 Eccles. 12. 7.
2 Luke 23. 46.
3 Acts 7. 59.

fountain of life. Lastly, the many noble faculties with which the human mind is adorned, and which loudly proclaim that something divine is inscribed on it, are so many testimonies of its immortal essence. For the sense which the brutes have does not extend beyond the body, or at most not beyond the objects near it. But the agility of the human mind—looking through heaven and earth and the secrets of nature, and comprehending in its intellect and memory all ages, digesting everything in proper order, and concluding future events from those which are past—clearly demonstrates that there is concealed within man something distinct from the body. In our minds we form conceptions of the invisible God and of angels to which the body is not at all competent. We apprehend what is right, just, and honest, which is concealed from the corporeal senses. The spirit, therefore, must be the seat of this intelligence. Even sleep itself, which, stupefying man, seems to divest him even of life, is no obscure proof of immortality, since it not only suggests to us ideas of things which never happen, but also presages of future events. I briefly touch those things which even profane writers magnificently extol in a more splendid and ornamented diction; but with the pious reader the simple mention of them will be sufficient. Now, unless the soul were something essentially distinct from the body, the Scripture would not inform us that we dwell in houses of clay [4] and at death quit the tabernacle of the flesh,[5] that we put off the corruptible [6] to receive a reward at the last day according to the respective conduct of each individual in the body.[7] For certainly these and similar passages, which often occur, not only manifestly distinguish the soul from the body, but, by transferring to it the name of "man," indicate that it is the principal part of our nature. When Paul exhorts the faithful to cleanse themselves from all filthiness of the flesh and of the spirit,[8] he points out two parts in which the defilement of sin resides. Peter also, when he called Christ the shep-

---

[4] Job 4. 19.
[5] II Cor. 5. 4.
[6] II Pet. 1. 13, 14.

[7] II Cor. 5. 10.
[8] II Cor. 7. 1.

herd and bishop of souls,[9] would have spoken improperly if
there were no souls over whom he could exercise that office.
Nor would there be any consistency in what he says concerning the eternal salvation of souls, or in his injunction to purify
the souls, or in his assertion that fleshly lusts war against the
soul,[10] or in what the author of the Epistle to the Hebrews
says—that pastors watch to give an account of our souls [11]—
unless souls had a proper essence. To the same purpose is the
place where Paul "calls God for a record upon his soul," [12]
because it could not be amenable to God if it were not capable of punishment; which is also more clearly expressed in
the words of Christ where he commands us to fear him who,
after having killed the body, is able to cast the soul into hell.[13]
Where the author of the Epistle to the Hebrews distinguishes
between the fathers of our flesh and God, who is the only
Father of spirits,[14] he could not assert the essence or existence
of the soul in more express terms. Besides, unless the soul
survived after its liberation from the prison of the body, it was
absurd for Christ to represent the soul of Lazarus as enjoying
happiness in the bosom of Abraham, and the soul of the rich
man as condemned to dreadful torments.[15] Paul confirms the
same point by informing us that we are absent from God as
long as we dwell in the body, but that when absent from the
body we are present with the Lord.[16] Not to be too prolix on
a subject of so little obscurity, I shall only add this from Luke:
that it is reckoned among the errors of the Sadducees that they
did not believe the existence of the angels or of spirits.[17]

*The argument moves to an exposition of the image of
God in man's soul, which though defaced may be renewed
by Christ; a refutation of certain opinions of Servetus and
Osiander; remarks on the teachings of philosophers on*

[9] I Pet. 2. 25.
[10] I Pet. 1. 9, 22; 2. 11.
[11] Heb. 13. 17.
[12] II Cor. 1. 23.
[13] Matt. 10. 28; Luke 12. 4, 5.

[14] Heb. 12. 9.
[15] Luke 16. 22.
[16] II Cor. 5. 6, 8.
[17] Acts 23. 8.

the soul; and an assertion of man's loss of freedom in the fall of Adam.

Chapter 16 is on "God's Preservation and Support of the World by His Power, and His Government of Every Part of It by His Providence." In setting forth the doctrine of divine providence Calvin assails the teaching of each of the schools of ancient philosophy and vigorously asserts from Scripture a doctrine of "special providence" which allows for nothing fortuitous or merely contingent. Chapter 17, "The Proper Application of This Doctrine to Render It Useful to Us," suggests a variety of inferences from it for our conduct and our consolation. Chapter 18, "God Uses the Agency of the Impious . . . ," gives Scripture proofs that God for his good purposes makes use of the intentions of wicked men.

BOOK II

ON THE KNOWLEDGE OF GOD THE REDEEMER IN CHRIST
WHICH WAS REVEALED FIRST TO THE FATHERS
UNDER THE LAW AND SINCE TO US
IN THE GOSPEL

*The Fall of Adam entails man's inherited corruption or
original sin, which leaves us depraved and incapacitated.*

1. 8. *Definition of original sin*

To remove all uncertainty and misunderstanding on this
subject, let us define original sin. It is not my intention to
discuss all the definitions given by writers; I shall only produce one, which I think perfectly consistent with the truth.
Original sin, therefore, appears to be a hereditary depravity
and corruption of our nature, diffused through all the parts
of the soul, rendering us obnoxious to the divine wrath and
producing in us those works which the Scripture calls "works
of the flesh." [1] And this is indeed what Paul frequently denominates "sin." The works which proceed thence, such as
adulteries, fornications, thefts, hatreds, murders, revelings, he
calls in the same manner "fruits of sin," although they are
also called "sins" in many passages of Scripture and even by
himself. These two things, therefore, should be distinctly observed: first, that our nature being so totally vitiated and depraved, we are, on account of this very corruption, considered
as convicted and justly condemned in the sight of God, to
whom nothing is acceptable but righteousness, innocence, and
purity. And this liableness to punishment does not arise from
the delinquency of another; for when it is said that the sin of
Adam renders us obnoxious to the divine judgment, it is not

[1] Gal. 5. 19.

42

to be understood as if we, though innocent, were undeservedly loaded with the guilt of his sin, but, because we are all subject to a curse in consequence of his transgression, he is therefore said to have involved us in guilt. Nevertheless we derive from him not only the punishment but also the pollution to which the punishment is justly due. Wherefore Augustine, though he frequently calls it the sin of another the more clearly to indicate its transmission to us by propagation, yet at the same time also asserts it properly to belong to every individual. And the Apostle himself expressly declares that "death has therefore passed upon all men, for that all have sinned" [2]—that is, have been involved in original sin and defiled with its blemishes. And therefore infants themselves, as they bring their condemnation into the world with them, are rendered obnoxious to punishment by their own sinfulness, not by the sinfulness of another. For though they have not yet produced the fruits of their iniquity, yet they have the seed of it within them; even their whole nature is, as it were, a seed of sin, and therefore cannot but be odious and abominable to God. Whence it follows that it is properly accounted sin in the sight of God because there could be no guilt without crime. The other thing to be remarked is that this depravity never ceases in us but is perpetually producing new fruits, those works of the flesh which we have before described, like the emission of flame and sparks from a heated furnace or like the streams of water from a never-failing spring. Wherefore those who have defined original sin as a privation of the original righteousness which we ought to possess, though they comprise the whole of the subject, yet have not used language sufficiently expressive of its operation and influence. For our nature is not only destitute of all good, but is so fertile in all evils that it cannot remain inactive. Those who have called it "concupiscence" have used an expression not improper, if it were only added, which is far from being conceded by most persons, that everything in man—the understanding and will, the soul and body—is polluted and

2 Rom. 5. 12.

engrossed by this concupiscence; or, to express it more briefly, that man is of himself nothing else but concupiscence.

1. 9. *Its devastation of the soul*

Wherefore I have asserted that sin has possessed all the powers of the soul since Adam departed from the fountain of righteousness. For man has not only been ensnared by the inferior appetites, but abominable impiety has seized the very citadel of his mind, and pride has penetrated into the inmost recesses of his heart; so that it is weak and foolish to restrict the corruption which has proceeded thence to what are called the sensual affections, or to call it an incentive which allures, excites, and attracts to sin only what they style the sensual part. In this the grossest ignorance has been discovered by Peter Lombard, who, when investigating the seat of it, says that it is in the flesh, according to the testimony of Paul,[1] not indeed exclusively, but because it principally appears in the flesh; as though Paul designated only a part of the soul and not the whole of our nature, which is opposed to supernatural grace. Now Paul removes every doubt by informing us that the corruption resides not in one part only, but that there is nothing pure and uncontaminated by its mortal infection. For, when arguing respecting corrupt nature, he not only condemns the inordinate motions of the appetites, but principally insists on the blindness of the mind and the depravity of the heart;[2] and the third chapter of his Epistle to the Romans is nothing but a description of original sin. This appears more evident from our renovation. For "the Spirit," which is opposed to "the old man" and "the flesh," not only denotes the grace which corrects the inferior or sensual part of the soul, but comprehends a complete reformation of all its powers. And therefore Paul not only enjoins us to mortify our sensual appetites but exhorts us to be renewed in the spirit of our

1 Rom. 7. 18.
2 Eph. 4. 17, 18.

mind;[3] and in another place he directs us to be transformed by the renewing of our mind.[4] Whence it follows that that part which principally displays the excellence and dignity of the soul is not only wounded but so corrupted that it requires not merely to be healed but to receive a new nature. How far sin occupies both the mind and the heart we shall presently see. My intention here was only to hint, in a brief way, that man is so totally overwhelmed, as with a deluge, that no part is free from sin; and therefore that whatever proceeds from him is accounted sin; as Paul says that all the affections or thoughts of the flesh are enmity against God, and therefore death.[5]

1. 10. *We, not God, to be blamed for this*

Now let us dismiss those who dare to charge God with their corruptions because we say that men are naturally corrupt. They err in seeking for the work of God in their own pollution, whereas they should rather seek it in the nature of Adam while yet innocent and uncorrupted. Our perdition therefore proceeds from the sinfulness of our flesh, not from God, it being only a consequence of our degenerating from our primitive condition. And let no one murmur that God might have made a better provision for our safety by preventing the fall of Adam. For such an objection ought to be abominated, as too presumptuously curious, by all pious minds; and it also belongs to the mystery of predestination, which shall afterwards be treated in its proper place. Wherefore let us remember that our ruin must be imputed to the corruption of our nature that we may not bring an accusation against God himself, the author of nature. That this fatal wound is inherent in our nature is indeed a truth; but it is an important question whether it was in it originally or was derived from any

[3] Eph. 4. 23.
[4] Rom. 12. 2.
[5] Rom. 8. 6, 7.

extraneous cause. But it is evident that it was occasioned by sin. We have therefore no reason to complain but of ourselves, which in the Scripture is distinctly remarked. For the Preacher says, "This only have I found, that God hath made man upright; but they have sought out many inventions." [1] It is clear that the misery of man must be ascribed solely to himself, since he was favored with rectitude by the divine goodness but has lapsed into vanity through his own folly.

1. 11. *Natural depravity, a depravity of nature not originating in nature*

We say, therefore, that man is corrupted by a natural depravity, but which did not originate from nature. We deny that it proceeded from nature to signify that it is rather an adventitious quality or accident than a substantial property originally innate. Yet we call it natural that no one may suppose it to be contracted by every individual from corrupt habit whereas it prevails over all by hereditary right. Nor is this representation of ours without authority. For the same reason the Apostle says that we are all by nature the children of wrath.[1] How could God, who is pleased with all his meanest works, be angry with the noblest of all his creatures? But he is angry rather with the corruption of his work than with his work itself. Therefore, if, on account of the corruption of human nature, man be justly said to be naturally abominable to God, he may also be truly said to be naturally depraved and corrupt; as Augustine, in consequence of the corruption of nature, does not hesitate to call those sins natural which necessarily predominate in our flesh where they are not prevented by the grace of God. Thus vanishes the foolish and nugatory system of the Manichaeans, who, having imagined in man a substantial wickedness, presumed to invent for him a new creator, that they might not appear to assign the cause and origin of evil to a righteous God.

[1] Eccles. 7. 29.
[1] (1. 11) Eph. 2. 3.

In chapter 2, Calvin argues at length that man is now despoiled of freedom of will and subjected to a wretched slavery. Here he criticizes not only the philosophers but the Church Fathers, Augustine excepted, for admitting human freedom to do good.

In chapter 3 Calvin affirms that, man's nature being corrupted, all that proceeds from it is to be condemned. As frequently elsewhere, he here claims the support of Augustine and Bernard as well as of Scripture. The will of man, Bernard said, is in some strange way "the author of the necessity of which it is the subject" (sec. 5). But Calvin rejects Chrysostom's "Quem trahit volentem trahit"—whom God draws he draws willing—as taking away the divine initiative (sec. 10).

3. 12. Bad theology from a bad translation

And to this purpose they falsely and ignorantly pervert that observation of the Apostle, "I labored more abundantly than they all; yet not I, but the grace of God which was with me." [1] For they understand it in this manner: that because his preference of himself to all others might appear rather too arrogant, he corrects it by referring the praise to the grace of God, but yet so as to denominate himself a co-operator with grace. It is surprising that so many men, not otherwise erroneous, have stumbled at this imaginary difficulty. For the Apostle does not say that the grace of God labored with him to make himself a partner in the labor; but rather by that correction ascribes the whole praise of the labor to grace alone. "It is not I," says he, "that have labored, but the grace of God which was with me." They have been deceived by an ambiguity of expression, but still more by a preposterous translation in which the force of the Greek article is omitted. For if you translate it literally he says, not that grace was co-operative with him, but that the grace which was with him was the author of all. And the same is maintained by Augustine,

[1] I Cor. 15. 10.

though briefly, yet without obscurity, when he thus expresses himself: "The good will of man precedes many of the gifts of God, but not all. But of those which it precedes it is itself one." Then follows this reason: "Because it is written, 'The God of my mercy shall prevent me.' [2] And, 'Mercy shall follow me.' [3] It prevents the unwilling, that he may will; it follows the willing, that he may not will in vain." [4] With this agrees Bernard, who introduces the Church, saying, "Draw me unwilling, to make me willing; draw me inactive, to make me run." [5]

3. 13. *Augustine bears testimony*

Now, let us hear Augustine speak in his own words, lest the sophists of the Sorbonne, those Pelagians of the present age, according to their usual custom, accuse us of opposing the whole current of antiquity. In this they imitate their father Pelagius, by whom Augustine was formerly obliged to enter into the same field of controversy. In his treatise *On Correction and Grace,* addressed to Valentine, he treats very much at large what I shall recite briefly, but in his own words: "That to Adam was given the grace of persevering in good if he chose; that grace is given to us to will, and by willing to overcome concupiscence. That Adam therefore had the power if he had the will, but not the will that he might have the power; but that it is given to us to have both the will and the power. That the primitive liberty was a power to abstain from sin, but that ours is much greater, being an inability to commit sin." And lest he should be supposed to speak of the perfection to be enjoyed after the attainment of a state of im-

[2] Ps. 59. 10.

[3] Ps. 23. 6.

[4] [Augustine, *Enchiridion* 32; text in Migne, *PL*, XL, 243. A. C. Outler has translated this work, using later critical editions, in *Augustine: Confessions and Enchiridion* (Philadelphia, 1955). For this passage see p. 359.]

[5] [Bernard of Clairvaux, *Sermones in Cantica Canticorum* XXI. 9; in Migne, *PL*, CLXXXIII, 876.]

mortality, as Lombard misinterprets his meaning, he presently removes this difficulty. For he says, "The will of the saints is so inflamed by the Holy Spirit that they therefore have an ability because they have such a will; and that their having such a will proceeds from the operations of God." For if, amidst such great weakness—which still requires "strength" to be "made perfect" [1] for the repressing of pride—they were left to their own will, so as to have ability, through the divine assistance, if they were willing, and God did not operate in them to produce that will, among so many temptations and infirmities their will would fail, and therefore they could not possibly persevere. The infirmity of the human will, then, is succored, that it may be invariably and inseparably actuated by divine grace and so, notwithstanding all its weakness, may not fail. He afterwards discusses more at large how our hearts necessarily follow the impulse of God; and he asserts that the Lord draws men with their own wills, but that those wills are such as he himself has formed. Now we have a testimony from the mouth of Augustine to the point which we are principally endeavoring to establish: that grace is not merely offered by the Lord to be either received or rejected according to the free choice of each individual, but that it is grace which produces both the choice and the will in the heart; so that every subsequent good work is the fruit and effect of it, and that it is obeyed by no other will but that which it has produced. For this is his language also in another place—that it is grace alone which performs every good work in us.

3. 14. *"Not grace by liberty, but liberty by grace"*

When he observes that the will is not taken away by grace but only changed from a bad one into a good one, and when it is good, assisted, he only intends that man is not drawn in such a manner as to be carried away by an external impulse, without any inclination of his mind, but that he is internally so disposed as to obey from his very heart. That grace is spe-

[1] II Cor. 12. 9.

cially and gratuitously given to the elect he maintains in an epistle to Boniface in the following language: "We know that the grace of God is not given to all men; and that to them to whom it is given it is given neither according to the merits of works, nor according to the merits of will, but by gratuitous favor; and to those to whom it is not given, we know that it is not given by the righteous judgment of God." [1] And in the same epistle he strenuously combats that opinion which supposes that subsequent grace is given to the merits of men because, by not rejecting the first grace, they showed themselves worthy of it. For he wishes Pelagius to allow that grace is necessary to us for every one of our actions and is not a retribution of our works, that it may be acknowledged to be pure grace. But the subject cannot be comprised in a more concise summary than in the eighth chapter of his treatise addressed to Valentine, where he teaches that the human will obtains, not grace by liberty, but liberty by grace; that, being impressed by the same grace with a disposition of delight, it is formed for perpetuity; that it is strengthened with invincible fortitude; that while grace reigns it never falls, but deserted by grace falls immediately; that by the gratuitous mercy of the Lord it is converted to what is good and, being converted, perseveres in it; that the first direction of the human will to that which is good, and its subsequent constancy, depend solely on the will of God and not on any merit of man. Thus there is left to man such a free will, if we choose to give it that appellation, as he describes in another place, that he can neither be converted to God nor continue in God but by grace, and that all the ability which he has is derived from grace.

1 [This letter was in fact addressed to Vitalis of Carthage. Augustine, *Epistolae* 217. 5. 16; in Migne, *PL*, XXXIII, 984; Eng. tr. by Sister Wilfred Parsons in *Saint Augustine, Letters* (New York, 1956), V, 75-96, at 86.]

4. 1. *Augustine's figure of the human will ridden by the devil*

It has now, I apprehend, been sufficiently proved that man is so enslaved by sin as to be of his own nature incapable of an effort, or even an aspiration, toward that which is good. We have also laid down a distinction between coaction and necessity from which it appears that, while he sins necessarily, he nevertheless sins voluntarily. But since, while he is devoted to the servitude of the devil, he seems to be actuated by his will rather than by his own, it remains for us to explain the nature of both kinds of influence. There is also this question to be resolved: whether anything is to be attributed to God in evil actions in which the Scripture intimates that some influence of his is concerned. Augustine somewhere [1] compares the human will to a horse obedient to the direction of his rider, and God and the devil he compares to riders. "If God rides it, he, like a sober and skillful rider, manages it in a graceful manner: stimulates its tardiness, restrains its immoderate celerity, represses its wantonness and wildness, tames its perverseness, and conducts it into the right way. But if the devil has taken possession of it, he, like a foolish and wanton rider, forces it through pathless places, hurries it into ditches, drives it down over precipices, and excites it to obstinacy and ferocity." With this similitude, as no better occurs, we will at present be content. When the will of a natural man is said to be subject to the power of the devil so as to be directed by it, the meaning is not that it resists and is compelled to a reluctant submission, as masters compel slaves to an unwilling performance of their commands, but that, being fascinated by the fallacies of Satan, it necessarily submits itself to all his directions. For those whom the Lord does not favor with the government of his Spirit he abandons, in righteous judgment, to the influence of Satan. Wherefore the Apostle says that "the god of this world hath blinded the minds of them which believe not,"

---

[1] [Scholars have been unable to find this passage in the works of St. Augustine. Calvin may have been in error in attributing it to him.]

who are destined to destruction, "lest the light of the gospel should shine unto them." [2] And in another place, that he "worketh in the children of disobedience." [3] The blinding of the wicked, and all those enormities which attend it, are called the works of Satan, the cause of which must nevertheless be sought only in the human will, from which proceeds the root of evil and in which rests the foundation of the kingdom of Satan—that is, sin.

4. 2. *Satan may be the instrument of God's wrath*

Very different, in such instances, is the method of the divine operation. And that we may have a clearer view of it, let us take as an example the calamity which holy Job suffered from the Chaldeans.[1] The Chaldeans massacred his shepherds and committed hostile depredations on his flock. Now the wickedness of their procedure is evident; yet in these transactions Satan was not unconcerned, for with him the history states the whole affair to have originated. But Job himself recognizes in it the work of the Lord, whom he asserts to have taken from him those things of which he had been plundered by the Chaldeans. How can we refer the same action to God, to Satan, and to man, as being each the author of it, without either excusing Satan by associating him with God or making God the author of evil? Very easily, if we examine, first, the end for which the action was designed, and secondly, the manner in which it was effected. The design of the Lord is to exercise the patience of his servant by adversity; Satan endeavors to drive him to despair; the Chaldeans, in defiance of law and justice, desire to enrich themselves by the property of another. So great a diversity of design makes a great distinction in the action. There is no less difference in the manner. The Lord permits his servant to be afflicted by Satan; the Chaldeans, whom he commissions to execute his purpose, he permits and

2 II Cor. 4. 4.
3 Eph. 2. 2.
1 Job 1.

resigns to be impelled by Satan; Satan, with his envenomed stings, instigates the minds of the Chaldeans, otherwise very depraved, to perpetrate the crime: they furiously rush into the act of injustice and overwhelm themselves in criminality. Satan therefore is properly said to work in the reprobate, in whom he exercises his dominion—that is, the kingdom of iniquity. God also is said to work in a way proper to himself because Satan, being the instrument of his wrath, turns himself hither and thither at his appointment and command to execute his righteous judgments. Here I allude not to the universal influence of God, by which all creatures are sustained and from which they derive an ability to perform whatever they do. I speak only of that special influence which appears in every particular act. We see, then, that the same action is without absurdity ascribed to God, to Satan, and to man; but the variety in the end and in the manner causes the righteousness of God to shine without the least blemish, and the iniquity of Satan and of man to betray itself to its own disgrace.

4. 3. *The Fathers hesitate where the Scripture is plain*

The Fathers are sometimes too scrupulous on this subject and afraid of a simple confession of the truth, lest they should afford an occasion to impiety to speak irreverently and reproachfully of the works of God. Though I highly approve this sobriety, yet I think we are in no danger if we simply maintain what the Scripture delivers. Even Augustine at one time was not free from this scrupulosity, as when he says that hardening and blinding belong not to the operation but to the prescience of God. But these subtleties are inconsistent with numerous expressions of the Scripture which evidently import some intervention of God beyond mere foreknowledge. And Augustine himself, in his fifth book against Julian, contends very largely that sins proceed not only from the permission or the prescience but from the power of God, in order that former sins may thereby be punished. So also what they advance concerning permission is too weak to be supported.

God is very frequently said to blind and harden the reprobate
and to turn, incline, and influence their hearts, as I have elsewhere more fully stated. But it affords no explication of the
nature of this influence to resort to prescience or permission.
We answer, therefore, that it operates in two ways. For since,
when his light is removed, nothing remains but darkness and
blindness; since, when his Spirit is withdrawn, our hearts
harden into stones; since, when his direction ceases, they are
warped into obliquity—he is properly said to blind, harden,
and incline those whom he deprives of the power of seeing,
obeying, and acting aright. The second way, which is much
more consistent with strict propriety of language, is when,
for the execution of his judgments, he, by means of Satan,
the minister of his wrath, directs their counsels to what he
pleases and excites their wills and strengthens their efforts.
Thus when Moses relates that Sihon the king would not grant
a free passage to the people because God had "hardened his
spirit, and made his heart obstinate," he immediately subjoins
the end of God's design: "That he might deliver him into thy
hand." [1] Since God willed his destruction, the obduration of
his heart, therefore, was the divine preparation for his ruin.

*Numerous passages from the Old Testament are employed
to support these views and to show that God controls
men's choices according to his providence.*

*Chapter 5 is entitled "A Refutation of Objections Com-
monly Urged in Support of Free Will." Objections are
cited not only from Pelagius and his supporters, but from
Erasmus, Cochlaeus, and others of the sixteenth century.*

*In Chapter 6, "Redemption for Lost Man to be Sought
in Christ," Calvin turns to positive aspects of the theme
of Book II. He argues that God's favor to his ancient
people was associated with the work of Christ as mediator. This short chapter concludes as follows.*

[1] Deut. 2. 30.

6. 4. *The Jews instructed in these prophecies by Christ*

It was the will of God that the Jews should be instructed by these prophecies so that they might direct their eyes to Christ whenever they wanted deliverance. Nor, indeed, notwithstanding their shameful degeneracy, could the memory of this general principle ever be obliterated—that God would be the deliverer of the Church by the hand of Christ, according to his promise to David; and that in this manner the covenant of grace, in which God had adopted his elect, would at length be confirmed. Hence it came to pass that when Christ, a little before his death, entered into Jerusalem, that song was heard from the mouths of children, "Hosanna to the Son of David." [1] For the subject of their song appears to have been derived from a sentiment generally received and avowed by the people that there remained to them no other pledge of the mercy of God but in the advent of the Redeemer. For this reason Christ commands his disciples to believe in him that they may distinctly and perfectly believe in God: "Ye believe in God, believe also in me." [2] For though, strictly speaking, faith ascends from Christ to the Father, yet he suggests that though it were even fixed on God, yet it would gradually decline unless he interposed to preserve its stability. The majesty of God is otherwise far above the reach of mortals, who are like worms crawling upon the earth. Wherefore, though I do not reject that common observation that God is the object of faith, yet I consider it as requiring some correction. For it is not without reason that Christ is called "the image of the invisible God"; [3] but by this appellation we are reminded that, unless God reveal himself to us in Christ, we cannot have that knowledge of him which is necessary to salvation. For although among the Jews the scribes had by false glosses ob-

[1] Matt. 21. 9.
[2] John 14. 1.
[3] Col. 1. 15.

scured the declarations of the prophets concerning the Redeemer, yet Christ assumed it for granted, as if allowed by common consent, that there was no other remedy for the confusion into which the Jews had fallen, nor any other mode of deliverance for the Church, but the exhibition of the Mediator. There was not, indeed, such a general knowledge as there ought to have been of the principle taught by Paul, that "Christ is the end of the law"; [4] but the truth and certainty of this evidently appears both from the law itself and from the prophets. I am not yet treating of faith; there will be a more suitable place for that subject in another part of the work. Only let this be well fixed in the mind of the reader: that the first step to piety is to know that God is our Father, to protect, govern, and support us till he gathers us into the eternal inheritance of his kingdom; that hence it is plain, as we have before asserted, that there can be no saving knowledge of God without Christ, and consequently that from the beginning of the world he has always been manifested to all the elect, that they might look to him, and repose all their confidence in him. In this sense Irenaeus says that the Father, who is infinite in himself, becomes finite in the Son because he has accommodated himself to our capacity, that he may not overwhelm our minds with the infinity of his glory.[5] And fanatics, not considering this, pervert a useful observation into an impious reverie, as though there were in Christ merely a portion of deity, an emanation from the infinite perfection; whereas the sole meaning of that writer is that God is apprehended in Christ, and in him alone. The assertion of John has been verified in all ages: "Whosoever denieth the Son, the same hath not the Father." [6] For though many in ancient times gloried in being worshipers of the Supreme Deity, the Creator of heaven and earth, yet, because they had no Mediator, it was impossible for them to have any real acquaintance with the mercy of God or persuasion that he was their Father.

[4] Rom. 10. 4.
[5] Irenaeus 4, 8.
[6] I John 2. 23.

Therefore, as they did not hold the head—that is, Christ—all their knowledge of God was obscure and unsettled; whence it came to pass that, degenerating at length into gross and vile superstitions, they betrayed their ignorance, like the Turks in modern times who, though they boast of having the Creator of heaven and earth for their God, yet only substitute an idol instead of the true God as long as they remain enemies to Christ.

In chapter 7 the theme is the purpose of the Old Testament law, which was "to encourage their hope of salvation in Christ, till the time of his coming." Chapter 8 is an exposition of the moral law. This extends to fifty-eight sections and is mainly a penetrating interpretation of the Ten Commandments. Chapter 9 has the heading: "Christ, Though Known to the Jews Under the Law, Yet Clearly Revealed Only in the Gospel." There is a comment on the intermediate position of John the Baptist.
  Chapter 10 is entitled "The Similarity of the Old and New Testaments."

10. 1. Reasons for discussing the relations of the Old and New Testaments

From the preceding observations it may now be evident that all those persons, from the beginning of the world, whom God has adopted into the society of his people have been federally connected with him by the same law and the same doctrine which are in force among us; but because it is of no small importance that this point be established, I shall show, by way of appendix, since the fathers were partakers with us of the same inheritance and hoped for the same salvation through the grace of our common Mediator, how far their condition in this connection was different from ours. For though the testimonies we have collected from the law and the prophets in proof of this render it sufficiently evident that the people of God have never had any other rule of religion and piety, yet because some writers have raised many disputes concerning the difference of the Old and New Testaments, which may occasion doubts in the mind of an undiscerning reader, we shall assign a particular chapter for the better and more accurate discussion of this subject. Moreover, what would otherwise have been very useful has now been rendered necessary for us by Servetus and some madmen of the sect of the Anabaptists who entertain no other ideas of the Israelitish nation than of a herd of swine whom they pretend to have been pampered by the Lord in this world without the least hope of a future immortality in heaven. To defend the pious mind, therefore, from this pestilent error, and at the same time to remove all difficulties which may arise from the mention of a diversity between the Old and New Testaments, let us, as we proceed, examine what similarity there is between them, and what difference; what covenant the Lord made with the Israelites in ancient times before the advent of Christ, and what he has entered into with us since his manifestation in the flesh.

There follows a statement of their points of agreement: the hope of immortality, the covenant founded not on merit but on mercy, and the mediation of Christ. In the light of these, various passages employed by objectors are reviewed.

10. 7. *The Jews had a real participation in God and eternal life*

But if the reader would prefer a recital of testimonies from the law and the prophets to show him that the spiritual covenant was common also to the fathers, as we have heard from Christ and his apostles, I will attend to this wish, and that with the greater readiness because our adversaries will thereby be more decisively confuted and will have no pretense for any future cavil. I will begin with that demonstration which, though I know the Anabaptists will superciliously deem it

futile and almost ridiculous, yet will have considerable weight
with persons of docility and good understanding. And I take
it for granted that there is such a vital efficacy in the divine
word as to quicken the souls of all those whom God favors
with a participation of it. For the assertion of Peter has ever
been true that it is "an incorruptible seed, which abideth forever," [1] as he also concludes from the words of Isaiah.[2] Now
when God anciently united the Jews with himself in this sacred bond, there is no doubt that he separated them to the
hope of eternal life. For when I say that they embraced the
word which was to connect them more closely with God, I
advert not to that general species of communication with him
which is diffused through heaven and earth and all the creatures in the universe, which although it animates all things
according to their respective natures, yet does not deliver from
the necessity of corruption. I refer to that particular species of
communication by which the minds of the pious are enlightened into the knowledge of God, and in some measure united
to him. Since Adam, Abel, Noah, Abraham, and the other
patriarchs were attached to God by such an illumination of his
word, I maintain there can be no doubt that they had an entrance into his immortal kingdom. For it was a real participation of God, which cannot be separated from the blessing of
eternal life.

*In sections 8 to 19 the patriarchs are described as exam-
ples of the elect of God who suffer adversity on earth,
keeping in view the blessedness of the future state. This
expectation is expressed by Job.*

10. 20. *Progressive revelation in Scripture*

If we descend to the later prophets, there we may freely
expatiate as quite at home. For if it was not difficult to prove
our point from David, Job, and Samuel, we shall do it there

[1] I Pet. 1. 23, 25.
[2] Isa. 40. 8.

with much greater facility. For this is the order and economy which God observed in dispensing the covenant of his mercy: that as the course of time accelerated the period of its full exhibition, he illustrated it from day to day with additional revelations. Therefore, in the beginning, when the first promise was given to Adam, it was like the kindling of some feeble sparks. Subsequent accessions caused a considerable enlargement of the light, which continued to increase more and more, and diffused its splendor through a wide extent, till at length, every cloud being dissipated, Christ, the Sun of Righteousness, completely illuminated the whole world. There is no reason to fear, therefore, if we want the suffrages of the prophets in support of our cause, that they will fail us. But as I perceive it would be a very extensive field, which would engross more of our attention than the nature of our design will admit—for it would furnish matter for a large volume—and as I also think that by what has been already said I have prepared the way even for a reader of small penetration to proceed without any difficulties, I shall abstain from a prolixity which at present is not very necessary. I shall only caution the reader to advance with the clue which we have put into his hand—namely, that whenever the prophets mention the blessedness of the faithful, scarcely any vestiges of which are discernible in the present life, he should recur to this distinction: that in order to the better elucidation of the divine goodness, the prophets represented it to the people in a figurative manner, but that they gave such a representation of it as would withdraw the mind from earth and time and the elements of this world, all which must ere long perish, and would necessarily excite to a contemplation of the felicity of the future spiritual life.

The chapter ends with a section (23) in which we are told that "Christ promises to his people no other kingdom of heaven than that where they may sit down with Abraham, Isaac, and Jacob."

In chapter 11, "The Differences of the Two Testaments," Calvin points out that in the Old Testament the future hope is represented by the figures of terrestrial blessings. Its images and shadows anticipate the New Testament revelation, but dimly.

11. 8. *Five differences of the New Testament from the Old*

Now let us explain the comparison of the Apostle in all its branches. In the first place, the Old Testament is literal, because it was promulgated without the efficacy of the Spirit; the New is spiritual, because the Lord has engraved it in a spiritual manner on the hearts of men. The second contrast, therefore, serves as an elucidation of the first. The Old Testament is the revelation of death, because it can only involve all mankind in a curse; the New is the instrument of life, because it delivers us from the curse and restores us to favor with God. The former is the ministry of condemnation, because it convicts all the children of Adam of unrighteousness; the latter is the ministry of righteousness, because it reveals the mercy of God, by which we are made righteous. The last contrast must be referred to the legal ceremonies. The law having an image of things that were at a distance, it was necessary that in time it should be abolished and disappear. The gospel, exhibiting the body itself, retains a firm and perpetual stability. Jeremiah calls even the moral law a weak and frail covenant, but for another reason — namely, because it was soon broken by the sudden defection of an ungrateful people. But as such a violation arises from the fault of the people, it cannot be properly attributed to the Testament. The ceremonies, however, which at the advent of Christ were abolished by their own weakness, contained in themselves the cause of their abrogation. Now this difference between the "letter" and the "spirit" is not to be understood as if the Lord had given his law to the Jews without any beneficial result, without one of them being converted to him; but it is used in a way of comparison, to display the plenitude of grace with which the same Legislator, assuming as it were a new character, has honored the preaching of the gospel. For if we survey the multitude of those, from among all nations, whom, by the influence of his Spirit in the preaching of the gospel, the Lord has regenerated and gathered into communion with his Church, we shall say that those of the ancient Israelites who cordially and sincerely embraced the covenant of the Lord were extremely few, though, if estimated by themselves without any comparison, they amounted to a considerable number.

These differences are further discussed, and Calvin notes that with the advent of Christ God has not changed the doctrine but the way of imparting it.

Calvin then proceeds to argue that in order to act as our mediator with the Father it was necessary that Christ should become man (ch. 12); that he assumed real humanity, not the semblance of it (ch. 13); that he possessed the two natures, of God and of man, in one Person (ch. 14); and that he exercises the offices of prophet, king, and priest (ch. 15). An ample chapter (ch. 16) is given to Christ's specific work of redemption, his death, resurrection, and ascension. Not to lose us, his creatures, God discovers something in us to love and abolishes our guilt by the expiation of Christ's death. Calvin interprets Christ's "descent into Hell" to mean that Christ's agony was intensified in his death by the fact that he was contending for us with the power of eternal death. The resurrection and ascension are the triumphant completion of this redeeming work: "He has opened the way to the kingdom of heaven that had been closed by Adam" (sec. 16) and he will appear again in ineffable majesty. Chapter 17 has the theme that Christ has merited salvation for us, not, as absurdly suggested, for himself.

BOOK III

On the Manner of Receiving the Grace of Christ, the Benefits Which We Derive from It, and the Effects Which Follow It

Having dealt with the portions of the Creed which refer to the Father and the Son, Calvin in Book III expounds the work of the Holy Spirit in making the grace of Christ available to men. In chapter 1, on the secret operation of the Spirit, faith is called the Spirit's "principal work" (sec. 4). Chapter 2 has the title: "Faith Defined and Its Properties Described." Faith, says Calvin, "consists not in ignorance but in knowledge," knowledge of God and of his will. It is not reverence for the Church (secs. 3-4).

2. 6. *Faith as knowledge of his will for us*

This, then, is the true knowledge of Christ: to receive him as he is offered by the Father, that is, invested with his gospel; for, as he is appointed to be the object of our faith, so we cannot advance in the right way to him without the guidance of the gospel. The gospel certainly opens to us those treasures of grace without which Christ would profit us little. Thus Paul connects faith as an inseparable concomitant with doctrine where he says, "Ye have not so learned Christ; if so be that ye have been taught by him, as the truth is in Jesus." [1] Yet I do not so far restrict faith to the gospel but that I admit Moses and the prophets to have delivered what was sufficient for its establishment; but because the gospel exhibits a fuller manifestation of Christ, it is justly styled by Paul "the words of faith and of good doctrine." [2] For the same reason, in an-

[1] Eph. 4. 20, 21.
[2] I Tim. 4. 6.

63

other place he represents the law as abolished by the coming of faith,[3] comprehending under this term the new kind of teaching by which Christ, since his appearance as our Master, has given a brighter display of the mercy of the Father and a more explicit testimony concerning our salvation. The more easy and convenient method for us will be to descend regularly from the genus to the species. In the first place, we must be apprised that faith has a perpetual relation to the word, and can no more be separated from it than the rays from the sun whence they proceed. Therefore God proclaims by Isaiah, "Hear, and your souls shall live." [4] And that the word is the fountain of faith is evident from this language of John: "These are written, that ye might believe." [5] The Psalmist also, intending to exhort the people to faith, says, "Today, if ye will hear his voice" [6]—and "to hear" generally means "to believe." Lastly, it is not without reason that in Isaiah God distinguishes the children of the Church from strangers by this character: that they shall all be his disciples and be taught by him; [7] for if this were a benefit common to all, why should he address himself to a few? Correspondent with this is the general use of the words "believers" and "disciples" as synonymous, by the evangelists on all occasions, and by Luke in particular very frequently in the Acts of the Apostles, in the ninth chapter of which he extends the latter epithet even to a woman. Wherefore, if faith decline in the smallest degree from this object, toward which it ought to be directed, it no longer retains its own nature but becomes an uncertain credulity and an erroneous excursion of the mind. The same divine word is the foundation by which faith is sustained and supported, from which it cannot be moved without an immediate downfall. Take away the word, then, and there will be no faith left. We are not here disputing whether the ministry of men be necessary to disseminate the word of God, by which faith

3 Gal. 3. 23-25.
4 Isa. 55. 3.
5 John 20. 31.
6 Ps. 95. 7.
7 Isa. 54. 13.

is produced, which we shall discuss in another place; but we assert that the word itself, however it may be conveyed to us, is like a mirror in which faith may behold God. Whether, therefore, God in this instance use the agency of men, or whether he operate solely by his own power, he always discovers himself by his word to those whom he designs to draw to himself.[8] Whence Paul defines faith as an obedience rendered to the gospel, and praises the service of faith.[9] For the apprehension of faith is not confined to our knowing that there is a God, but chiefly consists in our understanding what is his disposition toward us. For it is not of so much importance to us to know what he is in himself as what he is willing to be to us. We find, therefore, that faith is a knowledge of the will of God respecting us, received from his word. And the foundation of this is a previous persuasion of the divine veracity, any doubt of which being entertained in the mind, the authority of the word will be dubious and weak, or rather it will be of no authority at all. Nor is it sufficient to believe that the veracity of God is incapable of deception or falsehood, unless you also admit, as beyond all doubt, that whatever proceeds from him is sacred and inviolable truth.

The discussion of faith continues. Calvin rejects the scholastic distinction between "formed" and "unformed" faith. Faith is temporary in the reprobate. Its certainty and fruits are discussed, and the definition is further explained.

2. 28. *Faith does not secure for us worldly comfort but assures us of God's fatherly love*

Now in the divine benevolence, which is affirmed to be the object of faith, we apprehend the possession of salvation and everlasting life to be obtained. For if no good can be wanting when God is propitious, we have a sufficient certainty of salva-

8 Rom. 1. 5.
9 Phil. 2. 17.

tion when he himself assures us of his love. "O God, cause thy face to shine, and we shall be saved," [1] says the Psalmist. Hence the Scriptures represent this as the sum of our salvation: that he has "abolished" all "enmity" [2] and received us into his favor. In which they imply that, since God is reconciled to us, there remains no danger, but that all things will prosper with us. Wherefore faith, having apprehended the love of God, has promises for the present life and the life to come, and a solid assurance of all blessings; but it is such an assurance as may be derived from the divine word. For faith certainly promises itself neither longevity nor honor nor wealth in the present state—since the Lord has not been pleased to appoint any of these things for us—but is contented with this assurance: that whatever we may want of the conveniences or necessaries of this life, yet God will never leave us. But its principal security consists in an expectation of the future life, which is placed beyond all doubt by the word of God. For whatever miseries and calamities may on earth await those who are the objects of the love of God, they cannot prevent the divine benevolence from being a source of complete felicity. Therefore, when we meant to express the perfection of blessedness, we have mentioned the grace of God as the fountain from which every species of blessings flows down to us. And we may generally observe in the Scriptures that when they treat not only of eternal salvation but of any blessing we enjoy, our attention is recalled to the love of God. For which reason David says that "the loving-kindness of God," when experienced in a pious heart, "is better" and more desirable "than life" itself.[3] Finally, if we have an abundance of all things to the extent of our desires, but are uncertain of the love or hatred of God, our prosperity will be cursed and therefore miserable. But if the paternal countenance of God shine on us, even our miseries will be blessed, because they will be

1 Ps. 80. 3.
2 Eph. 2. 14, 15.
3 Ps. 63. 3.

converted into aids of our salvation.[4] Thus Paul, after an enumeration of all possible adversities, glories that they can never separate us from the love of God; and in his prayers he always begins with the grace of God, from which all prosperity proceeds. David likewise opposes the divine favor alone against all the terrors which disturb us: "Though I walk through the valley of the shadow of death," says he, "I will fear no evil, for thou art with me." [5] And we always feel our minds wavering unless, contented with the grace of God, they seek their peace in it and are deeply impressed with the sentiment of the Psalmist: "Blessed is the nation whose God is the Lord; and the people whom he hath chosen for his own inheritance." [6]

Faith is in necessary harmony with Scripture and is sealed on our hearts by the Holy Spirit. Believers may have their faith disturbed but not destroyed. The chapter closes with a discussion of the relation of faith and hope (secs. 42-45).

In chapter 3 Calvin treats repentance and regeneration, and the relation of these to faith. Repentance, a conversion to God (sec. 3), involves mortification of the flesh and vivification of the spirit (sec. 8). The implication of these terms, and the fruits of repentance, are examined. Repentance continues until death (sec. 20). Calvin discusses the nature of the sin against the Holy Spirit, citing instances in Scripture of the impenitence of the reprobate. He deals severely with scholastic teachings on penance and confession in chapter 4. He argues for secret confession to God and, where useful, voluntary confession before men, especially to a minister. In chapter 5 we find an attack on the doctrine of purgatory and indulgences. Calvin associates with the treatment of regeneration the ensuing five chapters (6-10) on the Christian life.

[4] Rom. 8. 39.
[5] Ps. 23. 4.
[6] Ps. 33. 12.

6. 2. *Love of righteousness and holiness*

This Scripture plan, of which we are now treating, consists chiefly in these two things: the first, that a love of righteousness, to which we have otherwise no natural propensity, be instilled and introduced into our hearts; the second, that a rule be prescribed to us to prevent our taking any devious steps in the race of righteousness. Now, in the recommendation of righteousness, it uses a great number of very excellent arguments, many of which we have before noticed on different occasions, and some we shall briefly touch on in this place. With what better foundation can it begin than when it admonishes us that we ought to be holy because *our God is holy?* [1] For when we were dispersed like scattered sheep, and lost in the labyrinth of the world, he gathered us together again that he might associate us to himself. When we hear any mention of our union with God, we should remember that holiness must be the bond of it; not that we attain communion with him by the merit of holiness (since it is rather necessary for us, in the first place, to adhere to him, in order that, being endowed with his holiness, we may follow whither he calls), but because it is a peculiar property of his glory not to have any intercourse with iniquity and uncleanness. Wherefore also it teaches that this is the end of our vocation, which it is requisite for us always to keep in view if we desire to correspond to the design of God in calling us. For to what purpose was it that we were delivered from the iniquity and pollution of the world, in which we had been immerged, if we permit ourselves to wallow in them as long as we live? Besides, it also admonishes us that, to be numbered among the people of God, we must inhabit the holy city of Jerusalem,[2] which, he having consecrated it to himself, cannot without impiety be profaned by impure inhabitants. Whence these expressions: "He shall abide in the tabernacle of the Lord, that walketh uprightly and worketh

1 Lev. 19. 2; I Pet. 1. 16.
2 Isa. 35. 10.

righteousness," etc.,[3] because it is very unbecoming the sanctuary which he inhabits to be rendered as filthy as a stable.

6. 3. *Christ our example*

And as a further incitement to us, it shows that as God the Father has reconciled us to himself in Christ, so he has exhibited to us in him a pattern to which it is his will that we should be conformed.[1] Now let those who are of opinion that the philosophers have the only just and orderly systems of moral philosophy show me, in any of their works, a more excellent economy than that which I have stated. When they intend to exhort us to the sublimest virtue, they advance no argument but that we ought to live agreeably to nature; but the Scripture deduces its exhortation from the true source when it not only enjoins us to refer our life to God the author of it, to whom it belongs, but, after having taught us that we are degenerated from the original state in which we were created, adds that Christ, by whom we have been reconciled to God, is proposed to us as an example, whose character we should exhibit in our lives. What can be required more efficacious than this one consideration? Indeed, what can be required besides? For if the Lord has adopted us as his sons on this condition—that we exhibit in our life an imitation of Christ, the bond of our adoption—unless we addict and devote ourselves to righteousness, we not only most perfidiously revolt from our Creator but also abjure him as our Saviour. The Scripture derives matter of exhortation from all the blessings of God which it recounts to us, and from all the parts of our salvation. It argues that since God has discovered himself as a Father to us, we must be convicted of the basest ingratitude unless we, on our part, manifest ourselves to be his children; that since Christ has purified us in the laver of his blood, and has communicated this purification by baptism, it does not become us to be defiled with fresh pollution; that since he has united us

3 Ps. 15. 1, 2; 24. 3, 4.
1 Rom. 6. 4 ff.; 8. 29.

to his body, we should, as his members, solicitously beware lest we asperse ourselves with any blemish or disgrace; that since he who is our Head has ascended to heaven, we ought to divest ourselves of all terrestrial affection and aspire thither with all our soul; that since the Holy Spirit has dedicated us as temples to God, we should use our utmost exertions that the glory of God may be displayed by us and ought not to allow ourselves to be profaned with the pollution of sin; that since both our soul and our body are destined to heavenly incorruption and a never-fading crown, we ought to exert our most strenuous efforts to preserve them pure and uncorrupt till the day of the Lord. These, I say, are the best foundations for the proper regulation of the life, such as we cannot find in the philosophers, who, in the recommendation of virtue, never rise above the natural dignity of man.

6. 4. *A doctrine not of the tongue but of the heart and life*

This is a proper place to address those who have nothing but the name and the symbol of Christ and yet would be denominated Christians. But with what face do they glory in his sacred name? For none have any intercourse with Christ but those who have received the true knowledge of him from the word of the gospel. Now, the Apostle denies that any have rightly learned Christ who have not been taught that they must put off the old man, which is corrupt according to the deceitful lusts, and put on Christ.[1] Their knowledge of Christ, then, is proved to be a false and injurious pretense, with whatever eloquence and volubility they may talk concerning the gospel. For it is a doctrine not of the tongue but of the life; and is not apprehended merely with the understanding and memory, like other sciences, but is then only received when it possesses the whole soul and finds a seat and residence in the inmost affection of the heart. Let them, therefore, either cease to insult God by boasting themselves to be what they are not, or show themselves disciples not unworthy of Christ,

1 Eph. 4. 20 ff.

their Master. We have allotted the first place to the doctrine which contains our religion because it is the origin of our salvation; but that it may not be unprofitable to us, it must be transfused into our breast, pervade our manners, and thus transform us into itself. If the philosophers are justly incensed against, and banish with disgrace from their society, those who, while they profess an art which ought to be a rule of life, convert it into a sophistical loquacity, with how much better reason may we detest those sophists who are contented to have the gospel on their lips when its efficacy ought to penetrate the inmost affections of the heart, to dwell in the soul and to affect the whole man with a hundred times more energy than the frigid exhortations of the philosophers!

6. 5. *Perfection not to be demanded, but progress*

Yet I would not insist upon it as absolutely necessary that the manners of a Christian should breathe nothing but the perfect gospel—which, nevertheless, ought both to be wished and to be aimed at. But I do not so rigorously require evangelical perfection as not to acknowledge as a Christian one who has not yet attained to it; for then all would be excluded from the Church, since no man can be found who is not still at a great distance from it, and many have hitherto made but a very small progress whom it would, nevertheless, be unjust to reject. What then? Let us set before our eyes that mark to which alone our pursuit must be directed. Let that be prescribed as the goal toward which we must earnestly tend. For it is not lawful for you to make such a compromise with God as to undertake a part of the duties prescribed to you in his word and to omit part of them at your own pleasure. For, in the first place, he everywhere recommends integrity as a principal branch of his worship, by which he intends a sincere simplicity of heart, free from all guile and falsehood, the opposite of which is a double heart; as though it had been said that the beginning of a life of uprightness is spiritual, when the internal affection of the mind is unfeignedly devoted to God in the cultivation of holiness and righteousness. But since no man in this terrestrial and corporeal prison has strength sufficient to press forward in his course with a due degree of alacrity, and the majority are oppressed with such great debility that they stagger and halt and even creep on the ground, and so make very inconsiderable advances—let us everyone proceed according to our small ability and prosecute the journey we have begun. No man will be so unhappy but that he may every day make some progress, however small. Therefore let us not cease to strive, that we may be incessantly advancing in the way of the Lord; nor let us despair on account of the smallness of our success; for however our success may not correspond to our wishes, yet our labor is not lost when this day surpasses the preceding one; provided that, with sincere simplicity, we keep our end in view, and press forward to the goal, not practicing self-adulation nor indulging our own evil propensities, but perpetually exerting our endeavors after increasing degrees of amelioration, till we shall have arrived at a perfection of goodness, which, indeed, we seek and pursue as long as we live, and shall then attain, when, divested of all corporeal infirmity, we shall be admitted by God into complete communion with him.

Chapters 7 and 8 deal in moving terms with self-denial for our neighbor's sake and the bearing of the cross.

9. 1. *The religious view of life's vicissitudes*

With whatever kind of tribulation we may be afflicted, we should always keep this end in view: to habituate ourselves to a contempt of the present life, that we may thereby be excited to meditation on that which is to come. For the Lord, well knowing our strong natural inclination to a brutish love of the world, adopts a most excellent method to reclaim us and rouse us from our insensibility, that we may not be too tenaciously attached to that foolish affection. There is not one of us who is not desirous of appearing, through the whole course of his life, to aspire and strive after celestial immortality. For we are ashamed of excelling in no respect the brutal herds, whose condition would not be at all inferior to ours unless there remained to us a hope of eternity after death. But if you examine the designs, pursuits, and actions of every individual, you will find nothing in them but what is terrestrial. Hence that stupidity, that the mental eyes, dazzled with the vain splendor of riches, power, and honors, cannot see to any considerable distance. The heart also, occupied and oppressed with avarice, ambition, and other inordinate desires, cannot rise to any eminence. In a word, the whole soul, fascinated by carnal allurements, seeks its felicity on earth. To oppose this evil, the Lord, by continual lessons of miseries, teaches his children the vanity of the present life. That they may not promise themselves profound and secure peace in it, therefore he permits them to be frequently disquieted and infested with wars or tumults, with robberies or other injuries. That they may not aspire with too much avidity after transient and uncertain riches, or depend on those which they possess—sometimes by exile, sometimes by the sterility of the land, sometimes by a conflagration, sometimes by other means, he reduces them to indigence, or at least confines them within the limits of mediocrity. That they may not be too complacently delighted with conjugal blessings, he either causes them to be distressed with the wickedness of their wives, or humbles them with a wicked offspring, or afflicts them with want or loss of children. But if in all these things he is more indulgent to them, yet that they may not be inflated with vainglory or improper confidence, he shows them by diseases and dangers the unstable and transitory nature of all mortal blessings. We therefore truly derive advantage from the discipline of the cross only when we learn that this life, considered in itself, is unquiet, turbulent, miserable in numberless instances, and in no respect altogether happy, and that all its reputed blessings are uncertain, transient, vain, and adulterated with a mixture of many evils; and in consequence of this at once conclude that nothing can be sought or expected on earth but conflict, and that when we think of a crown we must raise our eyes toward heaven. For it must be admitted that the mind is never seriously excited to desire and meditate on the future life without having previously imbibed a contempt of the present.

9. 2. *We are prone to forget that we are mortal*

There is no medium between these two extremes: either the earth must become vile in our estimation, or it must retain our immoderate love. Wherefore, if we have any concern about eternity, we must use our most diligent efforts to extricate ourselves from these fetters. Now, since the present life has numerous blandishments to attract us, and much pleasure, beauty, and sweetness to delight us, it is very necessary to our highest interests that we should be frequently called off, that we may not be fascinated with such allurements. For what would be the consequence if we were perpetually happy in the enjoyment of the blessings of this life, since we cannot, even by the incessant stimulus of calamity after calamity, be sufficiently aroused to a consideration of its misery? That human life is like a vapor or a shadow is not only known to the learned, but even the vulgar have no proverb more common; and perceiving it to be a thing the knowledge of which would be eminently useful, they have represented it in many remarkable sentences. But there is scarcely anything which we more carelessly consider or sooner forget, for we undertake everything as though we were erecting for ourselves an immortality on earth. If a funeral pass by or we walk among the tombs, because the image of death is then presented to our eyes we philosophize, I confess, in an admirable manner concerning the vanity of the present life; although even that is not always the case, for frequently we are quite unaffected with all these things. But when this effect is produced, our philosophy is momentary, vanishing as soon as we withdraw, and leaving not even the smallest vestige behind it; in short, it passes away and is forgotten just like the plaudits of a theater at any entertaining exhibition. And forgetting not only death but mortality itself, as though no rumor concerning it had ever reached us, we relapse into a supine security of immortality on earth. If anyone, in the meantime, reminds us of the unwelcome proverb that man is a creature of a day, we acknowledge the truth of it indeed, but with such inattention that the idea of perpetually living here still remains fixed in our minds. Who, then, can deny that it is highly useful to us all, I do not say to be admonished by words, but by every possible evidence to be convinced of the miserable condition of the present life; since even after we are convinced of it, we scarcely cease to be besotted with a perverse and foolish admiration of it, as though it contained the greatest attainable blessings? But if it be necessary for God to instruct us, it is, on the other hand, our duty to listen to him when he calls and rebukes our sluggishness, in order that, despising the world, we may apply ourselves with our whole heart to meditate on the life which is to come.

Section 3 stresses the value of this life as prelude to the heavenly.

9. 4. *Hope of the enjoyment of God's presence makes this life bearable*

Now whatever is abstracted from the corrupt love of this life should be added to the desire of a better. I grant, indeed, the correctness of their opinion who considered it as the greatest blessing not to be born, and as the next to die immediately. For, being heathens, destitute of the knowledge of God and of true religion, what could they see in it but unhappiness and misery? Nor was there anything irrational in the conduct of those who mourned and wept at the births of their relations and solemnly rejoiced at their funerals. But they practiced this without any advantage; for, destitute of the true doctrine of faith, they did not perceive how that can conduce to the benefit of the pious which in itself is neither blessed nor desirable; and so their views terminated in despair. It should be the object of believers, therefore, in judging of this mortal life, that, understanding it to be of itself nothing but misery, they may apply themselves wholly, with increasing cheerfulness and readiness, to meditate on the future and eternal life. When we come to this comparison, then indeed the former may be not only securely neglected but, in competition with the latter, altogether despised and abhorred. For if heaven is our country, what is the earth but a place of exile? If the departure out of the world is an entrance into life, what is the world but a sepulcher? What is a continuance in it but an absorption in death? If deliverance from the body is an introduction into complete liberty, what is the body but a prison? If to enjoy the presence of God is the summit of felicity, is it not misery to be destitute of it? But till we escape out of the world, "we are absent from the Lord." [1] Therefore, if the terrestrial life be compared with the celestial, it should undoubtedly be despised and accounted of no value. It certainly is never to be hated, except inasmuch as it keeps us obnoxious to sin, although even that hatred is not properly to be applied to life itself. It becomes us, however, to be so affected with weariness or hatred of it as to desire its end, but to be also prepared to remain in it during the divine pleasure; that is to say, our weariness should be remote from all murmuring and impatience. For it is a post at which the Lord has placed us, to be retained by us till he call us away. Paul, indeed, bewails his lot, that he is kept in bondage by the fetters of the body longer than he would wish, and sighs with an ardent desire of deliverance; [2] nevertheless, obedient to the divine authority, he professes himself prepared for both, for he acknowledges himself under an obligation to God to glorify his name either by life or by death,[3] but that it belongs to the

1 II Cor. 5. 6.
2 Rom. 7. 24.
3 Phil. 1. 20.

Lord to determine what will conduce most to his glory. Therefore, if it becomes us "to live and to die to the Lord," [4] let us leave the limits of our life and death to his decision; yet in such a manner as ardently to desire and continually to meditate on the latter, but to despise the former in comparison with future immortality, and on account of the servitude of sin to wish to forsake it whenever it shall please the Lord.

It is monstrous for Christians to fear death: their state would be deplorable if they did not look toward heaven.

10. 1. *On pilgrimage, we use his blessings required for our journey*

By such principles, the Scripture also fully instructs us in the right use of terrestrial blessings—a thing that ought not to be neglected in a plan for the regulation of life. For if we must live, we must also use the necessary supports of life; nor can we avoid even those things which appear to subserve our pleasures rather than our necessities. It behooves us, therefore, to observe moderation, that we may use them with a pure conscience, whether for necessity or for pleasure. This the Lord prescribes in his word when he teaches us that to his servants the present life is like a pilgrimage, in which they are traveling toward the celestial kingdom. If we are only to pass through the earth, we ought undoubtedly to make such a use of its blessings as will rather assist than retard us in our journey. It is not without reason, therefore, that Paul advises us to use this world as though we used it not, and to buy with the same disposition with which we sell.[1] But as this is a difficult subject, and there is danger of falling into one of two opposite errors, let us endeavor to proceed on safe ground, that we may avoid both extremes. For there have been some, in other respects good and holy men, who, seeing that intemperance and luxury, unless restrained with more

4 Rom. 14. 7, 8.
1 I Cor. 7. 30, 31.

than ordinary severity, would perpetually indulge the most extravagant excesses, and desiring to correct such a pernicious evil, have adopted the only method which occurred to them by permitting men to use corporeal blessings no further than their necessity should absolutely require. This advice was well intended, but they were far too austere. For they committed the very dangerous error of imposing on the conscience stricter rules than those which are prescribed to it by the word of the Lord. By restriction within the demands of necessity they meant an abstinence from everything from which it is possible to abstain; so that, according to them, it would scarcely be lawful to eat or drink anything but bread and water. Others have discovered still greater austerity, like Crates the Theban, who is said to have thrown his wealth into the sea from an apprehension that, unless it were destroyed, he should himself be destroyed by it. On the contrary, many in the present day who seek a pretext to excuse intemperance in the use of external things, and at the same time desire to indulge the licentiousness of the flesh, assume as granted, what I by no means concede to them, that this liberty is not to be restricted by any limitation, but that it ought to be left to the conscience of every individual to use as much as he thinks lawful for himself. I grant, indeed, that it is neither right nor possible to bind the conscience with the fixed and precise rules of law in this case, but since the Scripture delivers general rules for the lawful use of earthly things, our practice ought certainly to be regulated by them.

10. 2. *God's gifts not for necessity only, but for delight*

It must be laid down as a principle that the use of the gifts of God is not erroneous when it is directed to the same end for which the Creator himself has created and appointed them for us, since he has created them for our benefit, not for our injury. Wherefore no one will observe a more proper rule than he who shall diligently regard this end. Now if we consider for what end he has created the various kinds of aliment, we shall find that he intended to provide not only for our necessity but likewise for our pleasure and delight. So in clothing, he has had in view not mere necessity but propriety and decency. In herbs, trees, and fruits, beside their various uses, his design has been to gratify us by graceful forms and pleasant odors. For if this were not true, the Psalmist would not recount among the divine blessings "wine that maketh glad the heart of man, and oil to make his face to shine"; [1] nor would the Scriptures universally declare, in commendation of his goodness, that he has given all these things to men. And even the natural properties of things sufficiently indicate for what end, and to what extent, it is lawful to use them. But shall the Lord have endowed flowers with such beauty to present itself to our eyes, with such sweetness of smell to impress our sense of smelling, and shall it be unlawful for our eyes to be affected with the beautiful sight, or our olfactory nerves with the agreeable odor? What! has he not made such a distinction of colors as to render some more agreeable than others? Has he not given to gold and silver, to ivory and marble, a beauty which makes them more precious than other metals or stones? In a word, has he not made many things worthy of our estimation, independently of any necessary use?

10. 3. *Neither inhuman austerity nor indulgence*

Let us discard, therefore, that inhuman philosophy which, allowing no use of the creatures but what is absolutely necessary, not only malignantly deprives us of the lawful enjoyment of the divine beneficence, but which cannot be embraced till it has despoiled man of all his senses and reduced him to a senseless block. But, on the other hand, we must with equal diligence oppose the licentiousness of the flesh, which, unless it be rigidly restrained, transgresses every bound. And, as I have observed, it has its advocates who, under the pretext of liberty, allow it everything. In the first place, it will be one check to it if it be concluded that all things are made for us in

[1] Ps. 104. 15.

order that we may know and acknowledge their Author and
celebrate his goodness toward us by giving him thanks. What
will become of thanksgiving if you overcharge yourself with
dainties or wine so as to be stupefied or rendered unfit for
the duties of piety and the business of your station? Where
is any acknowledgment of God if your body, in consequence
of excessive abundance being inflamed with the vilest passions,
infects the mind with its impurity, so that you cannot discern
what is right or virtuous? Where is gratitude toward God for
clothing if, on account of our sumptuous apparel, we admire
ourselves and despise others? If, with the elegance and beauty
of it, we prepare ourselves for unchastity? Where is our acknowledgment of God if our minds be fixed on the splendor
of our garments? For many so entirely devote all their senses
to the pursuit of pleasure that the mind is, as it were, buried
in it; many are so delighted with marble, gold, and pictures
that they become like statues—are, as it were, metamorphosed
into metal, and resemble painted images. The flavor of meats
or the sweetness of odors so stupefies some that they have no
relish for anything spiritual. The same may be observed in
other cases. Wherefore it is evident that this principle lays
some restraint on the license of abusing the divine bounties
and confirms the rule given us by Paul, that we "make not
provision for the flesh, to fulfill the lusts thereof"; [1] which, if
they are allowed too much latitude, will transgress all the
bounds of temperance and moderation.

Warnings against misuse of temporal blessings follow.

10. 6. *The Christian in his vocation*

Lastly, it is to be remarked that the Lord commands every
one of us, in all the actions of life, to regard his vocation.
For he knows with what great inquietude the human mind
is inflamed, with what desultory levity it is hurried hither and
thither, and how insatiable is its ambition to grasp different

[1] Rom. 13. 14.

things at once. Therefore, to prevent universal confusion
being produced by our folly and temerity, he has appointed
to all their particular duties in different spheres of life. And
that no one might rashly transgress the limits prescribed, he
has styled such spheres of life "vocations," or "callings." Every
individual's line of life, therefore, is, as it were, a post assigned
him by the Lord, that he may not wander about in uncertainty all his days. And so necessary is this distinction that
in his sight all our actions are estimated according to it, and
often very differently from the sentence of human reason and
philosophy. There is no exploit esteemed more honorable,
even among philosophers, than to deliver our country from
tyranny; but the voice of the celestial Judge openly condemns
the private man who lays violent hands on a tyrant. It is not
my design, however, to stay to enumerate examples. It is sufficient if we know that the principle and foundation of right
conduct in every case is the vocation of the Lord, and that he
who disregards it will never keep the right way in the duties
of his station. He may sometimes, perhaps, achieve something
apparently laudable; but however it may appear in the eyes
of men, it will be rejected at the throne of God; besides which,
there will be no consistency between the various parts of his
life. Our life, therefore, will then be best regulated when it is
directed to this mark, since no one will be impelled by his own
temerity to attempt more than is compatible with his calling,
because he will know that it is unlawful to transgress the
bounds assigned him. He that is in obscurity will lead a private life without discontent so as not to desert the station in
which God has placed him. It will also be no small alleviation
of his cares, labors, troubles, and other burdens when a man
knows that in all these things he has God for his guide. The
magistrate will execute his office with greater pleasure, the
father of a family will confine himself to his duty with more
satisfaction, and all, in their respective spheres of life, will
bear and surmount the inconveniences, cares, disappointments,
and anxieties which befall them, when they shall be persuaded
that every individual has his burden laid upon him by God.

Hence also will arise peculiar consolation, since there will be no employment so mean and sordid (provided we follow our vocation) as not to appear truly respectable and be deemed highly important in the sight of God.

Chapters 11 to 18 are occupied with various facets of the doctrine of justification.

11. 2. *Terms of discussion explained*

But that we may not stumble at the threshold (which would be the case were we to enter on a disputation concerning a subject not understood by us), let us first explain the meaning of these expressions: "to be justified in the sight of God," "to be justified by faith" or "by works." He is said to be "justified in the sight of God" who in the divine judgment is reputed righteous and accepted on account of his righteousness; for as iniquity is abominable to God, so no sinner can find favor in his sight, as a sinner or so long as he is considered as such. Wherever sin is, therefore, it is accompanied with the wrath and vengeance of God. He is justified who is considered not as a sinner, but as a righteous person, and on that account stands in safety before the tribunal of God, where all sinners are confounded and ruined. As, if an innocent man be brought under an accusation before the tribunal of a just judge, when judgment is passed according to his innocence, he is said to be justified or acquitted before the judge, so he is justified before God who, not being numbered among sinners, has God for a witness and asserter of his righteousness. Thus he must be said, therefore, to be "justified by works" whose life discovers such purity and holiness as to deserve the character of righteousness before the throne of God, or who, by the integrity of his works, can answer and satisfy the divine judgment. On the other hand, he will be "justified by faith" who, being excluded from the righteousness of works, apprehends by faith the righteousness of Christ, invested in which he appears in the sight of God not as a sinner but as a righteous man. Thus we simply explain justification to be an acceptance, by which God receives us into his favor and esteems us as righteous persons; and we say that it consists in the remission of sins and the imputation of the righteousness of Christ.

After some further exposition, Calvin gives considerable space to a refutation of the opinions of Andrew Osiander, who taught that in justification we benefit by Christ's eternal righteousness rather than, as Calvin holds, by Christ's righteousness acquired through his death and resurrection. He also assails the teaching on works of Peter Lombard and other schoolmen (14-19) and asserts justification by faith alone.

11. 21. *Summary statement on justification*

Now let us examine the truth of what has been asserted in the definition—that the righteousness of faith is a reconciliation with God which consists solely in remission of sins.[1] We must always return to this axiom: that the divine wrath remains on all men as long as they continue to be sinners. This Isaiah has beautifully expressed in the following words: "The Lord's hand is not shortened, that it cannot save; neither is his ear heavy, that it cannot hear; but your iniquities have separated between you and your God, and your sins have hid his face from you, that he will not hear." [2] We are informed that sin makes a division between man and God and turns the divine countenance away from the sinner. Nor can it be otherwise, because it is incompatible with his righteousness to have any communion with sin. Hence the Apostle teaches that man is an enemy to God till he be reconciled to him through Christ.[3] Whom, therefore, the Lord receives into fellowship, him he is said to justify, because he cannot receive anyone into

1 See above, III. 11. 2 (p. 82).
2 Isa. 59. 1, 2.
3 Rom. 5. 8-10.

favor or into fellowship with himself without making him
from a sinner to be a righteous person. This, we add, is accomplished by the remission of sins. For if they whom the
Lord has reconciled to himself be judged according to their
works, they will still be found actually sinners, who, notwithstanding, must be absolved and free from sin. It appears,
then, that those whom God receives are made righteous no
otherwise than as they are purified by being cleansed from
all their defilements by the remission of their sins, so that
such a righteousness may, in one word, be denominated a remission of sins.

Calvin concludes this chapter with emphasis upon the
righteousness of Christ. In chapters 12 and 13 he enlarges
upon the abandonment of self before the righteousness of
God, and links the recognition of God's glory with peace
of conscience.
   Chapter 14, on the beginning and progress of justifica-
tion, distinguishes classes of men as: those merely dead in
sin; hypocritical and nominal Christians; and the regener-
ate. The latter still have defects and are not justified by
their works.

14. 16. *Confidence in works is excluded*

On this subject our minds require to be guarded chiefly
against two pernicious principles: that we place no confidence
in the righteousness of our works, and that we ascribe no
glory to them. The Scriptures everywhere drive us from all
confidence when they declare that all our righteousnesses are
odious in the divine view unless they are perfumed with the
holiness of Christ, and that they can only excite the vengeance of God unless they are supported by his merciful pardon. Thus they leave us nothing to do but to deprecate the
wrath of our Judge with the confession of David, "Enter not
into judgment with thy servant; for in thy sight shall no man

living be justified." [1] And where Job says, "If I be wicked,
woe unto me; and if I be righteous, yet will I not lift up my
head," [2] though he refers to that consummate righteousness of
God compared to which even the angels are deficient, yet he
at the same time shows that, when God comes to judgment,
all men must be dumb. For he not only means that he would
rather freely recede than incur the danger of contending with
the rigor of God, but signifies that he experiences in himself
no other righteousness than what would instantaneously van-
ish before the divine presence. When confidence is destroyed,
all boasting must of necessity be relinquished. For who can
give the praise of righteousness to his works, in which he is
afraid to confide in the presence of God? We must therefore
have recourse to the Lord, in whom we are assured, by Isaiah,
that "all the seed of Israel shall be justified, and shall glory"; [3]
for it is strictly true, as he says in another place, that we are
"the planting of the Lord, that he might be glorified." [4] Our
minds therefore will then be properly purified when they shall
in no degree confide nor glory in our works. But foolish men
are led into such a false and delusive confidence by the error
of always considering their works as the cause of their salvation.

14. 17. *The material cause of salvation is Christ, the instrumental cause, faith*

But if we advert to the four kinds of causes which the
philosophers direct us to consider in the production of effects,
we shall find none of them consistent with works in the accomplishment of our salvation. For the Scripture everywhere
proclaims that the efficient cause of eternal life being procured
for us was the mercy of our heavenly Father and his gratuitous
love toward us; that the material cause is Christ and his obedience, by which he obtained a righteousness for us; and what
shall we denominate the formal and instrumental cause, un-

1 Ps. 143. 2.   3 Isa. 45. 25.
2 Job 10. 15.   4 Isa. 61. 3.

less it be faith? These three John comprehends in one sentence when he says that "God so loved the world that he gave his only begotten Son, that whosoever believeth in him should not perish, but have everlasting life." [1] The final cause the Apostle declares to be both the demonstration of the divine righteousness and the praise of the divine goodness, in a passage in which he also expressly mentions the other three causes. For this is his language to the Romans: "All have sinned, and come short of the glory of God, being justified freely by his grace"; [2] here we have the original source of our salvation, which is the gratuitous mercy of God toward us. There follows "through the redemption that is in Christ Jesus": here we have the matter of our justification. "Through faith in his blood": here he points out the instrumental cause by which the righteousness of Christ is revealed to us. Lastly, he subjoins the end of all when he says, "To declare his righteousness; that he might be just, and the justifier of him which believeth in Jesus." And to suggest, by the way, that this righteousness consists in reconciliation or propitiation, he expressly asserts that Christ was "set forth to be a propitiation." So also in the first chapter to the Ephesians he teaches that we are received into the favor of God through his mere mercy; that it is accomplished by the mediation of Christ; that it is apprehended by faith; and that the end of all is that the glory of the divine goodness may be fully displayed.[3] When we see that every part of our salvation is accomplished without us, what reason have we to confide or to glory in our works? Nor can even the most inveterate enemies of divine grace raise any controversy with us concerning the efficient or the final cause, unless they mean altogether to renounce the authority of the Scripture. Over the material and formal causes they superinduce a false coloring; as if our own works were to share the honor of them with faith and the righteousness of Christ.

1 John 3. 16.
2 Rom. 3. 23 ff.
3 Eph. 1. 5-7, 13.

But this also is contradicted by the Scripture, which affirms that Christ is the sole author of our righteousness and life, and that this blessing of righteousness is enjoyed by faith alone.

There follows a further argument in rejection of the alleged merit of works (ch. 15) and the charges made against the doctrine of unmerited grace (ch. 16). "The harmony between the promises of the Law and those of the Gospel" is affirmed in chapter 17, and in chapter 18 "rewards" are dissociated from any fruits of good works. Chapter 19 is Calvin's treatment of Christian liberty, which has importance for his ethics and politics (see John T. McNeill [ed.], John Calvin on God and Political Duty ["The Library of Liberal Arts," No. 23; New York: The Liberal Arts Press, 1956]).

20. 1. *Faith implies prayer*

From the subjects already discussed, we clearly perceive how utterly destitute man is of every good and in want of all the means of salvation. Wherefore, if he seek for relief in his necessities, he must go out of himself and obtain it from some other quarter. It has been subsequently stated that the Lord voluntarily and liberally manifests himself in his Christ, in whom he offers us all felicity instead of our misery, and opulence instead of our poverty; in whom he opens to our view the treasures of heaven, that our faith may be wholly engaged in the contemplation of his beloved Son, that all our expectation may depend upon him, and that in him all our hope may rest and be fully satisfied. This, indeed, is that secret and recondite philosophy which cannot be extracted from syllogisms but is well understood by those whose eyes God has opened, that in his light they may see light. But since we have been taught by faith to acknowledge that whatever we want for the supply of our necessities is in God and our Lord Jesus Christ, in whom it has pleased the Father all the fullness of his bounty should dwell that we may all draw from it as from a most copious fountain, it remains for us to seek in him, and by prayers to implore of him, that which we have been informed resides in him. Otherwise to know God as the Lord and giver of every good who invites us to supplicate him, but neither to approach him nor to supplicate him, would be equally unprofitable as for a man to neglect a treasure discovered to him buried in the earth. Wherefore the Apostle, to show that true faith cannot but be engaged in calling upon God, has laid down this order: that, as faith is produced by the gospel, so by faith our hearts are brought to invoke the name of the Lord.[1] And this is the same as he had a little before said, that the "Spirit of adoption," who seals the testimony of the gospel in our hearts, encourages our spirits so that they venture to pour out their desires before God, excite "groanings that cannot be uttered," and cry with confidence, "*Abba,* Father." [2] This last subject, therefore, having been before only cursorily mentioned and slightly touched, requires now to be treated more at large.

Prayer is "a communication between God and men" and is not superfluous though our needs are already known to God. It requires a reverent concentration (secs. 2-4).

20. 5. *The conditions of true prayer*

Both these things are highly worthy of observation: first, that whoever engages in prayer should apply all his faculties and attention to it and not be distracted, as is commonly the case, with wandering thoughts, nothing being more contrary to a reverence for God than such levity, which indicates a licentious spirit wholly unrestrained by fear. In this case our exertions must be great in proportion to the difficulty we experience. For no man can be so intent on praying but he may

1 Rom. 10. 13, 14, 17.
2 Rom. 8. 15, 26.

perceive many irregular thoughts intruding on him, and either interrupting or by some oblique digression retarding the course of his devotions. But here let us consider what an indignity it is, when God admits us to familiar intercourse with him, to abuse such great condescension by a mixture of things sacred and profane, while our thoughts are not confined to him by reverential awe; but as if we were conversing with a mean mortal, we quit him in the midst of our prayer and make excursions on every side. We may be assured, therefore, that none are rightly prepared for the exercise of prayer but those who are so affected by the divine majesty as to come to it divested of all earthly cares and affections. And this is indicated by the ceremony of lifting up the hands, that men may remember that they are at a great distance from God unless they lift up their thoughts on high. As it is also expressed in the psalm, "Unto thee do I lift up my soul." [1] And the Scripture frequently uses this mode of expression, "to lift up one's prayer," that they who desire to be heard by God may not sink into lethargic inactivity. To sum up the whole, the greater the liberality of God toward us in gently inviting us to disburden ourselves of our cares by casting them on him, the less excusable are we, unless his signal and incomparable favor preponderate with us beyond everything else and attract us to him in a serious application of all our faculties and attention to the duty of prayer; which cannot be done unless our mind by strenuous exertion rise superior to every impediment. Our second proposition is that we must pray for no more than God permits. For though he enjoins us to pour out our hearts before him,[2] yet he does not carelessly give the reins to affections of folly and depravity; and when he promises to "fulfill the desire" [3] of believers, he does not go to such an extreme of indulgence as to subject himself to their caprice. But offenses against both these rules are common and great; for most men not only presume, without

1 Ps. 25. 1.
2 Ps. 62. 8.
3 Ps. 145. 19.

modesty or reverence, to address God concerning their follies and impudently to utter at his tribunal whatever has amused them in their reveries or dreams, but so great is their folly or stupidity that they dare to obtrude upon God all their foulest desires, which they would be exceedingly ashamed to reveal to men. Some heathens have ridiculed and even detested this presumption, but the vice itself has always prevailed; and hence it was that the ambitious chose Jupiter as their patron; the avaricious, Mercury; the lovers of learning, Apollo and Minerva; the warlike, Mars; and the libidinous, Venus; just as in the present age (as I have lately hinted) men indulge a greater license to their unlawful desires in their prayers than if they were conversing in a jocular manner with their equals. God suffers not his indulgence to be so mocked, but asserts his power and subjects our devotions to his commands. Therefore we ought to remember this passage in John: "This is the confidence that we have in him, that, if we ask anything according to his will, he heareth us." [4] But as our abilities are very unequal to such great perfection, we must seek some remedy to relieve us. As the attention of the mind ought to be fixed on God, so it is necessary that it should be followed by the affection of the heart. But they both remain far below this elevation; or rather, to speak more consistently with truth, they grow weary and fail in the ascent, or are carried a contrary course. Therefore, to assist this imbecility, God gives us the Spirit to be the director of our prayers, to suggest what is right, and to regulate our affections. For "the Spirit helpeth our infirmities; for we know not what we should pray for as we ought; but the Spirit itself maketh intercession for us with groanings which cannot be uttered"; [5] not that he really prays or groans, but he excites within us confidence, desires, and sighs to the conception of which our native powers were altogether inadequate. Nor is it without reason that Paul terms those "groanings" which arise from believers under the influence of the Spirit "unutterable," because they who are

4 I John 5. 14.
5 Rom. 8. 26.

truly engaged in prayers are not ignorant that they are so
perplexed with dubious anxieties that they can scarcely decide
what it is expedient to utter; and even while they are attempting to lisp, they stammer and hesitate; whence it follows that the ability of praying rightly is a peculiar gift.
These things are not said in order that we may indulge our
own indolence, resigning the office of prayer to the Spirit of
God and growing torpid in that negligence to which we are
too prone; according to the impious errors of some, that we
should wait in indolent supineness till he call our minds from
other engagements and draw them to himself; but rather that,
wearied with our sloth and inactivity, we may implore such
assistance of the Spirit. Nor does the Apostle, when he exhorts
us to "pray in the Holy Ghost," [6] encourage us to remit our
vigilance, signifying that the inspiration of the Spirit operates
in the formation of our prayers so as not in the least to impede
or retard our own exertions, since it is the will of God to
prove in this instance the efficacious influence of faith on our
hearts.

*The discussion of prayer in general, including the prayer
of common worship, is followed by an extended and impressive exposition of the petitions of the Lord's Prayer.*

*In chapter 21, entitled "Eternal Election, or God's
Predestination of Some to Salvation and of Others to Destruction," Calvin begins the formal treatment of the doctrine of election. He notes at the outset as a matter of
observation that some never hear the gospel preached and
that those who do respond variously. He warns against
both presumption and timid silence in this field (secs. 1-4).*

21. 5. *The eternal decree of God*

Predestination, by which God adopts some to the hope of
life and adjudges others to eternal death, no one, desirous of
the credit of piety, dares absolutely to deny. But it is involved

[6] Jude 20; I Cor. 14. 15.

in many cavils, especially by those who make foreknowledge the cause of it. We maintain that both belong to God; but it is preposterous to represent one as dependent on the other. When we attribute foreknowledge to God, we mean that all things have ever been, and perpetually remain, before his eyes, so that to his knowledge nothing is future or past, but all things are present; and present in such a manner that he does not merely conceive of them from ideas formed in his mind, as things remembered by us appear present to our minds, but really beholds and sees them as if actually placed before him. And this foreknowledge extends to the whole world and to all the creatures. Predestination we call the eternal decree of God by which he has determined in himself what he would have to become of every individual of mankind. For they are not all created with a similar destiny, but eternal life is foreordained for some and eternal damnation for others. Every man, therefore, being created for one or the other of these ends, we say he is predestined either to life or to death. This God has not only testified in particular persons, but has given a specimen of it in the whole posterity of Abraham, which should evidently show the future condition of every nation to depend upon his decision. "When the Most High divided the nations, when he separated the sons of Adam, the Lord's portion was his people; Jacob was the lot of his inheritance." [1] The separation is before the eyes of all: in the person of Abraham, as in the dry trunk of a tree, one people is peculiarly chosen to the rejection of others; no reason for this appears, except that Moses, to deprive their posterity of all occasion of glorying, teaches them that their exaltation is wholly from God's gratuitous love. . . .

The theme is continued, with Old Testament examples. In chapter 22, "Testimonies of Scripture in Support of This Doctrine," Calvin disputes the notion that election depends on "foreknowledge of merit": it is the gratuitous gift of grace. Chapter 23 is mainly designed to refute those

1 Deut. 32. 8, 9.

who deny reprobation and deals with a series of objec-
tions to this doctrine (secs. 1-12). Calvin's reliance upon
Augustine is illustrated in the next selection.

23. 13. *Augustine on the preaching of predestination*

This doctrine is maliciously and impudently calumniated
by others as subversive of all exhortations to piety of life. This
formerly brought great odium upon Augustine, which he removed by his treatise *On Correction and Grace,* addressed to
Valentine, the perusal of which will easily satisfy all pious and
teachable persons. Yet I will touch on a few things which I
hope will convince such as are honest and not contentious.
How openly and loudly gratuitous election was preached by
Paul we have already seen; was he therefore cold in admonitions and exhortations? Let these good zealots compare his
vehemence with theirs; theirs will be found ice itself in comparison with his incredible fervor. And certainly every scruple
is removed by this principle, that "God hath not called us to
uncleanness, but that everyone should know how to possess his
vessel in sanctification and honor"; [1] and again, that "we are
his workmanship, created in Christ Jesus unto good works,
which God hath before ordained, that we should walk in
them." [2] Indeed, a slight acquaintance with Paul will enable
anyone to understand, without tedious arguments, how easily
he reconciles things which they pretend to be repugnant to
each other. Christ commands men to believe in him. Yet his
limitation is neither false nor contrary to his command when
he says, "No man can come unto me, except it were given unto
him of my Father." [3] Let preaching therefore have its course
to bring men to faith, and by a continual progress to promote
their perseverance. Nor let the knowledge of predestination
be prevented, that the obedient may not be proud as of anything of their own but may glory in the Lord. Christ had some

[1] I Thess. 4. 4, 7.
[2] Eph. 2. 10.
[3] John 6. 65.

particular meaning in saying, "Who hath ears to hear, let him hear." [4] Therefore when we exhort and preach, persons endowed with ears readily obey; and those who are destitute of them exhibit an accomplishment of the Scripture, that hearing they hear not.[5] "But why," says Augustine, "should some have ears, and others not? 'Who hath known the mind of the Lord?' [6] Must that which is evident be denied, because that which is concealed cannot be comprehended?" [7] These observations I have faithfully borrowed from Augustine; but as his words will perhaps have more authority than mine, I will proceed to an exact quotation of them. "If, on hearing this, some persons become torpid and slothful, and, exchanging labor for lawless desire, pursue the various objects of concupiscence, must what is declared concerning the foreknowledge of God be therefore accounted false? If God foreknew that they would be good, will they not be so, in whatever wickedness they now live? And if he foreknew that they would be wicked, will they not be so, in whatever goodness they now appear? Are these, then, sufficient causes why the truths which are declared concerning the foreknowledge of God should be either denied or passed over in silence, especially when the consequence of silence respecting these would be the adoption of other errors? The reason of concealing the truth," he says, "is one thing, and the necessity of declaring it is another. It would be tedious to inquire after all the reasons for passing the truth over in silence, but this is one of them: lest those who understand it not should become worse, while we wish to make those who understand it better informed—who, indeed, are not made wiser by our declaring any such thing, nor are they rendered worse. But since the truth is of such a nature that, when we speak of it, he becomes worse who cannot understand it, and when we are silent about it, he who can un-

4 Matt. 13. 9.

5 Isa. 6. 9.

6 Rom. 11. 34.

7 [Augustine, *De dono perseverantiae* XIV. 37; in Migne, *PL*, XLV, 1016; Eng. tr. in *NPNF*, V, 540.]

derstand it becomes worse, what do we think ought to be done? Should not the truth rather be spoken, that he who is capable may understand it, than buried in silence; the consequence of which would be, not only that neither would know it, but even the more intelligent of the two would become worse, who, if he heard and understood it, would also teach it to many others? And we are unwilling to say what we are authorized to say by the testimony of Scripture. For we are afraid, indeed, lest by speaking we may offend him who cannot understand, but are not afraid lest, in consequence of our silence, he who is capable of understanding the truth may be deceived by falsehood." And condensing this sentiment afterwards into a smaller compass, he places it in a still stronger light. "Wherefore, if the apostles and the succeeding teachers of the Church both piously treated of God's eternal election, and held believers under the discipline of a pious life, what reason have these our opponents, when silenced by the invincible force of truth, to suppose themselves right in maintaining that what is spoken of predestination, although it be true, ought not to be preached to the people? But it must by all means be preached, that he who has ears to hear may hear. But who has them, unless he receives them from him who has promised to bestow them? Certainly he who receives not may reject, provided he who receives takes and drinks, drinks and lives. For as piety must be preached that God may be rightly worshiped, so also must predestination, that he who has ears to hear of the grace of God may glory in God and not in himself." [8]

23. 14. *Man's will cannot resist God's. We desire every man's salvation and leave the result to God*

And yet, being peculiarly desirous of edification, that holy man regulates his mode of teaching the truth so that offense may as far as possible be prudently avoided. For he suggests

8 [Augustine, *op. cit.*, XV, XVI, XX; Migne, *PL*, XLV, 1016-1018, 1026 f.; *NPNF*, V, 541, 546-547.]

that whatever is asserted with truth may also be delivered in a suitable manner. If anyone address the people in such a way as this: "If you believe not, it is because you are by a divine decree already destined to destruction"—he not only cherishes slothfulness, but even encourages wickedness. If anyone extend the declaration to the future—that they who hear will never believe because they are reprobated—this would be rather imprecation than instruction. Such persons, therefore, as foolish teachers or inauspicious, ominous prophets Augustine charges to depart from the Church.[1] In another place, indeed, he justly maintains "that a man then profits by correction when he, who causes whom he pleases to profit even without correction, compassionates and assists. But why some in one way and some in another? Far be it from us to ascribe the choice to the clay instead of the potter."[2] Again afterwards: "When men are either introduced or restored into the way of righteousness by correction, who works salvation in their hearts but he who gives the increase, whoever plants and waters, he whose determination to save is not resisted by any free will of man? It is beyond all doubt, therefore, that the will of God, who has done whatever he has pleased in heaven and in earth, and who has done even things that are yet future, cannot possibly be resisted by the will of man so as to prevent the execution of his purposes since he controls the wills of men according to his pleasure."[3] Again: "When he designs to bring men to himself, does he bind them by corporeal bonds? He acts inwardly; he inwardly seizes their hearts; he inwardly moves their hearts and draws them by their wills, which he has wrought in them." But he immediately subjoins, what must by no means be omitted, "that because we know not who belongs, or does not belong, to the number of the predestinated, it becomes us affectionately to desire the salvation of all. The consequence

---

[1] [Cf. Augustine, *op. cit.*, XXII; Migne, *PL*, XLV, 1028 ff.; *NPNF*, V, 549 f.]

[2] [Augustine, *De correptione et gratia* V. 8; Migne, *PL*, XLIV, 920; *NPNF*, V, 474.]

[3] [Augustine, *op. cit.*, XIV. 43; Migne, *PL*, XLIV, 1942; *NPNF*, V, 489.]

will be that whomsoever we meet we shall endeavor to make him a partaker of peace. But our peace shall rest upon the sons of peace. On our part, therefore, salutary and severe reproof, like a medicine, must be administered to all, that they may neither perish themselves nor destroy others; but it will be the province of God to render it useful to them whom he had foreknown and predestinated." [4]

Chapter 24, "Election Confirmed by the Divine Call. The Destined Destruction of the Reprobate Procured by Themselves," presents Calvin's doctrine of effectual calling and resumes the argument for reprobation. "Let our conclusion be to stand astonished with Paul at so great a mystery" (sec. 17). Book III ends with a chapter (15) on "the final resurrection." Belief in the future resurrection of the dead is based on the resurrection of Christ. There is included a discussion of "eternal felicity" (sec. 10) and of the misery of the reprobate in everlasting estrangement from God (sec. 12).

4 [Augustine, *op. cit.*, XVI. 49; Migne, *PL*, XLIV, 946; *NPNF*, V, 491.]

BOOK IV

On the External Means or Aids by Which God Calls Us into Communion with Christ and Retains Us in It

The "external means" consist of the ministries of the Church, and Book IV is really on "the Holy Catholic Church" of the Creed. Chapter 1 deals with "the true church."

1. 1. *The Church our Mother*

That by the faith of the gospel Christ becomes ours, and we become partakers of the salvation procured by him and of eternal happiness, has been explained in the preceding Book. But as our ignorance and slothfulness—and, I may add, the vanity of our minds—require external aids for the production of faith in our hearts and its increase and progressive advance even to its completion, God has provided such aids in compassion to our infirmity; and that the preaching of the gospel might be maintained, he has deposited this treasure with the Church. He has appointed pastors and teachers, that his people might be taught by their lips; he has invested them with authority; in short, he has omitted nothing that could contribute to a holy unity of faith and to the establishment of good order.[1] First of all, he has instituted sacraments, which we know by experience to be means of the greatest utility for the nourishment and support of our faith. For as, during our confinement in the prison of our flesh, we have not yet attained to the state of angels, God has, in his wonderful providence, accommodated himself to our capacity by prescribing a way in which we might approach him, notwithstanding our

[1] Eph. 4. 11-16.

immense distance from him. Wherefore the order of instruction requires us now to treat of the Church and its government, orders, and power; secondly, of the sacraments; and lastly, of civil government; and at the same time to call off the pious readers from the abuses of the Papacy, by which Satan has corrupted everything that God had appointed to be instrumental to our salvation. I shall begin with the Church, in whose bosom it is God's will that all his children should be collected, not only to be nourished by her assistance and ministry during their infancy and childhood, but also to be governed by her maternal care till they attain a mature age and at length reach the end of their faith. For it is not lawful to "put asunder" those things "which God hath joined together"; [2] that the Church is the mother of all who have him for their Father; and that not only under the law, but since the coming of Christ also, according to the testimony of the Apostle, who declares the new and heavenly Jerusalem to be "the mother of us all." [3]

1. 2. *Catholic, as comprising all the elect*

That article of the Creed in which we profess to believe "the Church" refers not only to the visible Church of which we are now speaking, but likewise to all the elect of God, including the dead as well as the living. The word "believe" is used because it is often impossible to discover any difference between the children of God and the ungodly, between his peculiar flock and wild beasts. The particle "in," interpolated by many, is not supported by any probable reason. I confess that it is generally adopted at present, and is not destitute of the suffrage of antiquity, being found in the Nicene Creed as it is transmitted to us in ecclesiastical history. Yet it is evident from the writings of the Fathers that it was anciently admitted without controversy to say "I believe the Church," not "*in* the Church." For not only is this word not used by Augustine and

2 Mark 10. 9.
3 Gal. 4. 26.

the ancient writer of the work *On the Exposition of the Creed*, which passes under the name of Cyprian, but they particularly remark that there would be an impropriety in the expression if this preposition were inserted, and they confirm their opinion by no trivial reason. For we declare that we believe *in* God because our mind depends upon him as true and our confidence rests in him. But this would not be applicable to the Church, any more than to "the remission of sins" or the "resurrection of the body." Therefore, though I am averse to contentions about words, yet I would rather adopt a proper phraseology adapted to express the subject than affect forms of expression by which the subject would be unnecessarily involved in obscurity. The design of this clause is to teach us that though the devil moves every engine to destroy the grace of Christ, and all the enemies of God exert the most furious violence in the same attempt, yet his grace cannot possibly be extinguished, nor can his blood be rendered barren so as not to produce some fruit. Here we must regard both the secret election of God and his internal vocation, because he alone "knoweth them that are his" and keeps them enclosed under his "seal," to use the expression of Paul,[1] except that they bear his impression, by which they may be distinguished from the reprobate. But because a small and contemptible number is concealed among a vast multitude, and a few grains of wheat are covered with a heap of chaff, we must leave to God alone the knowledge of his Church whose foundation is his secret election. Nor is it sufficient to include in our thoughts and minds the whole multitude of the elect unless we conceive of such a unity of the Church, into which we know ourselves to be truly ingrafted. For unless we are united with all the other members under Christ our Head, we can have no hope of the future inheritance. Therefore the Church is called "catholic," or universal, because there could not be two or three churches without Christ being divided, which is impossible. But all the elect of God are so connected with each other

[1] II Tim. 2. 19.

in Christ that, as they depend upon one head, so they grow up together as into one body, compacted together like members of the same body—being made truly one, as living by one faith, hope, and charity, through the same divine Spirit, being called not only to the same inheritance of eternal life, but also to a participation of one God and Christ. Therefore, though the melancholy desolation which surrounds us seems to proclaim that there is nothing left of the Church, let us remember that the death of Christ is fruitful, and that God wonderfully preserves his Church as it were in hiding-places, according to what he said in Elijah: "I have reserved to myself seven thousand men, who have not bowed the knee to Baal." [2]

1. 3. *The communion of saints*

This article of the Creed, however, relates in some measure to the external Church, that every one of us may maintain a brotherly agreement with all the children of God, may pay due deference to the authority of the Church, and, in a word, may conduct himself as one of the flock. Therefore we add "the communion of saints"—a clause which, though generally omitted by the ancients, ought not to be neglected, because it excellently expresses the character of the Church; as though it had been said that the saints are united in the fellowship of Christ on this condition, that whatever benefits God confers upon them they should mutually communicate to each other. This does not destroy the diversity of grace, for we know that the gifts of the Spirit are variously distributed; nor does it disturb the order of civil polity, which secures to every individual the exclusive enjoyment of his property, as it is necessary for the preservation of the peace of society that men should have peculiar and distinct possessions. But the community asserted is such as Luke describes, that "the multitude of them that believed were of one heart and of one soul"; [1] and Paul, when

2 Rom. 11. 4; I Kings 19. 18.
1 Acts 4. 32.

he exhorts the Ephesians to be "one body, and one spirit, even as they were called in one hope." [2] Nor is it possible, if they are truly persuaded that God is a common Father to them all and Christ their common Head, but that, being united in brotherly affection, they should mutually communicate their advantages to each other. Now it highly concerns us to know what benefit we receive from this. For we believe the Church in order to have a certain assurance that we are members of it. For thus our salvation rests on firm and solid foundations, so that it cannot fall into ruin though the whole fabric of the world should be dissolved. First, it is founded on the election of God, and can be liable to no variation or failure but with the subversion of his eternal providence. In the next place, it is united with the stability of Christ, who will no more suffer his faithful people to be severed from him than his members to be torn in pieces. Besides, we are certain, as long as we continue in the bosom of the Church, that we shall remain in possession of the truth. Lastly, we understand these promises to belong to us: "In mount Zion shall be deliverance"; [3] "God is in the midst of her; she shall not be moved." [4] Such is the effect of union with the Church, that it retains us in the fellowship of God. The very word "communion" likewise contains abundant consolation; for while it is certain that whatever the Lord confers upon his members and ours belongs to us, our hope is confirmed by all the benefits which they enjoy. But in order to embrace the unity of the Church in this manner, it is unnecessary, as we have observed, to see the Church with our eyes or feel it with our hands; on the contrary, from its being an object of faith, we are taught that it is no less to be considered as existing when it escapes our observation than if it were evident to our eyes. Nor is our faith the worse because it acknowledges the Church which we do not fully comprehend; for we are not commanded here to distinguish the

2 Eph. 4. 4.
3 Joel 2. 32; Obad. 17.
4 Ps. 46. 5.

reprobate from the elect, which is not our province, but that of God alone; we are only required to be assured in our minds that all those who, by the mercy of God the Father, through the efficacious influence of the Holy Spirit, have attained to the participation of Christ are separated as the peculiar possession and portion of God, and that, being numbered among them, we are partakers of such great grace.

1. 4. *We never outgrow the guidance of the Church*

But as our present design is to treat of the *visible* Church, we may learn even from the title of "mother" how useful and even necessary it is for us to know her; since there is no other way of entrance into life unless we are conceived by her, born of her, nourished at her breast, and continually preserved under her care and government till we are divested of this mortal flesh and "become like the angels." [1] For our infirmity will not admit of our dismission from her school; we must continue under her instruction and discipline to the end of our lives. It is also to be remarked that out of her bosom there can be no hope of remission of sins or any salvation, according to the testimony of Joel and Isaiah; [2] which is confirmed by Ezekiel [3] when he denounces that those whom God excludes from the heavenly life shall not be enrolled among his people. So, on the contrary, those who devote themselves to the service of God are said to inscribe their names among the citizens of Jerusalem. For which reason the Psalmist says, "Remember me, O Lord, with the favor that thou bearest unto thy people; O visit me with thy salvation that I may see the good of thy chosen, that I may rejoice in the gladness of thy nation, that I may glory with thine inheritance." [4] In these words the paternal favor of God and the peculiar testimony of the spiritual life are restricted to his flock to teach us that it is always fatally dangerous to be separated from the Church.

[1] Matt. 22. 30.
[2] Isa. 37. 35; Joel 2. 32.
[3] Ezek. 13. 9.
[4] Ps. 106. 4, 5.

*These considerations introduce an extended discussion
of: the Church invisible and visible; the marks of a true
visible Church; the sin of schism for insufficient cause; the
Keys of the Church; and the need of moderation in discipline.*

*Chapter 2, "The True and False Church Compared,"
offers a defense of the Reformation Churches against the
charge of schism: "Communion is not a bond to bind us
in idolatry" (sec. 2). In the papal Church only vestiges of
the true Church remain (sec. 11).*

2. 12. *The papal Church accused and rejected*

While we refuse, therefore, to allow to the papists the title
of the Church, without any qualification or restriction, we do
not deny that there are Churches among them. We only contend for the true and legitimate constitution of the Church,
which requires not only a communion in the sacraments,
which are the signs of a Christian profession, but above all an
agreement in doctrine. Daniel and Paul had predicted that
Antichrist would sit in the temple of God.[1] The head of that
cursed and abominable kingdom, in the Western Church, we
affirm to be the Pope. When his seat is placed in the temple of
God, it suggests that his kingdom will be such that he will not
abolish the name of Christ or the Church. Hence it appears
that we by no means deny that Churches may exist even under
his tyranny; but he has profaned them by sacrilegious impiety,
afflicted them by cruel despotism, corrupted and almost terminated their existence by false and pernicious doctrines, like
poisonous potions; in such Churches, Christ lies half buried,
the gospel is suppressed, piety exterminated, and the worship
of God almost abolished; in a word, they are altogether in
such a state of confusion that they exhibit a picture of Babylon rather than of the holy city of God. To conclude, I affirm
that they are Churches, inasmuch as God has wonderfully preserved among them a remnant of his people, though miserably

[1] Dan. 9. 27; II Thess. 2. 3, 4.

dispersed and dejected, and as there still remain some marks of the Church, especially those the efficacy of which neither the craft of the devil nor the malice of men can ever destroy. But, on the other hand, because those marks which we ought chiefly to regard in this controversy are obliterated, I affirm that the form of the legitimate Church is not to be found either in any one of their congregations or in the body at large.

Chapters 3 to 7 treat the ministry and government of the Church. Bishops, presbyters, pastors, and ministers are not differentiated in order (3. 8; 4. 3). Bishops were formerly chosen by the people and ordained in assemblies, but the ancient practice was later subverted and the ministry corrupted (ch. 5). In chapter 6, on "The Primacy of the Roman See," Calvin examines the claims connected with Peter (sec. 15). He traces the history of the rise of the Roman bishopric and of the advance of papal power in the Middle Ages with attendant loss of liberty (ch. 7). The assault on the Papacy is continued in chapters on the power of the Church and its perversion (ch. 8), the rightful authority of Church councils (ch. 9), and the tyrannical use of legislative power under the Papacy (ch. 10). In this last chapter Calvin charges that the traditions and ceremonies of the Papacy are contrary to Scripture and that man-made laws in worship are to be rejected.

10. 17. *The name of Church is falsely claimed where the Scripture rule is broken*

I hear the answer which they make—that their traditions are not from themselves, but from God; that the Church is directed by the Holy Spirit, so that it cannot err; and that they are in possession of his authority. When this point is gained, it immediately follows that their traditions are the revelations of the Holy Spirit, which cannot be despised without impiety and contempt of God. That they may not appear to attempt anything without high authorities, they wish it to be believed that the greatest part of their observances have descended from the apostles; and they contend that one example sufficiently shows what was the conduct of the apostles in other cases, when, being assembled together in a council, they determined and announced to all Gentiles that they should "abstain from meats offered to idols, and from blood, and from things strangled."[1] We have already exposed the falsehood of their pretensions in arrogating to themselves the title of the Church. With regard to the present argument, if, stripping off all false disguises, we confine our attention to what ought to be our chief concern and involves our highest interests, namely, what kind of a Church Christ requires, in order that we may conform ourselves to its standard—it will be sufficiently evident to us that the name of the Church does not belong to those who overleap all the limits of the word of God and exercise an unbounded license of enacting new laws. For does not that law which was once given to the Church remain forever in force? "What thing soever I command you, observe to do it: thou shalt not add thereto, nor diminish from it."[2] And again: "Add not thou unto his words, lest he reprove thee, and thou be found a liar."[3] Since they cannot deny these things to have been spoken to the Church, do they not declare the rebellion of the Church when they pretend that, notwithstanding such prohibitions, it has dared to mingle additions of its own with the doctrine of God? Far be it from us, however, to countenance their falsehoods, by which they do so great an injury to the Church; let us know that the assumption of the name of the Church is a false pretense in all who are so carried away by the violence of human presumption as to disregard all the restraints of the word of God and to introduce a torrent of their own inventions. There is nothing involved, nothing intricate, nothing ambiguous in these words

[1] Acts 15. 28, 29.
[2] Deut. 12. 32.
[3] Prov. 30.

by which the whole Church is forbidden to add anything to the word or to diminish anything from it in any question relating to the worship of God and his salutary precepts. But it will be alleged that this was spoken exclusively of the law, which has been succeeded by the prophecies and the whole dispensation of the gospel. This I certainly admit, and at the same time assert that these were accomplishments of the law rather than additions to it or retrenchments of it. But if the Lord suffered no enlargement or diminution of the ministry of Moses, notwithstanding it was enveloped in such great obscurity, till he dispensed a clearer doctrine by his servants the prophets, and finally by his beloved Son—why do not we consider ourselves far more severely prohibited from making any addition to the law, the prophets, the psalms, and the gospel? No change has taken place in the Lord, who long ago declared that nothing was so highly offensive to him as to attempt to worship him with the inventions of men. Hence those striking declarations in the prophets which ought to be continually sounding in our ears: "I spake not unto your fathers, nor commanded them in the day that I brought them out of the land of Egypt, concerning burnt-offerings or sacrifices; but this thing commanded I them, saying, Obey my voice, and I will be your God, and ye shall be my people: and walk ye in all the ways that I have commanded you." [4] Again: "I earnestly protested unto your fathers, saying, Obey my voice." [5] There are many other similar passages, but the most remarkable of all is the following: "Hath the Lord," says Samuel, "as great delight in burnt-offerings and sacrifices as in obeying the voice of the Lord? Behold, to obey is better than sacrifice, and to hearken than the fat of rams. For rebellion is as the sin of witchcraft, and stubbornness is as iniquity and idolatry." [6] Therefore, whatever human inventions relating to the worship of God may be defended by the authority of the

[4] Jer. 7. 22, 23.
[5] Jer. 11. 7.
[6] I Sam. 15. 22, 23.

Church, since it is impossible to vindicate them from impiety, it is easy to infer that the imputation of them to the Church has no foundation in truth.

10. 18. *The practices here censured were not apostolic*

For this reason we freely censure that tyranny of human traditions which is imposed upon the world under the name of the Church. Nor do we hold the Church in contempt, as our adversaries, in order to render us obnoxious, falsely assert. We allow it the praise of obedience than which no higher praise can be given. On the contrary, they are themselves the most outrageous violators of the Church, which they represent as guilty of rebellion against the Lord, when they pretend that it has gone beyond what was permitted by the word of God; to say nothing of the combination of impudence and wickedness discovered in their incessant vociferations respecting the authority of the Church, while they take no notice of the command of the Lord, or of the obedience due from the Church to that command. But if we desire, as we ought, to agree with the Church, it will be best for us to observe and remember what commands are given by the Lord, equally to us and to the whole Church, that we may all obey him with one consent. For there is no doubt that we shall fully agree with the Church if we show ourselves in all things obedient to the Lord. Now to attribute to the apostles the origin of the traditions which have hitherto oppressed the Church is a mere imposture, for the whole tendency of the doctrine of the apostles was that men's consciences should not be burdened with new observances, or the worship of God contaminated with human inventions. Besides, if there be any credit due to ancient histories and records, the apostles not only never knew, but never even heard of that which is ascribed to them. Nor let it be pretended that the greatest part of their constitutions were received in use and commonly practiced, which were never committed to writing—namely, those things which, during the life of Christ, they were not able to understand, but which after his ascension they learned from the revelation of the Holy Spirit. The meaning of that passage we have already examined. With respect to the present subject, we may observe, they make themselves truly ridiculous by maintaining that those great mysteries, which were so long unknown to the apostles, consisted partly of Jewish or heathen ceremonies, of which the former had long before been promulgated among the Jews and the latter among the heathen, and partly of foolish gesticulations and unmeaning rites, which stupid priests, who scarcely know how to walk or speak, perform with the greatest exactness, and which even infants and fools counterfeit so well that it might be thought there were no more suitable ministers of such solemnities. If there were no histories, yet men of sound judgment would conclude from the thing itself that such a vast multitude of rites and observances did not break into the Church all of a sudden, but that they must have been introduced by degrees. For when those holy bishops who were the immediate successors of the apostles had made some appointments relating to order and discipline, they were followed by a series of others who had too little consideration and too much curiosity and cupidity, of whom every one in succession vied with his predecessors from a foolish emulation to excel them in the invention of new observances. And because there was danger that their inventions, by which they desired to obtain the praises of posterity, might in a short time be disused, they were the more rigid in enforcing the observance of them. This foolish and perverse imitation has been the source of most of those rites which the Romanists urge upon us as apostolic. And this is also attested by various histories.

Chapter 11, on abuses of Church jurisdiction, has reference to the assertion of political mastery by medieval popes. This is contrasted with the modesty and civil obedience of the early bishops (secs. 15, 16).

Chapter 12 deals with Church discipline.

12. 1. *Discipline necessary: a bridle, a spur, and a rod*

The discipline of the Church, the discussion of which I have deferred to this place, must be despatched in a few words, that we may proceed to the remaining subjects. Now the discipline depends chiefly on the power of the keys, and the spiritual jurisdiction. To make this more easily understood, let us divide the Church into two principal orders—the clergy and the people. I use the word "clergy" as the common, though improper, appellation of those who execute the public ministry in the Church. We shall, first, speak of the common discipline to which all ought to be subject; and in the next place we shall proceed to the clergy, who, beside this common discipline, have a discipline peculiar to themselves. But as some have such a hatred of discipline as to abhor the very name, they should attend to the following consideration: that if no society, and even no house, though containing only a small family, can be preserved in a proper state without discipline, this is far more necessary in the Church, the state of which ought to be the most orderly of all. As the saving doctrine of Christ is the soul of the Church, so discipline forms the ligaments which connect the members together and keep each in its proper place. Whoever, therefore, either desires the abolition of all discipline or obstructs its restoration, whether they act from design or inadvertency, they certainly promote the entire dissolution of the Church. For what will be the consequence if every man be at liberty to follow his own inclinations? But such would be the case, unless the preaching of the doctrine were accompanied with private admonitions, reproofs, and other means to enforce the doctrine and prevent it from being altogether ineffectual. Discipline, therefore, serves as a bridle to curb and restrain the refractory, who resist the doctrine of Christ; or as a spur to stimulate the inactive; and sometimes as a father's rod, with which those who have grievously fallen may be chastised in mercy, and with the gentleness of the Spirit of Christ. Now when we see the approach of certain beginnings of a dreadful desolation in the Church, since there is no solicitude or means to keep the people in obedience to our Lord, necessity itself proclaims the want of a remedy; and this is the only remedy which has been commanded by Christ, or which has ever been adopted among believers.

12. 2. *Order to be followed in correction of an offender*

The first foundation of discipline consists in the use of private admonitions; that is to say, that if anyone be guilty of a voluntary omission of duty, or conduct himself in an insolent manner, or discover a want of virtue in his life, or commit any act deserving of reprehension, he should suffer himself to be admonished; and that everyone should study to admonish his brother, whenever occasion shall require; but that pastors and presbyters, beyond all others, should be vigilant in the discharge of this duty, being called by their office, not only to preach to the congregation, but also to admonish and exhort in private houses, if in any instances their public instructions may not have been sufficiently efficacious; as Paul inculcates, when he says that he "taught publicly and from house to house," and protests himself to be "pure from the blood of all men," having "ceased not to warn everyone night and day with tears." [1] For the doctrine then obtains its full authority and produces its due effect when the minister not only declares to all the people together what is their duty to Christ, but has the right and means of enforcing it upon them whom he observes to be inattentive or not obedient to the doctrine. If anyone either obstinately reject such admonitions or manifest his contempt of them by persisting in his misconduct, after he shall have been admonished a second time in the presence of witnesses, Christ directs him to be summoned before the tribunal of the Church—that is, the assembly of the elders —and there to be more severely admonished by the public authority, that if he reverence the Church he may submit and

[1] Acts 20. 20, 26, 31.

obey; but if this do not overcome him, and he still persevere in his iniquity, our Lord then commands him, as a despiser of the Church, to be excluded from the society of believers.[2]

Private and public, slight and grave faults are to be differentiated (secs. 3-4). The purposes of discipline are: to maintain the purity of communion; to prevent the corruption of good members; and to obtain the repentance of offenders (sec. 5). Severity is to be tempered with gentleness (secs. 8-11). Calvin also discusses fasting and Lent (secs. 14-21) and clerical celibacy (secs. 22-28).

Chapter 13 is entitled "Vows, the Misery of Rashly Making Them." It includes a discussion of monastic vows. In chapter 14 Calvin considers the sacraments.

14. 1. *Definition of a sacrament*

Connected with the preaching of the gospel, another assistance and support for our faith is presented to us in the sacraments; on the subject of which it is highly important to lay down some certain doctrine, that we may learn for what end they were instituted and how they ought to be used. In the first place, it is necessary to consider what a sacrament is. Now I think it will be a simple and appropriate definition if we say that it is an outward sign by which the Lord seals in our consciences the promises of his good will toward us to support the weakness of our faith; and we on our part testify our piety toward him, in his presence and that of angels, as well as before men. It may, however, be more briefly defined, in other words, by calling it a testimony of the grace of God toward us, confirmed by an outward sign, with a reciprocal attestation of our piety toward him. Whichever of these definitions be chosen, it conveys exactly the same meaning as that of Augustine, which states a sacrament to be "a visible sign of a sacred thing," or "a visible form of invisible grace"; but it expresses

2 Matt. 18. 15-17.

the thing itself with more clearness and precision, for as his conciseness leaves some obscurity, by which many inexperienced persons may be misled, I have endeavored to render the subject plainer by more words, that no room might be left for any doubt.

14. 2. Sacramentum *used to translate* mystērion

The reason why the ancient Fathers used this word in such a sense is very evident. For whenever the author of the old common version of the New Testament wanted to render the Greek word μυστηριον, "mystery," into Latin, especially where it related to divine things, he used the word *sacramentum,* "sacrament." Thus, in the Epistle to the Ephesians, "Having made known unto us the *mystery* of his will." [1] Again: "If ye have heard of the dispensation of the grace of God which is given me to you-ward; how that by revelation he made known unto me the *mystery*." [2] In the Epistle to the Colossians: "The *mystery* which hath been hid from ages and from generations, but now is made manifest to his saints; to whom God would make known what is the riches of the glory of this *mystery*." [3] Again, to Timothy: "Great is the *mystery* of godliness; God was manifest in the flesh." [4] In all these places, where the word "mystery" is used, the author of that version has rendered it "sacrament." He would not say "arcanum," or "secret," lest he should appear to degrade the majesty of the subject. Therefore he has used the word "sacrament" for a sacred or divine secret. In this signification it frequently occurs in the writings of the Fathers. And it is well known that baptism and the Lord's Supper, which the Latins denominate "sacraments," are called "mysteries" by the Greeks, a synonymous use of the terms which removes every doubt. And hence the word "sacrament" came to be applied to those signs which contained a representation of sublime and spiritual things; which is also

[1] Eph. 1. 9.
[2] Eph. 3. 2, 3.
[3] Col. 1. 26, 27.
[4] I Tim. 3. 16.

remarked by Augustine, who says, "It would be tedious to dispute respecting the diversity of signs, which, when they pertain to divine things, are called *sacraments*."

Calvin associates the sacraments closely with the Scripture and with the influence of the Holy Spirit. Like the Scripture, they present Christ to us (sec. 17).

14. 22. *What the two sacraments testify*

Our two sacraments present us with a clearer exhibition of Christ in proportion to the nearer view of him which men have enjoyed since he was really manifested by the Father in the manner in which he had been promised. For baptism testifies to us our purgation and ablution; the eucharistic supper testifies our redemption. Water is a figure of ablution, and blood of satisfaction. These things are both found in Christ, who, as John says, "came by water and blood" [1]—that is, to purify and redeem. Of this the Spirit of God is a witness; or, rather, "there are three that bear witness, the Spirit, the Water, and the Blood." [2] In the water and the blood we have a testimony of purgation and redemption; and the Spirit, as the principal witness, confirms and secures our reception and belief of this testimony. This sublime mystery was strikingly exhibited on the cross, when blood and water issued from Christ's sacred side; which, on this account, Augustine has justly called "the fountain of our sacraments"—of which we are yet to treat more at large. And there is no doubt, if we compare one time with another, but that the more abundant grace of the Spirit is also here displayed. For that belongs to the glory of the kingdom of Christ, as we gather from various places, and especially from the seventh chapter of John. In this sense we must understand that passage where Paul, speaking of the legal institutions, says, "which are a shadow of

1 I John 5. 8.
2 I John 5. 8.

things to come, but the body is of Christ." [3] His design in this declaration is not to deny the efficacy of those testimonies of grace, in which God was formerly pleased to attest his veracity to the Fathers, as he does to us now in baptism and the sacred supper, but to represent the comparative superiority of what has been given to us, that no one might wonder at the ceremonies of the law having been abolished at the advent of Christ.

Various objections to the argument are met (secs. 23-26). Chapters 15 and 16 are on baptism. By it is symbolized our death to sin, our ingrafting into Christ, and the initiation of infants into the Church.

15. 20. *Lay baptism of infants based on the doctrinal error that all who die unbaptized are lost*

It is also necessary to state that it is not right for private persons to take upon themselves the administration of baptism; for this, as well as the administration of the Lord's Supper, is a part of the public ministry of the Church. Christ never commanded women, or men in general, to baptize; he gave this charge to those whom he had appointed to be apostles. And when he enjoined his disciples, in the celebration of the supper, to do as they had seen done by him when he executed the office of a legitimate dispenser, he intended, without doubt, that they should imitate his example. The custom, which has been received and practiced for many ages past, and almost from the primitive times of the Church, for baptism to be performed by laymen in cases where death was apprehended and no minister was present in time, it appears to me impossible to defend by any good reason. Indeed, the ancients themselves who either observed or tolerated this custom were not certain whether it was right or not. Augustine betrays this uncertainty when he says, "And if a

[3] Col. 2. 17.

layman, compelled by necessity, has given baptism, I know not whether anyone may piously affirm that it ought to be repeated. For if it be done without the constraint of necessity, it is a usurpation of an office which belongs to another; but if necessity obliges, it is either no offense, or a venial one." [1] Respecting women, it was decreed without any exception, in the Council of Carthage, that they should not presume to baptize at all, on pain of excommunication. But, it is alleged, there is danger lest a child who is sick and dies without baptism should be deprived of the grace of regeneration. This I can by no means admit. God pronounces that he adopts our infants as his children, before they are born, when he promises that he will be a God to us and to our seed after us. This promise includes their salvation. Nor will any dare to offer such an insult to God as to deny the sufficiency of his promise to insure its own accomplishment. The mischievous consequences of that ill-stated notion, that baptism is necessary to salvation, are overlooked by persons in general, and therefore they are less cautious: for the reception of an opinion that all who happen to die without baptism are lost makes our condition worse than that of the ancient people, as though the grace of God were more restricted now than it was under the law; it leads to the conclusion that Christ came not to fulfill the promises but to abolish them, since the promise, which at that time was of itself sufficiently efficacious to insure salvation before the eighth day, would have no validity now without the assistance of the sign.

The children of believers are not aliens before their baptism but by baptism are solemnly received into the Church (sec 22). Chapter 16 is a closely argued treatment of the baptism of infants. They should not be denied baptism, Calvin asserts. "As the Lord does not exclude them from

1 [Augustine, *Contra epistolam Parmeniani* II. 13; Migne, *PL*, XLIII, 71. For a summary of this treatise, see C. D. Hartranft's "Introductory Essay" to the anti-Donatist writings of Augustine, *NPNF*, IV, 380 f.]

*the hope of mercy but rather assures them of it, why
should we refuse them the sign?" (sec. 22).
Chapter 17 is devoted to the Lord's Supper.*

17. 1. *A visible sign of that by which our souls are fed*

After God has once received us into his family—and not
only so as to admit us among his servants but to number us
with his children—in order to fulfill the part of a most excellent father, solicitous for his offspring, he also undertakes
to sustain and nourish us as long as we live; and not content
with this, he has been pleased to give us a pledge as a further
assurance of this never-ceasing liberality. For this purpose,
therefore, by the hand of his only begotten Son, he has favored
his Church with another sacrament, a spiritual banquet, in
which Christ testifies himself to be the bread of life, to feed
our souls for a true and blessed immortality. Now as the
knowledge of so great a mystery is highly necessary, and on
account of its importance requires an accurate explication;
and, on the other hand, as Satan, in order to deprive the
Church of this inestimable treasure, long ago endeavored,
first by mists and afterwards by thicker shades, to obscure its
luster, and then raised disputes and contentions to alienate the
minds of the simple from a relish for this sacred food, and in
our time also has attempted the same artifice—after having exhibited a summary of what relates to the subject, adapted to
the capacity of the unlearned, I will disentangle it from those
sophistries with which Satan has been laboring to deceive the
world. In the first place, the signs are bread and wine, which
represent to us the invisible nourishment which we receive
from the body and blood of Christ. For as in baptism God
regenerates us, incorporates us into the society of his Church,
and makes us his children by adoption, so we have said that
he acts toward us the part of a provident father of a family
in constantly supplying us with food, to sustain and preserve
us in that life to which he has begotten us by his word. Now

the only food of our souls is Christ; and to him, therefore, our heavenly Father invites us, that, being refreshed by a participation of him, we may gain fresh vigor from day to day till we arrive at the heavenly immortality. And because this mystery of the secret union of Christ with believers is incomprehensible by nature, he exhibits a figure and image of it in visible signs peculiarly adapted to our feeble capacity; and, as it were, by giving tokens and pledges, renders it equally as certain to us as if we beheld it with our eyes; for the dullest minds understand this very familiar similitude, that our souls are nourished by Christ just as the life of the body is supported by bread and wine. We see, then, for what end this mystical benediction is designed—namely, to assure us that the body of the Lord was once offered as a sacrifice for us, so that we may now feed upon it, and, feeding on it, may experience within us the efficacy of that one sacrifice; and that his blood was once shed for us, so that it is our perpetual drink. And this is the import of the words of the promise annexed to it: "Take, eat; this is my body, which is given for you." The body, therefore, which was once offered for our salvation, we are commanded to take and eat, that seeing ourselves made partakers of it, we may certainly conclude that the virtue of that life-giving death will be efficacious within us. Hence, also, he calls the cup "the new testament," or rather *covenant,* in his blood.[1] For the covenant which he once ratified with his blood he in some measure renews, or rather continues, as far as relates to the confirmation of our faith whenever he presents us that sacred blood to drink.

Calvin insists that the reality symbolized in the Lord's Supper is present as well as the symbols: we eat the body of Christ by faith. How this takes place is not to be stated explicitly; let those who are able go beyond the explanation offered (sec. 7). A consideration of objections to transubstantiation (secs. 12-19) is followed by an answer to the

[1] Matt. 26. 26, 28; Mark 14. 22, 24; Luke 22. 19, 20; I Cor. 11. 24, 25.

*(Lutheran) advocates of a strictly literal interpretation
of "is" in the words "This is my body" (I Cor. 11. 24) and
of the accompanying doctrine of ubiquity (secs. 20-30).*

17. 31. *The presence effected by the Spirit*

They are exceedingly deceived who cannot conceive of any
presence of the flesh of Christ in the supper except it be attached to the bread. For on this principle they leave nothing
to the secret operation of the Spirit, which unites us to Christ.
They suppose Christ not to be present unless he descends to
us, as though we cannot equally enjoy his presence if he ele-
vates us to himself. The only question between us, therefore,
respects the manner of this presence, because they place Christ
in the bread and we think it unlawful for us to bring him
down from heaven. Let the readers judge on which side the
truth lies. Only let us hear no more of that calumny that
Christ is excluded from the sacrament unless he be concealed
under the bread. For as this is a heavenly mystery, there is
no necessity to bring Christ down to the earth in order to be
united to us.

17. 32. *The manner of this is a mystery of faith*

If anyone inquire of me respecting the manner, I shall not
be ashamed to acknowledge that it is a mystery too sublime
for me to be able to express, or even to comprehend; and, to
be still more explicit, I rather experience it than understand
it. Here, therefore, without any controversy, I embrace the
truth of God, on which I can safely rely. He pronounces his
flesh to be the food and his blood the drink of my soul. I offer
him my soul to be nourished with such aliment. In his sacred
supper he commands me, under the symbols of bread and
wine, to take and eat and drink his body and blood. I doubt
not that he truly presents and that I receive them. Only I reject the absurdities which appear to be either degrading to
his majesty or inconsistent with the reality of his human na-

ture and are at the same time repugnant to the word of God, which informs us that Christ has been received into the glory of the celestial kingdom where he is exalted above every condition of the world, and which is equally careful to attribute to his human nature the properties of real humanity. Nor ought this to seem incredible or unreasonable, because, as the kingdom of Christ is wholly spiritual, so his communications with his Church are not at all to be regulated by the order of the present world; or, to use the words of Augustine, "This mystery, as well as others, is celebrated by man, but in a divine manner; it is administered on earth, but in a heavenly manner." [1] The presence of Christ's body, I say, is such as the nature of the sacrament requires, where we affirm that it appears with so much virtue and efficacy as not only to afford our minds an undoubted confidence of eternal life, but also to give us an assurance of the resurrection and immortality of our bodies. For they are vivified by his immortal flesh, and in some degree participate his immortality. Those who go beyond this in their hyperbolical representations merely obscure the simple and obvious truth by such intricacies. If any person be not yet satisfied, I would request him to consider that we are now treating of a sacrament, every part of which ought to be referred to faith. Now we feed our faith by this participation of the body of Christ which we have mentioned as fully as they do who bring him down from heaven. At the same time, I candidly confess that I reject that mixture of the flesh of Christ with our souls, or that transfusion of it into us, which they teach, because it is sufficient for us that Christ inspires life into our souls from the substance of his flesh, and even infuses his own life into us, though his flesh never actually enters into us. I may also remark that the analogy of faith, to which Paul directs us to conform every interpretation of the Scripture, is in this case, beyond all doubt, eminently in our favor. Let the adversaries of so clear a truth examine by what rule of faith they regulate themselves. "He that confesseth not that Jesus Christ is come in the flesh, is

1 [These words have not been found in Augustine.]

not of God." [2] Such persons, though they may conceal it, or may not observe it, do, in effect, deny the reality of his flesh.

Special points of doctrine and practice are discussed and the idea of the sacrament as "external confession" is raised.

17. 37. *To be received with thanksgiving*

Now as superstition, when it has once gone beyond the proper limits, proceeds in sinning without end, they have wandered still further; they have invented ceremonies altogether incompatible with the institution of the sacred supper for the sole purpose of giving divine honors to the sign. When we remonstrate with them, they reply that they pay this veneration to Christ. In the first place, if this were done in the supper, I would still say that that is the only legitimate adoration which terminates not in the sign but is directed to Christ enthroned in heaven. Now what pretense have they for alleging that they worship Christ in the bread when they have no promise of such a thing? They consecrate their "host," as they call it, to carry it about in procession, to display it in pomp, and to exhibit it in a box, to be seen, adored, and invoked by the people. I inquire how they consider it to be rightly consecrated. They immediately adduce these words: "This is my body." I object that it was said at the same time, "Take and eat." And I have sufficient reason for this, for when a promise is annexed to a precept, it is so included in the precept that, separated from it, it ceases to be a promise at all. This shall be further elucidated by a similar example. The Lord gave a command when he said, "Call upon me"; he added a promise, "I will deliver thee." [1] If anyone should invoke Peter or Paul, and boast of this promise, will not his conduct be universally condemned? And wherein would this differ from the conduct of those who suppress the command to eat and lay hold of the mutilated promise, "This is my

2 I John 4. 3.
1 Ps. 50. 15.

body," in order to misapply it to ceremonies foreign from the institution of Christ? Let us remember, then, that this promise is given to those who observe the commandment connected with it, but that they are entirely unsupported by the word of God who transfer the sacrament to any other usage. We have already shown how the mystery of the supper promotes our faith before God. But as God here not only recalls to our remembrance the vast exuberance of his goodness, but delivers it, as it were, into our hands, as we have already declared, and excites us to acknowledge it, so he also admonishes us not to be ungrateful for such a profusion of beneficence, but, on the contrary, to magnify it with the praises it deserves and to celebrate it with thanksgivings. Therefore, when he gave the institution of this sacrament to the apostles, he said to them, "This do in remembrance of me," [2] which Paul explains to be "showing the Lord's death" [3]—that is, publicly and all together, as with one mouth, to confess that all our confidence of life and salvation rests on the death of the Lord, that we may glorify him by our confession and by our example may exhort others to give him the same glory. Here again we see the object to which the sacrament tends, which is to exercise us in a remembrance of the death of Christ. For the command which we have received, to "show the Lord's death till he come" to judgment, is no other than to declare, by the confession of our lips, what our faith has acknowledged in the sacrament, that the death of Christ is our life. This is the second use of the sacrament, which relates to external confession.

17. 38. *The nature of communion*

In the third place, the Lord intended it to serve us as an exhortation, and no other could be better adapted to animate and influence us in the most powerful manner to purity and sanctity of life, as well as to charity, peace, and concord. For there the Lord communicates his body to us in such a manner

[2] Luke 22. 10.
[3] I Cor. 11. 26.

that he becomes completely one with us, and we become one with him. Now as he has only one body, of which he makes us all partakers, it follows of necessity that by such participation we also are all made one body; and this union is represented by the bread which is exhibited in the sacrament. For as it is composed of many grains, mixed together in such a manner that one cannot be separated or distinguished from another, in the same manner we ought, likewise, to be connected and united together by such an agreement of minds as to admit of no dissension or division between us. This I prefer expressing in the language of Paul: "The cup of blessing which we bless, is it not the communion of the blood of Christ? The bread which we break, is it not the communion of the body of Christ? For we, being many, are one bread and one body; for we are all partakers of that one bread." [1] We have derived considerable benefit from the sacrament if this thought be impressed and engraved upon our minds: that it is impossible for us to wound, despise, reject, injure, or in any way to offend one of our brethren but we at the same time wound, despise, reject, injure, and offend Christ in him; that we have no discord with our brethren without being, at the same time, at variance with Christ; that we cannot love Christ without loving him in our brethren; that such care as we take of our own body, we ought to exercise the same care of our brethren, who are members of our body; that as no part of our body can be in any pain without every other part feeling correspondent sensations, so we ought not to suffer our brother to be afflicted with any calamity without our sympathizing in the same. Wherefore, it is not without reason that Augustine so frequently calls this sacrament "the bond of charity." For what more powerful stimulus could be employed to excite mutual charity among us than when Christ, giving himself to us, not only invites us by his example mutually to devote ourselves to the promotion of one another's welfare, but also, by making himself common to all, makes us all to be one with himself?

[1] I Cor. 10. 16, 17.

17. 39. *The preaching of the word to accompany the sacrament*

This furnishes the best confirmation of what I have stated before—that there is no true administration of the sacrament without the word. For whatever advantage accrues to us from the sacred supper requires the word; whether we are to be confirmed in faith, exercised in confession, or excited to duty, there is need of preaching. Nothing more preposterous, therefore, can be done with respect to the supper than to convert it into a mute action as we have seen done under the tyranny of the pope. For they have maintained that all the validity of the consecration depends on the intention of the priests, as if it had nothing to do with the people, to whom the mystery ought principally to be explained. They fell into this error for want of observing that those promises on which the consecration rests are not directed to the elements themselves but to the persons who receive them. Christ does not address the bread to command it to become his body, but enjoins his disciples to eat and promises them the communication of his body and blood. Nor does Paul teach any other order than that the promises should be offered to believers together with the bread and the cup. And this is the truth. We are not to imagine any magical incantation, or think it sufficient to have muttered over the words, as if they were heard by the elements, but we are to understand those words by which the elements are consecrated to be a lively preaching, which edifies the hearers, which penetrates their minds, which is deeply impressed upon their hearts, which exerts its efficacy in the accomplishment of that which it promises. These considerations clearly show that the reservation of the sacrament, insisted upon by many persons, for the purpose of extraordinary distribution to the sick, is perfectly useless. For either they will receive it without any recital of the institution of Christ, or the minister will accompany the sign with a true explication of the mystery. If nothing be said, it is an abuse and corruption. If the promises are repeated and the mystery declared, that those who are about to receive it may communicate with advantage, we have no reason to doubt that this is the true consecration. What end will be answered, then, by the former consecration, which, having been pronounced when the sick persons were not present, is of no avail to them? But it will be alleged that those who adopt this practice have the example of the ancient Church in their favor. This I confess; but in a matter of such great importance, and in which any error must be highly dangerous, there is nothing so safe as to follow the truth itself.

The remainder of chapter 17 is concerned with: right and wrong ways of preventing unworthy participation; the duty of frequent communion (sec. 44); and the abuse of withholding the wine from the laity (secs. 47-50).

Chapter 18 assails the Mass as an unscriptural perversion of the Lord's Supper, but concludes more positively.

18. 19. *The two sacraments are sufficient, and none are to be added*

The readers may now see, collected into a brief summary, almost everything that I have thought important to be known respecting these two sacraments, the use of which has been enjoined on the Christian Church from the commencement of the New Testament until the end of time—that is to say, baptism, to be a kind of entrance into the Church and an initiatory profession of faith, and the Lord's supper, to be a continual nourishment with which Christ spiritually feeds his family of believers. Wherefore, as there is but "one God, one Christ, one faith," one Church, the body of Christ, so there is only "one baptism" and that is never repeated; but the supper is frequently distributed, that those who have once been admitted into the Church may understand that they are continually nourished by Christ. Besides these two, as no other sacrament has been instituted by God, so no other ought to be acknowledged by the Church of believers. For that it is not left to the will of man to institute new sacraments will be easily understood if we remember what has already been very plainly stated—that sacraments are appointed by God for the purpose of instructing us respecting some promise of his, and assuring us of his good will toward us—and if we also consider that no one has been the counselor of God, capable of affording us any certainty respecting his will [1] or furnishing us any assurance of his disposition toward us, what he chooses to give or to deny us. Hence it follows that no one can institute a sign to be a testimony respecting any determination or promise of his; he alone can furnish us a testimony respecting himself by giving a sign. I will express myself in terms more concise, and perhaps more homely, but more explicit—that there can be no sacrament unaccompanied with a promise of salvation. All mankind, collected in one assembly, can promise us nothing respecting our salvation. Therefore they can never institute or establish a sacrament.

In chapter 19 Calvin asserts that confirmation, extreme unction, penance, and matrimony are not sacraments.

With chapter 20, "On Civil Government," the work is concluded. (See John T. McNeill [ed.], John Calvin on God and Political Duty *["The Library of Liberal Arts," No. 23; New York: The Liberal Arts Press, 1956].)*

[1] Isa. 40. 14; Rom. 11. 34.

FROM THE COMMENTARIES

FROM THE COMMENTARIES

ON GENESIS

1. 26. And God said, Let us make man in our image, after our likeness: and let him have dominion over the fish of the sea, and over the fowl of the air, and over the cattle, and over all the earth, and over every creeping thing that creepeth upon the earth.

27. So God created man in his *own* image, in the image of God created he him; male and female created he them.

28. And God blessed them, and God said unto them, Be fruitful, and multiply, and replenish the earth, and subdue it: and have dominion over the fish of the sea, and over the fowl of the air, and over every living thing that moveth upon the earth.

29. And God said, Behold, I have given you every herb bearing seed, which *is* upon the face of all the earth, and every tree, in the which *is* the fruit of a tree yielding seed; to you it shall be for meat.

30. And to every beast of the earth, and to every fowl of the air, and to every thing that creepeth upon the earth, wherein *there is* life, *I have given* every green herb for meat: and it was so.

31. And God saw everything that he had made, and, behold, *it was* very good. And the evening and the morning were the sixth day.

26. *In our image, etc.* Interpreters do not agree concerning the meaning of these words. The greater part, and nearly all, conceive that the word *image* is to be distinguished from *likeness.* And the common distinction is that *image* exists in the substance, *likeness* in the accidents of anything. They who would define the subject briefly say that in the *image* are contained those endowments which God has conferred on human nature at large, while they expound *likeness* to mean gratuitous gifts. But Augustine, beyond all others, speculates with excessive refinement, for the purpose of fabricating a Trinity in

129

man. For in laying hold of the three faculties of the soul enumerated by Aristotle—the intellect, the memory, and the will—he afterwards out of one Trinity derives many. If any reader, having leisure, wishes to enjoy such speculations, let him read the tenth and fourteenth books on the Trinity, also the eleventh book of the "City of God." I acknowledge, indeed, that there is something in man which refers to the Father and the Son and the Spirit; and I have no difficulty in admitting the above distinction of the faculties of the soul, although the simpler division into two parts, which is more used in Scripture, is better adapted to the sound doctrine of piety; but a definition of the image of God ought to rest on a firmer basis than such subtleties. As for myself, before I define the image of God, I would deny that it differs from his likeness. For when Moses afterwards repeats the same thing, he passes over the *likeness* and contents himself with mentioning the *image.* Should anyone take the exception, that he was merely studying brevity, I answer that where he twice uses the word image, he makes no mention of the likeness. We also know that it was customary with the Hebrews to repeat the same thing in different words. Besides, the phrase itself shows that the second term was added for the sake of explanation: "Let us make," he says, "man in our image, according to our likeness"—that is, that he may be like God, or may represent the image of God. Lastly, in the fifth chapter, without making any mention of *image,* he puts likeness in its place (v. 1). Although we have set aside all difference between the two words, we have not yet ascertained what this image or likeness is. The Anthropomorphites were too gross in seeking this resemblance in the human body; let that reverie therefore remain entombed. Others proceed with a little more subtlety who, though they do not imagine God to be corporeal, yet maintain that the image of God is in the body of man because his admirable workmanship there shines brightly; but this opinion, as we shall see, is by no means consonant with Scripture. The exposition of Chrysostom is not more correct, who refers to the dominion which was given to man in order that he might, in a certain sense, act as God's vicegerent in the government of the world. This truly is some portion, though very small, of the image of God. Since the image of God has been destroyed in us by the fall, we may judge from its restoration what it originally had been. Paul says that we are transformed into the image of God by the gospel. And, according to him, spiritual regeneration is nothing else than the restoration of the same image (Col. 3. 10 and Eph. 4. 23). That he made this image to consist in "righteousness and true holiness" is by the figure *synecdoche*, for though this is the chief part, it is not the whole of God's image. Therefore by this word the perfection of our whole nature is designated, as it appeared when Adam was endowed with a right judgment, had affections in harmony with reason, had all his senses sound and well-regulated, and truly excelled in everything good. Thus the chief seat of the divine image was in his mind and heart, where it was eminent; yet was there no part of him in which some scintillations of it did not shine forth. For there was an attempering in the several parts of the soul which corresponded with their various offices. In the mind perfect intelligence flourished and reigned, uprightness attended as its companion, and all the senses were prepared and molded for due obedience to reason; and in the body there was a suitable correspondence with this internal order. But now, although some obscure lineaments of that image are found remaining in us, yet are they so vitiated and maimed that they may truly be said to be destroyed. For besides the deformity which everywhere appears unsightly, this evil also is added, that no part is free from the infection of sin.

And let them have dominion. Here he commemorates that part of dignity with which he decreed to honor man, namely, that he should have authority over all living creatures. He appointed man, it is true, lord of the world; but he expressly subjects the animals to him because they, having an inclination or instinct of their own, seem to be less under authority from without. The use of the plural number intimates that this authority was not given to Adam only, but to all his posterity as well as to him. And hence we infer what was the end for which all things were created, namely, that none of the conveniences and necessaries of life might be wanting to men. In the very order of the creation the paternal solicitude of God for man is conspicuous, because he furnished the world with all things needful, and even with an immense profusion of wealth, before he formed man. Thus man was rich before he was born. But if God had such care for us before we existed, he will by no means leave us destitute of food and of other necessaries of life now that we are placed in the world. Yet that he often keeps his hand as if closed is to be imputed to our sins.

27. *So God created man.* The reiterated mention of the image of God is not a vain repetition. For it is a remarkable instance of the divine goodness which can never be sufficiently proclaimed. And, at the same time, he admonishes us from what excellence we have fallen, that he may excite in us the desire of its recovery. When he soon afterwards adds that God created them "male and female," he commends to us that conjugal bond by which the society of mankind is cherished. For this form of speaking, "God created man, male and female created he them," is of the same force as if he had said that the man himself was incomplete. Under these circumstances, the woman was added to him as a companion that they both might be one, as he more clearly expresses it in the second chapter. Malachi also means the same thing when he relates (2. 15) that one man was created by God, while, nevertheless, he possessed the fullness of the Spirit. For he there treats of conjugal fidelity, which the Jews were violating by their polygamy. For the purpose of correcting this fault, he calls that pair, consisting of man and woman, which God in the beginning had joined together, *one man*, in order that everyone might learn to be content with his own wife.

28. *And God blessed them.* This blessing of God may be regarded as the source from which the human race has flowed. And we must so consider it not only with reference to the whole, but also, as they say, in every particular instance. For we are fruitful or barren in respect of offspring as God imparts his power to some and withholds it from others. But here Moses would simply declare that Adam with his wife was formed for the production of offspring in order that men might replenish the earth. God could himself indeed have covered the earth with a multitude of men; but it was his will that we should proceed from one fountain, in order that our desire of mutual concord might be the greater and that each might the more freely embrace the other as his own flesh. Besides, as men were created to occupy the earth, so we ought certainly to conclude that God has marked, as with a boundary, that space of earth which would suffice for the reception of men and would prove a suitable abode for them. Any inequality which is contrary to this arrangement is nothing else than a corruption of nature which proceeds from sin. In the meantime, however, the benediction of God so prevails that the earth everywhere lies open that it may have its inhabitants and that an immense multitude of men may find, in some part of the globe, their home. Now what I have said concerning marriage must be kept in mind—that God intends the human race to be multiplied by generation indeed, but not, as in brute animals, by promiscuous intercourse. For he has joined the man to his wife that they might produce a divine—that is, a legitimate—seed. Let us then mark whom God here addresses when he commands them to increase, and to whom he limits his benediction. Certainly he does not give the reins to human passions, but, beginning at holy and chaste marriage, he proceeds to speak of the production of offspring. For this is also worthy of notice—that Moses here briefly alludes to a subject which he afterwards means more fully to explain, and that the regular series of the history is inverted, yet in such a way as to make the true succession of events apparent. The question, however, is proposed whether

fornicators and adulterers become fruitful by the power of
God, which, if it be true, then whether the blessing of God
is in like manner extended to them? I answer, this is a corruption of the divine institute; and whereas God produces offspring from this muddy pool as well as from the pure fountain of marriage, this will tend to their greater destruction.
Still that pure and lawful method of increase which God ordained from the beginning remains firm; this is that law of
nature which common sense declares to be inviolable.

Subdue it. He confirms what he had before said respecting
dominion. Man had already been created with this condition,
that he should subject the earth to himself; but now, at
length, he is put in possession of his right when he hears what
has been given to him by the Lord; and this Moses expresses
still more fully in the next verse, when he introduces God
as granting to him the herbs and the fruits. For it is of great
importance that we touch nothing of God's bounty but what
we know he has permitted us to do, since we cannot enjoy
anything with a good conscience except we receive it as from
the hand of God. And therefore Paul teaches us that, in eating
and drinking, we always sin unless faith be present (Rom. 14.
23). Thus we are instructed to seek from God alone whatever
is necessary for us, and in the very use of his gifts we are
to exercise ourselves in meditating on his goodness and paternal care. For the words of God are to this effect: "Behold,
I have prepared food for thee before thou wast formed; acknowledge me, therefore, as thy Father, who have so diligently provided for thee when thou wast not yet created.
Moreover, my solicitude for thee has proceeded still further;
it was thy business to nurture the things provided for thee,
but I have taken even this charge also upon myself. Wherefore, although thou art, in a sense, constituted the father of the
earthly family, it is not for thee to be over-anxious about the
sustenance of animals."

Some infer from this passage that men were content with
herbs and fruits until the deluge, and that it was even un-

lawful for them to eat flesh. And this seems the more probable, because God confines in some way the food of mankind
within certain limits. Then, after the deluge, he expressly
grants them the use of flesh. These reasons, however, are not
sufficiently strong, for it may be adduced on the opposite
side that the first men offered sacrifices from their flocks. This,
moreover, is the law of sacrificing rightly: not to offer unto
God anything except what he has granted to our use. Lastly,
men were clothed in skins; therefore it was lawful for them
to kill animals. For these reasons, I think it will be better for
us to assert nothing concerning this matter. Let it suffice for us
that herbs and the fruits of trees were given them as their
common food; yet it is not to be doubted that this was abundantly sufficient for their highest gratification. For they judge
prudently who maintain that the earth was so marred by the
deluge that we retain scarcely a moderate portion of the
original benediction. Even immediately after the fall of man
it had already begun to bring forth degenerate and noxious
fruits, but at the deluge the change became still greater. Yet,
however this may be, God certainly did not intend that man
should be slenderly and sparingly sustained but rather, by
these words, he promises a liberal abundance, which should
leave nothing wanting to a sweet and pleasant life. For Moses
relates how beneficent the Lord had been to them in bestow-
ing on them all things which they could desire, that their ingratitude might have the less excuse.

31. *And God saw everything.* Once more, at the conclusion
of the creation, Moses declares that God approved of everything which he had made. In speaking of God as *seeing,* he
does it after the manner of men; for the Lord designed this his
judgment to be as a rule and example to us, that no one
should dare to think or speak otherwise of his works. For
it is not lawful for us to dispute whether that ought to be
approved or not which God has already approved, but it
rather becomes us to acquiesce without controversy. The
repetition also denotes how wanton is the temerity of man;

otherwise it would have been enough to have said, once for all, that God approved of his works. But God six times inculcates the same thing, that he may restrain, as with so many bridles, our restless audacity. But Moses expresses more than before, for he adds מאד (*meod*)—that is, *very*. On each of the days, simple approbation was given. But now, after the workmanship of the world was complete in all its parts, and had received, if I may so speak, the last finishing touch, he pronounces it perfectly good, that we may know that there is in the symmetry of God's works the highest perfection, to which nothing can be added.

22. 2. And he said, Take now thy son, thine only *son* Isaac, whom thou lovest, and get thee into the land of Moriah; and offer him there for a burnt-offering upon one of the mountains which I will tell thee of.

11. And the angel of the Lord called unto him out of heaven, and said, Abraham, Abraham: and he said, Here *am* I.

12. And he said, Lay not thine hand upon the lad, neither do thou any thing unto him: for now I know that thou fearest God, seeing thou hast not withheld thy son, thine only *son*, from me.

2. *Take now thy son.* Abraham is commanded to immolate his son. If God had said nothing more than that his son should die, even this message would have most grievously wounded his mind because whatever favor he could hope for from God was included in this single promise, "In Isaac shall thy seed be called." Whence he necessarily inferred that his own salvation, and that of the whole human race, would perish unless Isaac remained in safety. For he was taught, by that word, that God would not be propitious to man without a Mediator. For although the declaration of Paul that "all the promises of God in Christ are yea and Amen" (II Cor. I. 20) was not yet written, it was nevertheless engraved on the heart of Abraham. Whence, however, could he have had this hope but from Isaac? The matter had come to this: that God would appear to have done nothing but mock him. Yet not only is the death of his

son announced to him, but he is commanded with his own hand
to slay him—as if he were required, not only to throw aside,
but to cut in pieces, or cast into the fire, the charter of his
salvation and to have nothing left for himself but death and
hell. But it may be asked how, under the guidance of faith,
he could be brought to sacrifice his son, seeing that what was
proposed to him was in opposition to that word of God on
which it is necessary for faith to rely? To this question the
apostle answers that his confidence in the word of God remained unshaken because he hoped that God would be able
to cause the promised benediction to spring up, even out of
the dead ashes of his son (Heb. 11. 19). His mind, however,
must of necessity have been severely crushed and violently
agitated when the *command* and the *promise* of God were
conflicting within him. But when he had come to the conclusion that the God with whom he knew he had to do could
not be his adversary, although he did not immediately discover how the contradiction might be removed, he nevertheless, by hope, reconciled the command with the promise; because, being indubitably persuaded that God was faithful, he
left the unknown issue to divine providence. Meanwhile, as
with closed eyes, he goes whither he is directed. The truth
of God deserves this honor: not only that it should far tran-
scend all human means, or that it alone, even without means,
should suffice us, but also that it should surmount all ob-
stacles. Here, then, we perceive more clearly the nature of the
temptation which Moses has pointed out. It was difficult and
painful to Abraham to forget that he was a father and a
husband, to cast off all human affections, and to endure before the world the disgrace of shameful cruelty by becoming
the executioner of his son. But the other was a far more
severe and horrible thing—namely, that he conceives God to
contradict himself and his own word, and then that he supposes the hope of the promised blessing to be cut off from
him when Isaac is torn away from his embrace. For what
more could he have to do with God when the only pledge of
grace is taken away? But as before, when he expected seed

from his own dead body, he by hope rose above what it seemed possible to hope for, so now when, in the death of his son, he apprehends the quickening power of God in such a manner as to promise himself a blessing out of the ashes of his son, he emerges from the labyrinth of temptation; for, in order that he might obey God, it was necessary that he should tenaciously hold the promise which, had it failed, faith must have perished. But with him the promise always flourished, because he both firmly retained the love with which God had once embraced him and subjected to the power of God everything which Satan raised up to disturb his mind. But he was unwilling to measure by his own understanding the method of fulfilling the promise which he knew depended on the incomprehensible power of God. It remains for every one of us to apply this example to himself. The Lord, indeed, is so indulgent to our infirmity that he does not thus severely and sharply try our faith; yet he intended, in the father of all the faithful, to propose an example by which he might call us to a general trial of faith. For the faith, which is more precious than gold and silver, ought not to lie idle, without trial; and experience teaches that each will be tried by God according to the measure of his faith. At the same time, also, we may observe that God tempts his servants, not only when he subdues the affections of the flesh, but when he reduces all their senses to nothing, that he may lead them to a complete renunciation of themselves.

Thine only son Isaac, whom thou lovest. As if it were not enough to command in one word the sacrifice of his son, he pierces, as with fresh strokes, the mind of the holy man. By calling him his *only* son, he again irritates the wound recently inflicted by the banishment of the other son; he then looks forward into futurity, because no hope of offspring would remain. If the death of a first-born son is wont to be grievous, what must the mourning of Abraham be? Each word which follows is emphatical and serves to aggravate his grief. "Slay," he says, "him whom alone thou lovest." And he does not here

refer merely to his paternal love, but to that which sprang
from faith. Abraham loved his son, not only as nature dictates
and as parents commonly do who take delight in their children, but as beholding the paternal love of God in him; lastly,
Isaac was the mirror of eternal life and the pledge of all good
things. Wherefore God seems not so much to assail the paternal love of Abraham as to trample upon his own benevolence.
There is equal emphasis in the name *Isaac*, by which Abraham
was taught that nowhere besides did any joy remain for him.
Certainly, when he who had been given as the occasion
of joy was taken away, it was just as if God should condemn
Abraham to eternal torment. We must always remember that
Isaac was not a son of the common order, but one in whose
person the Mediator was promised.

11. *And the angel of the Lord called unto him.* The inward temptation had been already overcome when Abraham
intrepidly raised his hand to slay his son; and it was by the
special grace of God that he obtained so signal a victory. But
now Moses subjoins that suddenly, beyond all hope, his sorrow was changed into joy. Poets in their fables, when affairs
are desperate, introduce some god who unexpectedly appears
at the critical juncture. It is possible that Satan, by figments
of this kind, has endeavored to obscure the wonderful and
stupendous interpositions of God, when he has unexpectedly
appeared for the purpose of bringing assistance to his servants.
This history ought certainly to be known and celebrated
among all people; yet, by the subtlety of Satan, not only has
the truth of God been adulterated and turned into a lie, but
also distorted into materials for fable in order to render it
the more ridiculous. But it is our business with earnest minds
to consider how wonderfully God, in the very article of death,
both recalled Isaac from death to life and restored to Abraham
his son, as one who had risen from the tomb. Moses also describes the voice of the angel as having sounded out of heaven
to give assurance to Abraham that he had come from God,
in order that he might withdraw his hand under the direction

of the same faith by which he had stretched it out. For, in a cause of such magnitude, it was not lawful for him either to undertake or to relinquish anything, except under the authority of God. Let us, therefore, learn from his example by no means to pursue what our carnal sense may declare to be, probably, our right course; but let God, by his sole will, prescribe to us our manner of acting and of ceasing to act. And truly Abraham does not charge God with inconstancy, because he considers that there had been just cause for the exercising of his faith.

12. *Now I know that thou fearest God.* The exposition of Augustine, "I have caused thee to know," is forced. But how can anything become known to God, to whom all things have always been present? Truly, by condescending to the manner of men, God here says that what he has proved by experiment is now made known to himself. And he speaks thus with us, not according to his own infinite wisdom, but according to our infirmity. Moses, however, simply means that Abraham, by this very act, testified how reverently he feared God. It is, however, asked whether he had not already on former occasions given many proofs of his piety. I answer that when God had willed him to proceed thus far, he had, at length, completed his true trial; in other persons a much lighter trial might have been sufficient. And as Abraham showed that he feared God by not sparing his own and only begotten son, so a common testimony of the same fear is required from all the pious in acts of self-denial. Now, since God enjoins upon us a continual warfare, we must take care that none desires his release before the time.

37. 5. And Joseph dreamed a dream, and he told *it* his brethren: and they hated him yet the more.

8. And his brethren said to him, Shalt thou indeed reign over us? or shalt thou indeed have dominion over us? And they hated him yet the more for his dreams, and for his words.

9. And he dreamed yet another dream, and told it his brethren, and said, Behold, I have dreamed a dream more; and, be-

hold, the sun, and the moon, and the eleven stars, made obeisance to me.

5. *And Joseph dreamed a dream.* Moses, having stated what were the first seeds of this enmity, now ascends higher and shows that Joseph had been elected, by the wonderful purpose of God, to great things; that this had been declared to him in a dream; and that, therefore, the hatred of his brethren broke forth into madness. God, however, revealed in dreams what he would do, that afterwards it might be known that nothing had happened fortuitously but that what had been fixed by a celestial decree was at length, in its proper time, carried forward through circuitous windings to its completion. It had been predicted to Abraham that his seed should be wanderers from the land of Canaan. In order, then, that Jacob might pass over into Egypt, this method was divinely appointed—namely, that Joseph, being president over Egypt in a time of famine, might bring his father thither with his whole family and supply them with food. Now, from the facts first related, no one could have conjectured such a result. The sons of Jacob conspire to put the very person to death without whom they cannot be preserved; yea, he who was ordained to be the minister of salvation to them is thrown into a well and with difficulty rescued from the jaws of death. Driven about by various misfortunes, he seems to be an alien from his father's house. Afterwards, he is cast into prison, as into another sepulcher, where for a long time he languishes. Nothing, therefore, was less probable than that the family of Jacob should be preserved by his means when he was cut off from it and carried far away and not even reckoned among the living. Nor did any hope of his liberation remain, especially from the time in which he was neglected by the chief butler; but being condemned to perpetual imprisonment, he was left there to rot. God, however, by such complicated methods, accomplishes what he had purposed. Wherefore, in this history, we have not only a most beautiful example of divine providence, but also two other points are added

especially worthy of notice: first, that the Lord performs his work by wonderful and unusual modes; and secondly, that he brings forth the salvation of his Church, not from magnificent splendor, but from death and the grave. Besides, in the person of Joseph a lively image of Christ is presented, as will more fully appear from the context. But since these subjects will be often repeated, let us follow the thread of Moses' discourse. God, of his mere grace, conferred peculiar honor on the boy, who was the last but one among twelve, in giving him the priority among his brethren. For by what merit or virtue shall we say that he attained the lordship over his brethren? Afterwards he seemed, indeed, to acquire this by his own great beneficence; but from the dream we learn that it was the free gift of God, which in no way depended upon Joseph's beneficence. Rather, he was ordained to be chief by the mere good pleasure of God in order that he might show kindness to his brethren. Now, since the Lord was, at that time, wont to reveal his secrets by two methods—by visions and by dreams—one of these kinds is here noted. For no doubt Joseph had often dreamed in the common manner; but Moses shows that a dream was now divinely sent to him which might have the force and weight of an oracle. We know that dreams are often produced by our daily thoughts: sometimes they are indications of an unhealthy state of the body; but whenever God intends to make known his counsel by dreams, he engraves on them certain marks which distinguish them from passing and frivolous imaginations in order that their credibility and authority may stand firm. Thus Joseph, being certainly persuaded that he had not been deluded by an empty specter, fearlessly announced his dream as a celestial oracle. Now, although the dominion is promised to him under a rural symbol, it is one which does not seem suitable for instruction to the sons of Jacob, for we know that they were herdsmen, not plowmen. Since they had no harvest which they could gather in, it seems hardly congruous that homage should be paid to his *sheaf*. But perhaps God designedly chose this similitude to show that this prophecy was not founded upon the present fortunes of Joseph, and that the material of his dominion would not consist in those things which were at hand, but that it should be a future benefit, the cause of which was to be sought for elsewhere than at home.

8. *Shalt thou indeed reign over us?* Here it is plainly shown to us that the paternal favor of God toward the elect is like a fan to excite against them the enmity of the world. When the sons of Jacob heard that they were fighting in vain against God, their unjust hatred ought, by such means, to have been corrected. For it was as if God, setting himself in the midst, would repress their fury by these words, "Your impious conspiring will be fruitless; for although you boast, I have constituted as your chief the man whose ruin your wicked envy hurries you to seek." Perhaps, also, by this consolatory dream he intended to alleviate the trouble of the holy youth. Yet their obstinacy caused it to be the more increased. Let us then learn not to be grieved if, at any time, the shining of the grace of God upon us should cause us to be envied. The sons of Jacob, however, were but too acute interpreters of the dream; yet they deride it as a fable, because it was repugnant to their wishes. Thus it often happens that they who are ill-disposed quickly perceive what is the will of God, but because they feel no reverence, they despise it. To this contumacy, however, succeeds a stupor which destroys their former quick-sightedness.

9. *And he dreamed yet another dream.* The scope of this dream is the same. The only difference is that God, to inspire greater confidence in the oracle, presents him with a figure from heaven. The brethren of Joseph had despised what was said concerning the sheaves; the Lord now calls upon them to look toward heaven, where his august majesty shines forth. It may, however, be asked how it can be reconciled with fact that his mother, who was now dead, could come and bow down to him. The interpretation of certain Hebrews, who refer it to Bilhah, is frigid, and the sense appears plain with-

out such subterfuges; for the sun and moon designate the head of the family on each side; thus in this figure Joseph sees himself reverenced by the whole house of his father.

    45. 1. Then Joseph could not refrain himself before all them that stood by him; and he cried, Cause every man to go out from me. And there stood no man with him, while Joseph made himself known unto his brethren.
    3. And Joseph said unto his brethren, I *am* Joseph: doth my father yet live? And his brethren could not answer him; for they were troubled at his presence.
    4. And Joseph said unto his brethren, Come near to me, I pray you. And they came near. And he said, I *am* Joseph your brother, whom ye sold into Egypt.
    8. So now, *it was* not you *that* sent me hither, but God: and he hath made me a father to Pharaoh, and lord of all his house, and a ruler throughout all the land of Egypt.

    1. *Then Joseph could not refrain himself.* Moses relates in this chapter the manner in which Joseph made himself known to his brethren. In the first place, he declares that Joseph had done violence to his feelings as long as he presented to them an austere and harsh countenance. At length the strong fraternal affection, which he had suppressed during the time that he was breathing severe threatenings, poured itself forth with more abundant force, whence it appears that nothing severe or cruel had before been harbored in his mind. And whereas it thus bursts forth in tears, this softness or tenderness is more deserving of praise than if he had maintained an equable temper. Therefore the Stoics speak foolishly when they say that it is an heroic virtue not to be touched with compassion. Had Joseph stood inflexible, who would not have pronounced him to be a stupid or iron-hearted man? But now, by the vehemence of his feelings, he manifests a noble magnanimity as well as a divine moderation, because he was so superior both to anger and to hatred that he ardently loved those who had wickedly conspired to effect his ruin, though they had received no injury from him. He commands all men to depart, not because he was ashamed of his kindred (for he

does not afterwards dissemble the fact that they were his brethren, and he freely permits the report of it to be carried to the king's palace), but because he is considerate for their feelings, that he might not make known their detestable crime to many witnesses. And it was not the smallest part of his clemency to desire that their disgrace should be wholly buried in oblivion. We see, therefore, that witnesses were removed for no other reason than that he might more freely comfort his brethren; for he not only spared them by not exposing their crime; but when shut up alone with them he abstained from all bitterness of language and gladly administered to them friendly consolation.

3. *I am Joseph.* Although he had given them the clearest token of his mildness and his love, yet, when he told them his name, they were terrified, as if he had thundered against them; for while they revolve in their minds what they have deserved, the power of Joseph seems so formidable to them that they anticipate nothing for themselves but death. When, however, he sees them overcome with fear, he utters no reproach but only labors to calm their perturbation. Nay, he continues gently to soothe them, until he has rendered them composed and cheerful. By this example we are taught to take heed lest sadness should overwhelm those who are truly and seriously humbled under a sense of shame. So long as the offender is deaf to reproofs, or securely flatters himself, or wickedly and obstinately repels admonitions, or excuses himself by hypocrisy, greater severity is to be used toward him. But rigor should have its bounds, and as soon as the offender lies prostrate and trembles under the sense of his sin, let that moderation immediately follow which may raise him who is cast down by the hope of pardon. Therefore, in order that our severity may be rightly and duly attempered, we must cultivate this inward affection of Joseph, which will show itself at the proper time.

4. *Come near to me, I pray you*. This is more efficacious than any mere words, that he kindly invites them to his embrace. Yet he also tries to remove their care and fear by the most courteous language he can use. He so attempers his speech, indeed, that he mildly accuses and again consoles them; nevertheless, the consolation greatly predominates, because he sees that they are on the point of desperation unless he affords them timely relief. Moreover, in relating that he had been sold, he does not renew the memory of their guilt with the intention of expostulating with them but only because it is always profitable that the sense of sin should remain, provided that immoderate terror does not absorb the unhappy man after he has acknowledged his fault. And whereas the brethren of Joseph were more than sufficiently terrified, he insists the more fully on the second part of his purpose—namely, that he may heal the wound. This is the reason why he repeats that God had sent him for their preservation; that by the counsel of God himself he had been sent beforehand into Egypt to preserve them alive; and that, in short, he had not been sent into Egypt by them, but had been led thither by the hand of God.

8. *So now, it was not you that sent me hither*. This is a remarkable passage, in which we are taught that the right course of events is never so disturbed by the depravity and wickedness of men but that God can direct them to a good end. We are also instructed in what manner and for what purpose we must consider the providence of God. When men of inquisitive minds dispute concerning it, they not only mingle and pervert all things without regard to the end designed, but invent every absurdity in their power in order to sully the justice of God. And this rashness causes some pious and moderate men to wish this portion of doctrine to be concealed from view, for as soon as it is publicly declared that God holds the government of the whole world, and that nothing is done but by his will and authority, they who think with

little reverence of the mysteries of God break forth into various questions, not only frivolous but injurious. But as this profane intemperance of mind is to be restrained, so a just measure is to be observed on the other hand, lest we should encourage a gross ignorance of those things which are not only made plain in the word of God but are exceedingly useful to be known. Good men are ashamed to confess that what men undertake cannot be accomplished except by the will of God, fearing lest unbridled tongues should cry out immediately, either that God is the author of sin, or that wicked men are not to be accused of crime, seeing they fulfill the counsel of God. But although this sacrilegious fury cannot be effectually rebutted, it may suffice that we hold it in detestation. Meanwhile, it is right to maintain, what is declared by the clear testimonies of Scripture, that whatever men may contrive, yet, amidst all their tumult, God from heaven overrules their counsels and attempts, and, in short, does by their hands what he has himself decreed. Good men, who fear to expose the justice of God to the calumnies of the impious, resort to this distinction: that God *wills* some things, but *permits* others to be done. As if, truly, any degree of liberty of action, were he to cease from governing, would be left to men. If he had only *permitted* Joseph to be carried into Egypt, he had not *ordained* him to be the minister of deliverance to his father Jacob and his sons—which he is now expressly declared to have done. Away, then, with that vain figment that by the *permission* of God only, and not by his *counsel* or *will*, those evils are committed which he afterwards turns to a good account. I speak of evils with respect to men who propose nothing else to themselves but to act perversely. And as the vice dwells in them, so ought the whole blame also to be laid upon them. But God works wonderfully through their means in order that, from their impurity, he may bring forth his perfect righteousness. This method of acting is secret and far above our understanding. Therefore it is not wonderful that the licentiousness of our flesh should rise against it. But so much the more dili-

gently must we be on our guard, that we do not attempt to re-
duce this lofty standard to the measure of our own littleness.
Let this sentiment remain fixed with us, that while the lust of
men exults, and intemperately hurries them hither and thither, God is the ruler, and by his secret rein directs their motions whithersoever he pleases. At the same time, however, it
must also be maintained that God acts so far distinctly from
them that no vice can attach itself to his providence and that
his decrees have no affinity with the crimes of men. Of which
mode of procedure a most illustrious example is placed before
our eyes in this history. Joseph was sold by his brethren—for
what reason, but because they wished, by any means whatever,
to ruin and annihilate him? The same work is ascribed to
God, but for a very different end—namely, that in a time of
famine the family of Jacob might have an unexpected supply
of food. Therefore he willed that Joseph should be as one
dead for a short time in order that he might suddenly bring
him forth from the grave as the preserver of life. Whence it
appears that although he seems at the commencement to do
the same thing as the wicked, yet there is a wide distance between their wickedness and his admirable judgment. Let us
now examine the words of Joseph. For the consolation of his
brethren he seems to draw the veil of oblivion over their
fault. But we know that men are not exempt from guilt, although God may, beyond expectation, bring what they wickedly
attempt to a good and happy issue. For what advantage was it
to Judas that the redemption of the world proceeded from
his wicked treachery? Joseph, however, though he withdraws
in some degree the minds of his brethren from a consideration
of their own guilt until they can breathe again after their
immoderate terror, neither traces their fault to God as its
cause nor really absolves them from it, as we shall see more
clearly in the last chapter. And doubtless, it must be maintained that the deeds of men are not to be estimated according
to the event but according to the measure in which they may
have failed in their duty, or may have attempted something

contrary to the divine command and may have gone beyond
the bounds of their calling. Someone, for instance, has neglected his wife or children and has not diligently attended to
their necessities; and though they do not die unless God wills
it, yet the inhumanity of the father, who wickedly deserted
them when he ought to have relieved them, is not screened
or excused by this pretext. Therefore, they whose consciences
accuse them of evil derive no advantage from the pretense
that the providence of God exonerates them from blame. But
on the other hand, whenever the Lord interposes to prevent
the evil of those who desire to injure us—and not that only,
but turns even their wicked designs to our good—he subdues,
by this method, our carnal affections, and renders us more
just and placable. Thus we see that Joseph was a skillful interpreter of the providence of God when he borrowed from it
an argument for granting forgiveness to his brethren. The
magnitude of the crime committed against him might so have
incensed him as to cause him to burn with the desire of revenge; but when he reflects that their wickedness had been
overruled by the wonderful and unwonted goodness of God,
forgetting the injury received, he kindly embraces the men
whose dishonor God had covered with his grace. And truly,
charity is ingenious in hiding the faults of brethren, and
therefore she freely applies to this use anything which may
tend to appease anger and to set enmities at rest. Joseph also
is carried forward to another view of the case—namely, that
he had been divinely chosen to help his brethren. Whence it
happens that he not only remits their offense, but that, from
an earnest desire to discharge the duty enjoined upon him,
he delivers them from fear and anxiety as well as from want.
This is the reason why he asserts that he was ordained to
"put for them a remnant"—that is, to preserve a remaining
seed, or rather to preserve them alive—and that by an excellent and wonderful deliverance. In saying that he is a father
to Pharaoh, he is not carried away with empty boasting as
vain men are wont to be; nor does he make an ostentatious

display of his wealth; but he proves, from an event so great and incredible, that he had not obtained the post he occupied by accident nor by human means, but rather that, by the wonderful counsel of God, a lofty throne had been raised for him, from which he might succor his father and his whole family.

ON ISAIAH

40. 1. Comfort ye, comfort ye my people, saith your God.

1. *Comfort ye.* The Prophet introduces a new subject; for, leaving the people on whom no favorable impression was made either by threatenings or by admonitions on account of their desperate wickedness, he turns to posterity, in order to declare that the people who shall be humbled under the cross will experience no want of consolation even amidst the severest distresses. And it is probable that he wrote this prophecy when the time of the captivity was at hand, that he might not at his departure from life leave the Church of God overwhelmed by very grievous calamities, without the hope of restoration. Though he formerly mingled his predictions with threatenings and terrors for this purpose, yet he appears to have contemplated chiefly the benefit of those who lived at that time. What will afterwards follow will relate to the future Church, the revival of which was effected long after his death; for he will next lay down a perpetual doctrine, which must not be limited to a single period, and especially when he treats of the commencement and progress of the reign of Christ. And this prophecy must be of so much the greater importance to us because it addresses us in direct terms; for, although it may be a spiritual application of what goes before so as to be doctrine that is common both to the Jews and to us, yet, as he leaves the Jews of that age and addresses posterity down to the end of the world, it appears to belong more especially to us.

By this exhortation, therefore, the Lord intended to stir up the hearts of the godly, that they might not faint amidst heavy calamities. First he addresses the Jews, who were soon after to be carried into that hard captivity in which they should have neither sacrifices nor prophets, and would have been destitute of all consolation had not the Lord relieved their miseries by these predictions. Next he addresses all the godly that should live afterwards, or that shall yet live, to encourage their heart, even when they shall appear to be reduced very low and to be utterly ruined.

That this discourse might have greater weight and might more powerfully affect their minds, he represents God as raising up new prophets, whom he enjoins to soothe the sorrows of the people by friendly consolation. The general meaning is that, when he shall have appeared to have forsaken for a time the wretched captives, the testimony of his grace will again burst forth from the darkness, and that, when gladdening prophecies shall have ceased, their proper time will come round. In order to exhibit more strongly the ground of joy, he makes use of the plural number, *Comfort ye*, by which he intimates that he will send not one or another, but a vast multitude of prophets; and this he actually accomplished, by which we see more clearly his infinite goodness and mercy.

Will say. First, it ought to be observed that the verb is in the future tense; and those commentators who render it in the present or past tense both change the words and spoil the meaning. Indirectly he points out an intermediate period, during which the people would be heavily afflicted, as if God had been silent. Though even at that time God did not cease to hold out the hope of salvation by some prophets, yet, having for a long period cast them off, when they were wretchedly distressed and almost ruined, the consolation was less abundant, till it was pointed out, as it were with the finger, that they were at liberty to return. On this account the word *comfort* must be viewed as relating to a present favor; and the repetition of the word not only confirms the certainty of the prediction, but applauds its power and success, as if he had said that in this message there will be abundant, full, and unceasing cause of joy.

Above all, we must hold by the future tense of this verb because there is an implied contrast between that melancholy silence of which I have spoken and the doctrine of consola-

tion which afterwards followed. And with this prediction
agrees the complaint of the Church, "We do not see our signs;
there is no longer among us a prophet or anyone that knows
how long" (Ps. 74. 9). We see how she laments that she has been
deprived of the best kind of comfort, because no promise is
brought forward for soothing her distresses. It is as if the
Prophet had said, "The Lord will not suffer you to be deprived of prophets to comfort you amidst your severest distresses. At that time he will raise up men by whom he will
send to you the message that had been long desired, and at
that time also he will show that he takes care of you."

I consider the future tense, *will say*, as relating not only
to the captivity in Babylon, but to the whole period of deliverance, which includes the reign of Christ. To the verb
will say, we must supply "to the prophets," whom he will
appoint for that purpose; for in vain would they have spoken
if the Lord had not told them, and even put into their mouth,
what they should make known to others. Thus there is a
mutual relation between God and the prophets. In a word, the
Lord promises that the hope of salvation will be left, although
the ingratitude of men deserves that this voice shall be perpetually silenced and altogether extinguished.

These words, I have said, ought not to be limited to the
captivity in Babylon; for they have a very extensive meaning,
and include the doctrine of the gospel, in which chiefly lies
the power of "comforting." To the gospel it belongs to comfort
those who are distressed and cast down, to quicken those who
are slain and actually dead, to cheer the mourners, and, in
short, to bring all joy and gladness; and this is also the reason why it is called "the gospel," that is, good news. Nor did
it begin at the time when Christ appeared in the world, but
long before, since the time when God's favor was clearly revealed, and Daniel might be said to have first raised his banner that believers might hold themselves in readiness for re-
turning (Dan. 9. 2). Afterwards, Haggai, Zechariah, Malachi,
Nehemiah, Ezra, and others, down to the coming of Christ,
exhorted believers to cherish better and better hopes. Malachi,

the last of them that wrote, knowing that there would be few prophets, sends the people to the law of Moses, to learn from it the will of God and its threatenings and promises (Mal. 4. 4).

Your God. From this passage we learn what we ought chiefly to seek in the prophets, namely, to encourage the hopes of godly persons by exhibiting the sweetness of divine grace, that they may not faint under the weight of afflictions, but may boldly persevere in calling on God. But since it was difficult to be believed, he reminds them of the covenant; as if he had said that it was impossible for God ever to forget what he formerly promised to Abraham (Gen. 17. 7). Although, therefore, the Jews by their sins had fallen from grace, yet he affirms that he is *their God* and that they are his peculiar people, both of which depended on election; but as even in that nation there were many reprobates, the statement implies that to believers only is this discourse strictly directed, because he silently permits unbelievers, through constant languishment, to be utterly wasted and destroyed. But to believers there is held out an invaluable comfort that, although for a time they are oppressed by grief and mourning, yet because they hope in God, who is the Father of consolation, they shall know by experience that the promises of grace, like a hidden treasure, are laid up for them to cheer their hearts at the proper time. This is also a very high commendation of the prophetic office, that it supports believers in adversity that they may not faint or be discouraged; and, on the other hand, this passage shows that it is a very terrible display of God's vengeance when there are no faithful teachers from whose mouth may be heard in the Church of God the consolation that is fitted to raise up those who are cast down and to strengthen the feeble.

ON THE PSALMS

23. 1. Jehovah is my shepherd, I shall not want.
2. He maketh me to lie down in pastures of grass; he leadeth
me to gently flowing waters.
3. He restoreth my soul: he leadeth me by the paths of
righteousness for his name's sake.

1. *Jehovah is my shepherd.* Although God, by his benefits, gently allures us to himself, as it were, by a taste of his
fatherly sweetness, yet there is nothing into which we more
easily fall than into a forgetfulness of him when we are in
the enjoyment of peace and comfort. Yea, prosperity not
only so intoxicates many, as to carry them beyond all bounds
in their mirth, but it also engenders insolence, which makes
them proudly rise up and break forth against God. Accordingly, there is scarcely a hundredth part of those who enjoy in
abundance the good things of God who keep themselves in
his fear and live in the exercise of humility and temperance,
which would be so becoming. For this reason, we ought the
more carefully to mark the example which is here set before
us by David, who, elevated to the dignity of sovereign power,
surrounded with the splendor of riches and honors, possessed
of the greatest abundance of temporal good things, and in
the midst of princely pleasures, not only testifies that he is
mindful of God, but, calling to remembrance the benefits
which God had conferred upon him, makes them ladders by
which he may ascend nearer to him. By this means he not only
bridles the wantonness of his flesh, but also excites himself
with the greater earnestness to gratitude and the other exercises of godliness, as appears from the concluding sentence of
the psalm, where he says, "I shall dwell in the house of Jehovah for a length of days." In like manner, in the eighteenth
psalm, which was composed at a period of his life when he
was applauded on every side, by calling himself the servant
of God he showed the humility and simplicity of heart to

which he had attained and, at the same time, openly testified his gratitude by applying himself to the celebration of the praises of God.

Under the similitude of a shepherd, he commends the care which God in his providence had exercised toward him. His language implies that God had no less care of him than a shepherd has of the sheep who are committed to his charge. God, in the Scripture, frequently takes to himself the name and puts on the character of a shepherd, and this is no mean token of his tender love toward us. As this is a lowly and homely manner of speaking, he who does not disdain to stoop so low for our sake must bear a singularly strong affection toward us. It is therefore wonderful that, when he invites us to himself with such gentleness and familiarity, we are not drawn or allured to him that we may rest in safety and peace under his guardianship. But it should be observed that God is a shepherd only to those who, touched with a sense of their own weakness and poverty, feel their need of his protection, and who willingly abide in his sheepfold and surrender themselves to be governed by him. David, who excelled both in power and riches, nevertheless frankly confessed himself to be a poor sheep that he might have God for his shepherd. Who is there, then, among us who would exempt himself from this necessity, seeing our own weakness sufficiently shows that we are more than miserable if we do not live under the protection of this shepherd? We ought to bear in mind that our happiness consists in this: that his hand is stretched forth to govern us, that we live under his shadow, and that his providence keeps watch and ward over our welfare. Although, therefore, we have abundance of all temporal good things, yet let us be assured that we cannot be truly happy unless God vouchsafe to reckon us among the number of his flock. Besides, we then only attribute to God the office of a shepherd with due and rightful honor when we are persuaded that his providence alone is sufficient to supply all our necessities. As those who enjoy the greatest abundance of outward good things are empty and famished if God is not their shepherd, so it is beyond all doubt that those whom he has taken under his charge shall not want a full abundance of all good things. David, therefore, declares that he is not afraid of wanting anything, because God is his shepherd.

2. *He maketh me to lie down in pastures of grass.* With respect to the words, it is in the Hebrew *pastures* or *fields of grass*, for *grassy and rich grounds.* Some, instead of translating the word נאות (*neoth*), which we have rendered *pastures*, render it *shepherds' cotes* or *lodges.* If this translation is considered preferable, the meaning of the Psalmist will be that sheepcotes were prepared in rich pasture grounds, under which he might be protected from the heat of the sun. If even in cold countries the immoderate heat which sometimes occurs is troublesome to a flock of sheep, how could they bear the heat of the summer in Judea, a warm region, without sheepfolds? The verb רבץ (*rahats*), to *lie down* or *repose,* seems to have a reference to the same thing. David has used the phrase *the quiet waters* to express gently flowing waters, for rapid streams are inconvenient for sheep to drink in and are also for the most part hurtful. In this verse and in the verses following he explains the last clause of the first verse, *I shall not want.* He relates how abundantly God had provided for all his necessities, and he does this without departing from the comparison which he employed at the commencement. The amount of what is stated is that the heavenly Shepherd had omitted nothing which might contribute to make him live happily under his care. He therefore compares the great abundance of all things requisite for the purposes of the present life which he enjoyed to meadows richly covered with grass and to gently flowing streams of water; or he compares the benefit or advantage of such things to sheepcotes, for it would not have been enough to have been fed and satisfied in rich pasture had there not also been provided waters to drink and the shadow of the sheepcote to cool and refresh him.

3. *He restoreth my soul.* As it is the duty of a good shepherd to cherish his sheep, and when they are diseased or weak to nurse and support them, David declares that this was the manner in which he was treated by God. *The restoring of the soul,* as we have translated it, or *the conversion of the soul,* as it is literally rendered, is of the same import as *to make anew* or *to recover,* as has been already stated in the nineteenth psalm, at the seventh verse. By *the paths of righteousness* he means easy and plain paths. As he still continues his metaphor, it would be out of place to understand this as referring to the direction of the Holy Spirit. He has stated a little before that God liberally supplies him with all that is requisite for the maintenance of the present life, and now he adds that he is defended by him from all trouble. The amount of what is said is that God is in no respect wanting to his people, seeing he sustains them by his power, invigorates and quickens them, and averts from them whatever is hurtful, that they may walk at ease in plain and straight paths. That, however, he may not ascribe anything to his own worth or merit, David represents the goodness of God as the cause of so great liberality, declaring that God bestows all these things upon him *for his own name's sake.* And certainly his choosing us to be his sheep, and his performing toward us all the offices of a shepherd, is a blessing which proceeds entirely from his free and sovereign goodness, as we shall see in the sixty-fifth psalm.

84. 1. How amiable are thy tabernacles, O Jehovah of Hosts!

2. My soul longeth [or greatly desireth], yea, even fainteth after the courts of Jehovah: my heart and my flesh leap for joy towards the living God.

3. The sparrow also hath found a house for herself, and the swallow a nest for herself, where she may place her young ones, O thine altars! thou Jehovah of Hosts! my King, and my God.

4. Blessed are they who dwell in thy house: they will be ever praising thee. Selah.

1. *How amiable are thy tabernacles, O Jehovah of Hosts!*
David complains of his being deprived of liberty of access to
the Church of God, there to make a profession of his faith,
to improve in godliness, and to engage in the divine worship.
Some would understand by the *tabernacles of God* the kingdom of heaven, as if David mourned over his continuance in
this state of earthly pilgrimage; but they do not sufficiently
consider the nature of his present afflicted circumstances—that
he was debarred from the sanctuary. He knew that God had
not in vain appointed the holy assemblies, and that the godly
have need of such helps so long as they are sojourners in this
world. He was also deeply sensible of his own infirmity; nor
was he ignorant how far short he came of approaching the
perfection of angels. He had, therefore, good ground to la-
ment over his being deprived of those means, the utility of
which is well known to all true believers. His attention was, no
doubt, directed to the proper end for which the external
ritual was appointed; for his character was widely different
from that of hypocrites, who, while they frequent the solemn
assemblies with great pomp, and seem to burn with ardent
zeal in serving God, yet in all this aim at nothing more than
by an ostentatious display of piety to obtain the credit of
having performed their duty toward him. David's mind was
far from being occupied with this gross imagination. The end
he had in view in desiring so earnestly to enjoy free access
to the sanctuary was that he might there worship God with
sincerity of heart and in a spiritual manner. The opening
words are in the form of an exclamation, which is an indication of ardent affection; and this state of feeling is expressed
still more fully in the second verse. Hence we learn that those
are sadly deficient in understanding who carelessly neglect
God's instituted worship, as if they were able to mount up
to heaven by their own unaided efforts.

I have observed that in the second verse a more than ordinary ardor of desire is expressed. The first verb, כסף (*casaph*),
signifies *vehemently to desire;* but not contented with this

word, David adds that *his soul fainteth after the courts of the Lord,* which is equivalent to our pining away when, under the influence of extreme mental emotion, we are in a manner transported out of ourselves. He speaks only of the *courts* of the tabernacle because, not being a priest, it was not lawful for him to go beyond the outer court. None but the priests, as is well known, were permitted to enter into the inner sanctuary. In the close of the verse he declares that this longing extended itself even to his body—that is, manifested itself in the utterance of the mouth, the languor of the eyes, and the action of the hands. The reason why he longed so intensely to have access to the tabernacle was to enjoy *the living God;* not that he conceived of God as shut up in so narrow a place as was the tent of the ark, but he was convinced of the need he had of steps by which to rise up to heaven, and knew that the visible sanctuary served the purpose of a ladder because by it the minds of the godly were directed and conducted to the heavenly model. And assuredly, when we consider that the sluggishness of our flesh hinders us from elevating our minds to the height of the divine majesty, in vain would God call us to himself, did he not at the same time, on his part, come down to us, or did he not at least, by the interposition of means, stretch out his hand to us, so to speak, in order to lift us up to himself.

3. *The sparrow also hath found a house for herself, and the swallow a nest for herself.* Some read this verse as one continuous sentence, conveying the idea that the birds made their nests near the altars; from which it might the more evidently appear how hard and distressing his condition was in being kept at a distance from them. This opinion seems to be supported from the circumstance that immediately before the Hebrew word for *altars,* there is the particle את (*eth*), which is commonly joined with the accusative case. But as it is also sometimes used in exclamations, the prophet, I have no doubt, breaking off in the middle of his sentence all at once, exclaims that nothing would be more grateful to him than to behold

the altar of God. David then, in the first place, with the view of aggravating the misery of his condition, compares himself with the sparrows and swallows, showing how hard a case it was for the children of Abraham to be driven out of the heritage which had been promised them while the little birds found some place or other for building their nests. He might sometimes find a comfortable retreat, and might even dwell among unbelievers with some degree of honor and state; but so long as he was deprived of liberty of access to the sanctuary, he seemed to himself to be in a manner banished from the whole world. Undoubtedly, the proper end which we ought to propose to ourselves in living is to be engaged in the service of God. The manner in which he requires us to serve him is spiritual, but still it is necessary for us to make use of those external aids which he has wisely appointed for our observance. This is the reason why David all at once breaks forth into the exclamation, *O thine altars! thou Jehovah of Hosts!* Some might be ready to say in reference to his present circumstances that there were many retreats in the world where he might live in safety and repose, yea, that there were many who would gladly receive him as a guest under their roof, and that therefore he had no cause to be so greatly distressed. To this he answers that he would rather relinquish the whole world than continue in a state of exclusion from the holy tabernacle; that he felt no place delightful at a distance from God's altars; and, in short, that no dwelling place was agreeable to him beyond the limits of the Holy Land. This he would intimate by the appellations which he gives to God, *My King, and my God.* In speaking thus, he gives us to understand that his life was uncomfortable and embittered because he was banished from the kingdom of God. "Although all men," as if he had said, "should vie with each other in their eagerness to afford me shelter and entertainment, yet as thou art my King, what pleasure would it afford me to live in the world so long as I am excluded from the territory of the Holy Land? And again, as thou art my God, for what end do I live but to seek after thee? Now, when thou castest me off, should I not despise every place of retreat and shelter which is offered me, however pleasant and delightful it may be to my flesh?"

4. *Blessed are they who dwell in thy house.* Here the Psalmist expresses more distinctly the proper and legitimate use of the sanctuary; and thus he distinguishes himself from hypocrites, who are sedulously attentive to the observance of outward ceremonies but destitute of genuine heart godliness. David, on the contrary, testifies that the true worshipers of God offer to him the sacrifice of praise, which can never be dissociated from faith. Never will a man praise God from the heart unless, relying upon his grace, he is a partaker of spiritual peace and joy.

> 5. Blessed is the man whose strength is in thee; the ways are in their hearts.
> 6. They passing through the valley of weeping, will together make it a fountain; the rain also will cover the cisterns [or reservoirs].
> 7. They will go from strength to strength; the God of gods will be seen in Zion.

5. *Blessed is the man whose strength is in thee.* David again informs us that the purpose for which he desired liberty of access to the sanctuary was, not merely to gratify his eyes with what was to be seen there, but to make progress in faith. To lean with the whole heart upon God is to attain to no ordinary degree of advancement; and this cannot be attained by any man, unless all his pride is laid prostrate in the dust, and his heart truly humbled. In proposing to himself this way of seeking God, David's object is to borrow from him by prayer the strength of which he feels himself to be destitute. The concluding clause of the verse, *the ways are in their hearts*, is by some interpreted as meaning that those are happy who walk in the way which God has appointed, for nothing is more injurious to a man than to trust in his own understanding. It is not improperly said of the law, "This is the

way, walk ye in it" (Isa. 30. 21). Whenever then men turn aside, however little it may be, from the divine law, they go astray and become entangled in perverse errors. But it is more appropriate to restrict the clause to the scope of the passage and to understand it as implying that those are happy whose highest ambition it is to have God as the guide of their life, and who therefore desire to draw near to him. God, as we have formerly observed, is not satisfied with mere outward ceremonies. What he desires is to rule and keep in subjection to himself all whom he invites to his tabernacle. Whoever then has learned how great a blessedness it is to rely upon God will put forth all the desires and faculties of his mind, that with all speed he may hasten to him.

6. *They passing through the valley of weeping, will together make it a well.* The meaning of the Psalmist is that no impediments can prevent the enlightened and courageous worshipers of God from making conscience of waiting upon the sanctuary. By this manner of speaking, he confirms the statement which he had previously made that nothing is more desirable than to be daily engaged in the worship of God, showing, as he does, that no difficulties can put a stop to the ardent longings of the godly and prevent them from hastening with alacrity, yea, even though their way should be through dry and barren deserts, to meet together to solemnize the holy assemblies. As the Hebrew word הבכא (*habbacha*), when the final letter is ה (*he*), signifies *tears,* and when the final letter is א (*aleph*), *a mulberry tree,* some here read *valley of tears,* and others *valley of the mulberry.* The majority of interpreters adopt the first reading, but the other opinion is not destitute of probability. There is, however, no doubt that dry and barren deserts are here to be understood, in traveling through which much difficulty and privation must be endured, particularly from the want of water, drink being of all other articles the most necessary to persons when traveling. David intended this as an argument to prove the steadfastness of the godly, whom the scarcity of water, which often discourages

travelers from prosecuting their journey, will not hinder from hastening to seek God, though their way should be through sandy and arid vales. In these words, reproof is administered to the slothfulness of those who will not submit to any inconvenience for the sake of being benefited by the service of God. They indulge themselves in their own ease and pleasures, and allow nothing to interfere with these. They will, therefore, provided they are not required to make any exertion or sacrifice, readily profess themselves to be the servants of God; but they would not give a hair of their head, or make the smallest sacrifice, to obtain the liberty of hearing the gospel preached and of enjoying the sacraments. This slothful spirit, as is evident from daily observation, keeps multitudes fast bound to their nests, so that they cannot bear to forego in any degree their own ease and convenience. Yea, even in those places where they are summoned by the sound of the church bell to public prayers, to hear the doctrine of salvation or to partake of the holy mysteries, we see that some give themselves to sleep, some think only of gain, some are entangled with the affairs of the world, and others are engaged in their amusements. It is therefore not surprising if those who live at a distance and who cannot enjoy these religious services and means of salvation without making some sacrifice of their worldly substance remain lolling at home. That such may not live secure and self-satisfied in the enjoyment of outward prosperity, David declares that those who have true heart religion, and who sincerely serve God, direct their steps to the sanctuary of God not only when the way is easy and cheerful, under the shade and through delightful paths, but also when they must walk through rugged and barren deserts; and that they will rather make for themselves cisterns with immense toil, than be prevented from prosecuting their journey by reason of the drought of the country.

7. *They will go from strength to strength.* In this verse the same sentiment is repeated. Mount Zion being the place where, according to the appointment of the law, the holy

assemblies were observed after the ark of the covenant was removed thither, it is said that the people of God will come to Zion in great numbers, provoking one another to this good work. The word חיל (*chayil*) seldom signifies *a troop* or *band of men*, but most commonly *power* or *strength*. It will therefore be more in accordance with the ordinary use of the term to translate *They will go from strength to strength*, implying that the saints are continually acquiring fresh strength for going up to mount Zion, and continue to prosecute their journey without weariness or fatigue until they reach the wished-for place and behold the countenance of God. If the word *troop* is preferred, the meaning will be that not a few only will come, but numerous companies. The manner in which God manifested himself to his servants in the temple in old time, we have spoken of elsewhere, and especially on the twenty-seventh psalm, at the fourth and fifth verses. No visible image of God was there to be seen; but the ark of the covenant was a symbol of his presence, and genuine worshipers found from experience that by this means they were greatly aided in approaching him.

109. 4. On account of my love they have been opposed to me; but I gave myself to prayer.

4. *But I gave myself to prayer.* Some are of opinion that these words refer to David's pouring out a prayer for his enemies at the very moment when they were furiously assaulting him, and with this opinion corresponds that which we have stated in Psalm 35. 13. But the more plain and, to me, the preferable interpretation is that when he was attacked in a cruel and hostile manner he did not betake himself to such unlawful means as the rendering of evil for evil, but committed himself into the hand of God, fully satisfied that he alone could guard him from all ill. And it is assuredly a great and desirable attainment for a man so to restrain his passions as directly and immediately to make his appeal to God's tribunal at the very time when he is abused without a cause and

when the very injuries which he sustains are calculated to excite him to avenge them. For there are some persons who, while it is their aim to live in terms of friendship with the good, coming in contact with ill men imagine that they are at perfect liberty to return injury for injury; and to this temptation all the godly feel that they are liable. The Holy Spirit, however, restrains us, so that though oftimes provoked by the cruelty of our enemies to seek revenge, we yet abandon all fraudulent and violent means and betake ourselves by prayer to God alone. By this example, which David here sets before us, we are instructed that we must have recourse to the same means if we would wish to overcome our enemies through the power and protection of God. In Psalm 69. 13, we have a parallel passage: "They that sit in the gate spake against me; and I was the song of those who drink strong drink. But my prayer was made to thee, O Jehovah!" In that passage, as well as in the one under review, the mode of expression is elliptical. Besides, it is the design of David in these words to inform us that although he was aware that the whole world was opposed to him, yet he could cast all his cares upon God, and this was enough to render his mind calm and composed. And as the Holy Spirit taught David and all the godly to offer up prayers like these, it must follow that those who in this respect imitate them, will be promptly helped by God when he beholds them reproachfully and vilely persecuted.

6. Set thou over him a wicked person; and let the adversary stand at his right hand.

7. When he is judged, let him depart guilty, and let his prayer be turned into sin.

8. Let his days be few: and let another receive his office.

9. Let his children be fatherless, and his wife a widow:

10. And let his children wander without any settled habitation, and let them be beggars, and let them seek food out of their waste places.

11. Let the extortioner seize all that belongs to him, and let strangers spoil his labor.

6. *Set thou over him a wicked person.* Hitherto he poured out his complaint against a vast number of persons; now he seems to direct it against a single individual. Probably he speaks of each of them individually. It is, however, equally probable that he refers in very marked terms to some one in particular among these wicked persons, the most notorious transgressor of any of them. Some conjecture, and not without reason, that Doeg is the person here aimed at, who, by his treason and revolt, sought to bring ruin, not only upon David, but also upon all the holy priests; and we know that this psalm is applied by Peter to Judas (Acts 1. 20). But with equal propriety, and certainly not less forcibly, may this complaint be considered as applicable to some most intimate and particular friend of the Psalmist. Respecting the imprecations contained in this psalm, it will be proper to keep in mind what I have said elsewhere—that when David forms such maledictions, or expresses his desires for them, he is not instigated by any immoderate carnal propensity, nor is he actuated by zeal without knowledge, nor is he influenced by any private personal considerations. These three matters must be carefully weighed, for in proportion to the amount of self-esteem which a man possesses is he so enamored with his own interests as to rush headlong upon revenge. Hence it comes to pass that the more a person is devoted to selfishness he will be the more immoderately addicted to the advancement of his own individual interests. This desire for the promotion of personal interest gives birth to another species of vice. For no one wishes to be avenged upon his enemies because that such a thing would be right and equitable, but because it is the means of gratifying his own spiteful propensity. Some, indeed, make a pretext of righteousness and equity in the matter, but the spirit of malignity, by which they are inflamed, effaces every trace of justice and blinds their minds.

When these two vices, selfishness and carnality, are corrected, there is still another thing demanding correction—the repressing the ardor of foolish zeal, in order that we may follow the Spirit of God as our guide. Should anyone, under

the influence of perverse zeal, produce David as an example
of it, that would not be an example in point; for to such a
person may be very aptly applied the answer which Christ
returned to his disciples, "Ye know not what spirit ye are of"
(Luke 9. 55). How detestable a piece of sacrilege is it on the
part of the monks, and especially the Franciscan friars, to
pervert this psalm by employing it to countenance the most
nefarious purposes! If a man harbor malice against a neighbor, it is quite a common thing for him to engage one of these
wicked wretches to curse him, which he would do by daily
repeating this psalm. I know a lady in France who hired a
parcel of these friars to curse her own and only son in these
words.

But I return to David, who, free from all inordinate pas-
sion, breathed forth his prayers under the influence of the
Holy Spirit. Then, as to the ungodly, who live as the con-
temners of God and who are constantly plotting the overthrow of the unsuspecting and the good, casting off all restraint so that neither modesty nor honesty proves a check to
them, surely they are deserving of the punishment of *having
a wicked person set over them*. And since, by means of intrigue
and perfidy, they are constantly aiming at the extermination
of the good, they are most justly punished by God, who raises
up against them an adversary that should never depart from
their side. Only let believers be on their guard, lest they should
betray too much haste in their prayers, and let them rather
leave room for the grace of God to manifest itself in their
behalf; because it may turn out that the man who today bears
toward us a deadly enmity may by tomorrow through that
grace become our friend.

7. *When he is judged, let him depart guilty.* Another imprecation is that, being summoned to judgment, he might be
punished without mercy, and that, though he humbly crave
forgiveness, the judge should remain inexorable. This might
with propriety be understood to relate not merely to his being judged at the bar of men, but also at the tribunal of God.

But as it accords very well with the decisions awarded by an earthly judge, and as this is the commonly received interpretation, I have no wish to depart from it. There are two things which must be noticed here: that the wickedness of the wicked may be so palpable as to leave no room to escape from the execution of justice, and that all their entreaties for pardon may be disregarded. Accordingly, the Psalmist represents him as a condemned criminal leaving the presence of the judge, bearing the ignominy of the condemnation which he righteously merited, having his nefarious deeds disclosed and detected. With respect to the other interpretation which places the ungodly before God's judgment seat, it by no means appears absurd to say that their prayers should be turned against them to sin, the more especially as we know that all their sacrifices are an abomination unto him. And by how much they themselves are filthy, by so much do all their plausible virtues become offensive and displeasing to God. But as the scope of the passage is in favor of that interpretation which applies it to earthly judges, I do not consider it necessary to insist farther upon this point.

8. *Let his days be few.* Although this world is the scene of much toil and trouble, yet we know that these are pledges and proofs of God's loving-kindness, inasmuch as he frequently, and as a token of his love, promises to prolong the lives of men; not that it is absolutely necessary for us to remain long here, but that we may have an opportunity of sharing of God's fatherly love which he bears toward us, by which we may be led to cherish the hope of immortality. Now, in opposition to this, the brevity of human life is here introduced as a mark of God's disapprobation; for when he cuts off the wicked after a violent manner, he thus testifies that they did not deserve to breathe the breath of life. And the same sentiment is inculcated when, denuding them of their honor and dignity, he hurls them from the place of power and authority. The same thing may also happen to the children of God, for temporal evils are common to the good and to the bad; at the same

time, these are never so mingled and blended together but that one may perceive occasionally the judgments of God in a very manifest and marked manner. Peter, quoting this verse (Acts 1. 20), says it behooved to be fulfilled in Judas, because it is written here, "let another take his bishopric." And this he does on the assumed principle of interpretation that David here spoke in the person of Christ. To this it cannot be objected that the Hebrew term פְּקֻדָּה (*pekudah*) signifies generally *superintendence*, because Peter very properly applies it to the apostleship of Judas. In expounding this passage, sometimes in reference to a wife or to the soul (which is a precious jewel in man) or to wealth and property, there is good reason to believe that, in doing so, the Jewish interpreters are actuated by pure malice. What purpose can it serve to pervert the sense of a word, the meaning of which is so pointed and plain, unless that, under the influence of a malignant spirit, they endeavor so to obscure the passage as to make it appear not to be properly quoted by Peter? From these words we learn that there is no cause why the ungodly should be proud while their reputation is high in this world, seeing they cannot after all escape from that doom which the Holy Spirit here declares awaits them. Here, too, we are furnished with very valuable matter of comfort and patience when we hear that, however elevated may be their rank and reputation now, their downfall is approaching, and that they will soon be stripped of all their pomp and power. In the two succeeding verses the malediction is extended both to the wife and children; and the desire that she may be left a widow and they become fatherless depends upon the brevity of that life to which the prophet formerly adverted. Mention is likewise made of *beggary*, and the want of all the necessaries of life, which is a proof of the magnitude of their guilt; for assuredly the Holy Spirit would not denounce against them a punishment so grievous and heavy for a trivial offence. In delivering up his property as booty to the *extortioners*, David must be understood as alluding to the poverty which was to overtake his children; for he is not speaking of a poor and mean person who at his death can leave nothing to his family, but of one who, regardless of right or wrong, has amassed wealth to enrich his children but from whom God takes away the goods which he had unrighteously taken from others.

12. Let there be none prolonging mercy to him: and let there be none to pity his fatherless children.

13. Let his posterity be cut off; in the next generation let their name be effaced.

14. Let the iniquity of his fathers be remembered before Jehovah; and let not the sin of his mother be blotted out.

15. Let them be before Jehovah continually, and let him cut off their memorial from the earth.

16. Because he forgot to show mercy, but persecuted the afflicted and poor man, and the sorrowful in heart, that he might slay him.

12. *Let there be none prolonging mercy to him.* To continue to show humanity and mercy is, according to the Hebrew idiom, equivalent to constant and successive acts of kindness; and it also sometimes denotes pity, or the being moved to sympathy, when, through the lapse of years, anger is appeased and even one's calamity melts the heart of the man who bore hatred toward him. Accordingly, there are some who understand this clause to mean that there will be none to show kindness to his offspring, which interpretation is in conformity with the next clause of the verse. David, however, includes also the wicked man himself along with his children, as if he should say, "Though he visibly pine away under such calamities, and these descend to his children, yet let no one show pity toward them." We are aware it not unfrequently happens that the long-continued misfortune of an enemy either excites the sympathy of men of savage dispositions or else makes them forget all their hatred and malevolence. But in this part of the psalm, David expresses a desire that his enemy and all his posterity may be so hated and detested that the people may never be wearied with beholding the calamities which they endure but may become so familiarized with the spectacle as if their hearts were of iron. At the same

time, let it be remarked that David is not rashly excited by any personal anguish to speak in this manner, but that it is as God's messenger he declares the punishment which was impending over the ungodly. And verily the law accounts it as one of the judgments of God, his hardening men's hearts so that they who have been passionately and unmercifully cruel should find no sympathy (Deut. 2. 30). It is just that the same measure which they have used toward others should also be meted out to themselves.

13. *Let his posterity be cut off.* This is a continuation of the same subject upon the consideration of which the prophet had just now entered—that God would visit the iniquities of the fathers upon their children. And as he had to deal with the whole court of Saul and not with any single individual, he here employs the plural number. But as in deeds of wickedness, there are always some who are the prime movers and act as the ringleaders of others, we need not be surprised that, having spoken of one person, he next addresses the many and then returns to the same person. The more natural and simple mode of explanation is to refer it to his offspring, for the Hebrew term which signifies *posterity* is collective, implying a multitude and not a single individual only. This is a heavier imprecation than the former. It sometimes happens that a family, overthrown by an unexpected disaster, rises up again at a subsequent period; here, however, it is the wish of the prophet that the wicked may be so completely ruined as never to be able to regain their former state; for thus much is implied in *their name being effaced in the next generation,* or after the lapse of ages.

And as the destruction which he denounces against the houses and families of the wicked is so extensive that God punishes them in the person of their posterity, so he desires that *God may remember the iniquities of their fathers and mothers,* in order that their condemnation may be complete; and this is a principle in perfect accordance with the com-

monly received doctrine of Scripture. God, out of regard to
his covenant, which is in force to a thousand generations,
extends and continues his mercy toward posterity; but he
also punishes iniquity unto the third and fourth generation.
In doing this he does not involve the guiltless with the wicked
indiscriminately, but by withholding from the reprobate the
grace and illumination of his Spirit, he prepares the vessels
of wrath for destruction, even before they are born (Rom. 9.
21). To the common sense of mankind, the thought of such
severity is horrifying; but then we must recollect that if we
attempt to measure the secret and inscrutable judgments of
God by our finite minds we do him wrong. Struck with horror
at the severity of this threatening, let us improve it as the
means of filling us with reverence and godly fear. In reference
to the language of Ezekiel (18. 20), "The son shall not bear
the iniquity of the father, but the soul that sinneth, it shall
die," we know that in these words he disproves the ground-
less complaints of the people who, boasting that they were
guiltless, imagined that they were punished wrongfully. When,
however, God continues his vengeance from the father to the
children, he leaves them no room for palliation or complaint,
because they are all equally guilty. We have already said that
vengeance commences when God, in withdrawing his Spirit
both from the children and the fathers, delivers them over to
Satan. Some may inquire how it comes to pass that the prophet, in desiring that their sin *may be continually before God's
eyes,* does not likewise add, "Let their name be blotted out
from heaven," but merely wishes them *to be cut off, and to
perish in the world.* My reply is that he spoke agreeably to
the custom of the age in which he lived, when the nature of
spiritual punishments was not so well understood as in our
times because the period had not yet arrived when the revelation of God's will was to be full and complete. Besides, it is
the design of David that the vengeance of God may be so
manifest that the whole world may acquiesce in his equity as
a judge.

16. *Because he forgot to show mercy.* The prophet comes now to show that he had good reason for desiring such awful and direful calamities to be inflicted upon his enemies, whose thirst for cruelty was insatiable and who were transported with rage, no less cruel than obstinate, against the afflicted and poor man, persecuting him with as little scruple as if they were attacking a dead dog. Even philosophers look upon cruelty directed against the helpless and miserable as an act worthy only of a cowardly and groveling nature, for it is between equals that envy is cherished. For this reason the prophet represents the malignity of his enemies as being bitter in persecuting him when he was in *affliction and poverty.* The expression, *the sorrowful in heart,* is still more emphatic. For there are persons who, notwithstanding of their afflictions, are puffed up with pride; and as this conduct is unreasonable and unnatural, these individuals incur the displeasure of the powerful. On the other hand, it would be a sign of desperate cruelty to treat with contempt the lowly and dejected in heart. Would not this be to fight with a shadow? This insatiable cruelty is still further pointed out by the phrase *forgetting to show mercy,* the meaning of which is that the calamities with which he beheld this guiltless and miserable man struggling fail to excite his pity, so that, out of regard to the common lot of humanity, he should lay aside his savage disposition. In this passage, therefore, the contrast is equally balanced on the one side between such obstinate pride and, on the other, the strict and irrevocable judgment of God. And as David spoke only as he was moved by the Holy Spirit, this imprecation must be received as if God himself should thunder from his celestial throne. Thus, in the one case, by denouncing vengeance against the ungodly, he subdues and restrains our perverse inclinations, which might lead us to injure a fellow creature; and on the other, by imparting comfort to us, he mitigates and moderates our sorrow, so that we patiently endure the ills which they inflict upon us. The wicked may for a time revel with impunity in the gratification of their lusts; but this threatening shows that it is no vain protection which God

vouchsafes to the afflicted. But let the faithful conduct themselves meekly, that their humility and contrition of spirit may come up before God with acceptance. And as we cannot distinguish between the elect and the reprobate, it is our duty to pray for all who trouble us; to desire the salvation of all men; and even to be careful for the welfare of every individual. At the same time, if our hearts are pure and peaceful, this will not prevent us from freely appealing to God's judgment, that he may cut off the finally impenitent.

ON JOHN

2. 1. Three days after, there was a marriage in Cana of Galilee; and the mother of Jesus was there.
2. And Jesus also was invited, and his disciples, to the marriage.
3. And when the wine fell short, the mother of Jesus saith to him, They have no wine.

1. *There was a marriage in Cana of Galilee.* As this narrative contains the first miracle which Christ performed, it would be proper for us, were it on this ground alone, to consider the narrative attentively; though—as we shall afterwards see—there are other reasons which recommend it to our notice. But while we proceed, the various advantages arising from it will be more clearly seen. The Evangelist first mentions *Cana of Galilee*, not that which was situated toward Zarephath (I Kings 17. 9; Obad. 20; Luke 4. 26) or Sarepta, between Tyre and Sidon, and was called the greater in comparison of this latter *Cana*, which is placed by some in the tribe of Zebulun, and by others in the tribe of Asher. For Jerome too assures us that even in his time there existed a small town which bore that name. There is reason to believe that it was near the city of Nazareth, since the mother of Christ came there to attend the marriage. From the fourth chapter of this book it will be seen that it was not more than one day's journey distant from Capernaum. That it lay not far from the city of Bethsaida may also be inferred from the circumstance that *three days after* Christ had been in those territories, the marriage was celebrated—the Evangelist tells us—in *Cana of Galilee.* There may have been also a third *Cana* not far from Jerusalem and yet out of Galilee, but I leave this undetermined because I am unacquainted with it.

And the mother of Jesus was there. It was probably one of Christ's near relations who married a wife, for *Jesus* is mentioned as having accompanied *his mother.* From the fact that

176

the disciples also are invited, we may infer how plain and frugal was his way of living; for he lived in common with them. It may be thought strange, however, that a man who has no great wealth or abundance (as will be made evident from the scarcity of the wine) invites four or five other persons on Christ's account. But the poor are readier and more frank in their invitations because they are not, like the rich, afraid of being disgraced if they do not treat their guests with great costliness and splendor, for the poor adhere more zealously to the ancient custom of having an extended acquaintance.

Again, it may be supposed to show a want of courtesy, that the bridegroom allows his guests, in the middle of the entertainment, to be in want of wine; for it looks like a man of little thoughtfulness not to have a sufficiency of wine for his guests. I reply, nothing is here related which does not frequently happen, especially when people are not accustomed to the daily use of wine. Besides, the context shows that it was toward the conclusion of the banquet that *the wine fell short*, when, according to custom, it might be supposed that they had already drunk enough; for the master of the feast thus speaks: *Other men place worse wine before those who have drunk enough, but thou hast kept the best till now.* Besides, I have no doubt that all this was regulated by the providence of God, that there might be room for the miracle.

3. *The mother of Jesus saith to him.* It may be doubted if she expected or asked anything from her Son, since he had not yet performed any miracle; and it is possible that, without expecting any remedy of this sort, she advised him to give some pious exhortations which would have the effect of preventing the guests from feeling uneasiness and at the same time of relieving the shame of *the bridegroom*. I consider her words to be expressive of (συμπαθεία) earnest compassion; for the holy woman, perceiving that those who had been invited were likely to consider themselves as having been treated with disrespect and to murmur against the bridegroom, and that the entertainment might in that way be disturbed, wished that

some means of soothing them could be adopted. Chrysostom throws out a suspicion that she was moved by the feelings of a woman to seek I know not what favor for herself and her Son; but this conjecture is not supported by any argument.

15. 17. These things I command you, that you may love one another.
18. If the world hate you, you know that it hated me before it hated you.
19. If you were of the world, the world would love what was its own; but because you are not of the world, but I have chosen you out of the world, therefore the world hateth you.
20. Remember the word which I said to you, The servant is not greater than his master. If they have persecuted me, they will also persecute you; if they have kept my word, they will keep yours also.
21. But all these things they will do to you on account of my name, because they know not him who sent me.

17. *These things I command you.* This, too, was appropriately added, that the apostles might know that mutual love among ministers is demanded above all things, that they may be employed, with one accord, in building up the Church of God; for there is no greater hindrance than when everyone labors apart, and when all do not direct their exertions to the common good. If, then, ministers do not maintain brotherly intercourse with each other, they may possibly erect some large heaps, but utterly disjointed and confused; and all the while there will be no building of a Church.

18. *If the world hate you.* After having armed the apostles for the battle, Christ exhorts them likewise to patience; for the gospel cannot be published without instantly driving the world to rage. Consequently, it will never be possible for godly teachers to avoid the hatred of the world. Christ gives them early information of this, that they may not be instances of what usually happens to raw recruits, who, from want of experience, are valiant before they have seen their enemies but who tremble as soon as the battle is commenced. And not

only does Christ forewarn his disciples, that nothing may happen to them which is new and unexpected, but likewise confirms them by his example; for it is not reasonable that Christ should be *hated by the world* and that we, who represent his person, should have the world on our side, which is always like itself.

You know. I have translated the verb γινώσχετε in the indicative mood, *you know;* but if anyone prefer to translate it in the imperative mood, *know ye,* I have no objection, for it makes no change in the meaning. There is greater difficulty in the phrase which immediately follows, πρῶτον ὑμῶν, *before you;* for when he says that he is *before* the disciples, this may be referred either to *time* or to *rank.* The former exposition has been more generally received, namely, that Christ *was hated by the world* BEFORE the apostles were hated. But I prefer the second exposition, namely, that Christ, who is far exalted above them, was not exempted from the hatred of the world, and therefore his ministers ought not to refuse the same condition; for the phraseology is the same as that which we have seen twice before, in the twenty-seventh and thirtieth verses of the first chapter of this book, *He who cometh after me is preferred to me* (ὅτι πρῶτός μου ἦν), for *he was before me.*

19. *If you were of the world.* This is another consolation, that the reason why they are *hated by the world* is that they have been separated from it. Now, this is their true happiness and glory, for in this manner they have been rescued from destruction.

But I have chosen you out of the world. To choose means here *to separate.* Now, if they were *chosen out of the world,* it follows that they were a part *of the world,* and that it is only by the mercy of God that they are distinguished from the rest who perish. Again, by the term *the world,* Christ describes in this passage all who have not been regenerated by the Spirit of God; for he contrasts the Church with *the world,* as we shall see more fully under the seventeenth chapter. And yet this doctrine does not contradict the exhortation of Paul, *Be*

at peace with all men, as far as lieth in you (Rom. 12. 18);
for the exception which he adds amounts to saying that we
ought to see what is right and proper for us to do, that no
man, by seeking to please *the world,* may give himself up to
its corruptions.

But there is still another objection that may be urged; for
we see that it commonly happens that wicked men who are
of the world are not only *hated* but accursed by others. In
this respect, certainly, *the world loveth* not *what is its own.* I
reply, earthly men, who are regulated by the perception of
their flesh, never have a true hatred of sin, but only so far as
they are affected by the consideration of their own convenience or injury. And yet the intention of Christ was not to
deny that *the world* foams and rages within itself by internal
quarrels. He only intended to show that *the world hates*
nothing in believers but what is of God. And hence, too, it
plainly appears how foolish are the dreams of the Anabaptists,
who conclude from this single argument that they are the
servants of God because they displease the greater part of
men. For it is easy to reply that many who are *of the world*
favor their doctrine, because they are delighted at the thought
of having everything in shameful confusion; while many who
are *out of the world* hate it, because they are desirous that
the good order of the state should remain unbroken.

20. *Remember the word.* It might also be read in the indicative mood, *You remember the word,* and the meaning is
not very different; but I think that it is more suitable to read
it in the imperative mood, *Remember the word.* It is a confirmation of what Christ had spoken immediately before,
when he said that he was hated by the world, though he was
far more excellent than his disciples; for it is unreasonable
that the condition of *the servant* should be better than that of
his master. Having spoken of persons, he likewise makes mention of doctrine.

If they have kept my word, they will keep yours also. Nothing gives greater uneasiness to the godly than when they see

the doctrine, which is of God, haughtily despised by men; for it is truly shocking and dreadful, and the sight of it might shake the stoutest heart. But when we remember, on the other hand, that not less obstinate resistance was manifested against the Son of God himself, we need not wonder that the doctrine of God is so little reverenced among men. When he calls it *his doctrine* and *their doctrine*, this refers to the ministry. Christ is the only Teacher of the Church; but he intended that *his doctrine*, of which he had been the first Teacher, should be afterwards preached by the apostles.

21. *But all these things they will do to you.* As the fury of the world is monstrous when it is so enraged against the doctrine of its own salvation, Christ assigns the reason to be that it is hurried on by blind ignorance to its own destruction; for no man would deliberately engage in battle against God. It is blindness and ignorance of God, therefore, that hurries on the world, so that it does not hesitate to make war with Christ. We ought, then, always to observe the cause of this conduct, and the true consolation consists in nothing else than the testimony of a good conscience. It should also excite gratitude in our minds that, while the world perishes in its blindness, God has given to us his light. Yet let it be under-stood that hatred of Christ arises from stupidity of mind, when God is not known; for, as I have often said, unbelief is blind; not that wicked men do not understand or know anything, but because all the knowledge that they have is confused, and quickly vanishes away. On this subject I have elsewhere treated more largely.

ON ROMANS

2. 14. For when the Gentiles, which have not the law, do by nature the things contained in the law, these, having not the law, are a law unto themselves:

15. Which show the work of the law written in their hearts, their conscience also bearing witness, and *their* thoughts the meanwhile accusing or else excusing one another;

16. In the day when God shall judge the secrets of men by Jesus Christ, according to my gospel.

14. *For when the Gentiles, etc.* He now states what proves the former clause; for he did not think it enough to condemn us by mere assertion, and only to pronounce on us the just judgment of God; but he proceeds to prove this by reasons, in order to excite us to a greater desire for Christ and to a greater love toward him. He indeed shows that ignorance is in vain pretended as an excuse by the Gentiles, since they prove by their own deeds that they have some rule of righteousness; for there is no nation so lost to everything human that it does not keep within the limits of some laws. Since then all nations, of themselves and without a monitor, are disposed to make laws for themselves, it is beyond all question evident that they have some notions of justice and rectitude, which the Greeks call preconceptions, προληψεις, and which are implanted by nature in the hearts of men. They have then a law, though they are without law; for though they have not a written law, they are yet by no means wholly destitute of the knowledge of what is right and just; as they could not otherwise distinguish between vice and virtue; the first of which they restrain by punishment and the latter they commend, and manifest their approbation of it by honoring it with rewards. He sets nature in opposition to a written law, meaning that the Gentiles had the natural light of righteousness, which supplied the place of that law by which the Jews were instructed, so that they were a law to themselves.

15. *Who show the work of the law written, etc.;* that is,
they prove that there is imprinted on their hearts a discrimin-
ation and judgment by which they distinguish between what
is just and unjust, between what is honest and dishonest. He
means not that it was so engraved on their will, that they
sought and diligently pursued it, but that they were so mas-
tered by the power of truth that they could not disapprove of
it. For why did they institute religious rites, except that they
were convinced that God ought to be worshiped? Why were
they ashamed of adultery and theft, except that they deemed
them evils?

Without reason then is the power of the will deduced from
this passage, as though Paul had said that the keeping of the
law is within our power; for he speaks not of the power to
fulfill the law, but of the knowledge of it. Nor is the word
heart to be taken for the seat of the affections, but only for
the understanding, as it is found in Deut. 29. 4, "The Lord
hath not given thee a heart to understand"; and in Luke 24.
25, "O foolish men, and slow in heart to believe."

Nor can we conclude from this passage that there is in men
a *full* knowledge of the law, but that there are only some
seeds of what is right implanted in their nature, evidenced by
such acts as these: All the Gentiles alike instituted religious
rites, they made laws to punish adultery and theft and murder, they commended good faith in bargains and contracts.
They have thus indeed proved that God ought to be worshiped, that adultery and theft and murder are evils, that
honesty is commendable. It is not to our purpose to inquire
what sort of God they imagined him to be, or how many gods
they devised; it is enough to know that they thought that there
is a God, and that honor and worship are due to him. It matters not whether they permitted the coveting of another man's
wife, or of his possessions, or of anything which was his—
whether they connived at wrath and hatred—inasmuch as it
was not right for them to covet what they knew to be evil
when done.

Their conscience at the same time attesting, etc. He could not have more forcibly urged them than by the testimony of their own conscience, which is equal to a thousand witnesses. By the consciousness of having done good, men sustain and comfort themselves; those who are conscious of having done evil are inwardly harassed and tormented. Hence came these sayings of the heathens: "A good conscience is the widest sphere; but a bad one is the cruelest executioner, and more fiercely torments the ungodly than any furies can do." There is then a certain knowledge of the law by nature, which says, "This is good and worthy of being desired; that ought to be abhorred."

But observe how intelligently he defines conscience: he says that reasons come to our minds by which we defend what is rightly done, and that there are those which accuse and reprove us for our vices; and he refers this process of accusation and defense to the day of the Lord; not that it will then first commence, for it is now continually carried on, but that it will then also be in operation; and he says this, that no one should disregard this process as though it were vain and evanescent. And he has put *in the day* instead of *at the day*—a similar instance to what we have already observed.

16. *In which God shall judge the secrets of men.* Most suitable to the present occasion is this periphrastic definition of judgment; it teaches those who willfully hide themselves in the recesses of insensibility that the most secret thoughts and those now completely hid in the depths of their hearts shall then be brought forth to the light. So he speaks in another place: in order to show to the Corinthians what little value belongs to human judgment, which regards only the outward action, he bids them to wait until the Lord came who would bring to light the hidden things of darkness, and reveal the secrets of the heart (1 Cor. 4. 5). When we hear this, let it come to our minds that we are warned that if we wish to be really approved by our Judge, we must strive for sincerity of heart.

He adds *according to my gospel*, intimating that he announced a doctrine to which the judgments of men, naturally

implanted in them, gave a response; and he calls it *his* gospel
on account of the ministry, for the authority for setting forth
the gospel resides in the true God alone, and it was only
the dispensing of it that was committed to the apostles. It is
indeed no matter of surprise that the gospel is in part called
the messenger and the announcer of future judgment; for if
the fulfillment and completion of what it promises be deferred
to the full revelation of the heavenly kingdom, it must necessarily be connected with the last judgment; and further,
Christ cannot be preached without being a resurrection to
some and a destruction to others, and both these things have
a reference to the day of judgment. The words *through Jesus
Christ* I apply to the day of judgment, though they are regarded otherwise by some; and the meaning is that the Lord
will execute judgment by Christ, for he is appointed by the
Father to be the Judge of the living and of the dead, which the
apostles always mention among the main articles of the gospel.
Thus the sentence will be full and complete, which would
otherwise be defective.

8. 1. *There is* therefore now no condemnation to them which
are in Christ Jesus, who walk not after the flesh, but after the
Spirit.
2. For the law of the Spirit of life in Christ Jesus hath made
me free from the law of sin and death.

1. *There is then, etc.* After having described the contest
which the godly have perpetually with their own flesh, he
returns to the consolation which was very needful for them
and which he had before mentioned; and it was this: that
though they were still beset by sin, they were yet exempt
from the power of death and from every curse, provided they
lived not in the flesh but in the Spirit; for he joins together
these three things: the imperfection under which the faithful always labor, the mercy of God in pardoning and forgiving it, and the regeneration of the Spirit; and this indeed
in the last place, that no one should flatter himself with a vain
notion as though he were freed from the curse while securely

indulging in the meantime his own flesh. As then the carnal man flatters himself in vain when, in no way solicitous to reform his life, he promises to himself impunity under the pretense of having this grace, so the trembling consciences of the godly have an invincible fortress, for they know that while they abide in Christ they are beyond every danger of condemnation. We shall now examine the words.

After the Spirit. Those who walk after the Spirit are not such as have wholly put off all the emotions of the flesh, so that their whole life is redolent with nothing but celestial perfection; but they are those who sedulously labor to subdue and mortify the flesh, so that the love of true religion seems to reign in them. He declares that such walk not after the flesh; for wherever the real fear of God is vigorous, it takes away from the flesh its sovereignty, though it does not abolish all its corruptions.

2. *For the law of the Spirit of life, etc.* This is a confirmation of the former sentence; and that it may be understood, the meaning of the words must be noticed. Using a language not strictly correct, by the *law of the Spirit* he designates the Spirit of God, who sprinkles our souls with the blood of Christ, not only to cleanse us from the stain of sin with respect to its guilt, but also to sanctify us that we may be really purified. He adds that it is life-giving (for the genitive case, after the manner of the Hebrew, is to be taken as an adjective); it hence follows that they who detain man in the letter of the law expose him to death. On the other hand, he gives the name of the *law of sin* and *death* to the dominion of the flesh and to the tyranny of death, which thence follows: the law of God is set as it were in the middle, which by teaching righteousness cannot confer it, but on the contrary binds us with the strongest chains in bondage to sin and to death.

The meaning then is that the law of God condemns men, that this happens because as long as they remain under the bond of the law they are oppressed with the bondage of sin, and are thus exposed to death; but that the Spirit of Christ, while it abolishes the law of sin in us by destroying the prevailing desires of the flesh, does at the same time deliver us from the peril of death. If anyone objects and says that then pardon, by which our transgressions are buried, depends on regeneration, to this it may be easily answered that the reason is not here assigned by Paul, but that the manner only is specified in which we are delivered from guilt; and Paul denies that we obtain deliverance by the external teaching of the law, but intimates that when we are renewed by the Spirit of God we are at the same time justified by a gratuitous pardon, that the curse of sin may no longer abide on us. The sentence then has the same meaning as though Paul had said that the grace of regeneration is never disjoined from the imputation of righteousness.

I dare not, with some, take *the law of sin and death* for the law of God, because it seems a harsh expression. For though by increasing sin it generates death, yet Paul before turned aside designedly from this invidious language. At the same time I no more agree in opinion with those who explain the law of sin as being the lust of the flesh, as though Paul had said that he had become the conqueror of it. But it will appear very evident shortly, as I think, that he speaks of a gratuitous absolution, which brings to us tranquilizing peace with God. I prefer retaining the word *law*, rather than with Erasmus to render it *right* or *power*, for Paul did not without reason allude to the law of God.

12. Therefore, brethren, we are debtors, not to the flesh, to live after the flesh.
13. For if ye live after the flesh, ye shall die: but if ye through the Spirit do mortify the deeds of the body, ye shall live.
14. For as many as are led by the Spirit of God, they are the sons of God.

12. *So then, brethren, etc.* This is the conclusion of what has been previously said; for if we are to renounce the flesh, we ought not to consent to it; and if the Spirit ought to reign in us, it is inconsistent not to attend to his bidding.

Paul's sentence is here defective, for he omits the other part of the contrast—that we are debtors to the Spirit; but the meaning is in no way obscure. This conclusion has the force of an exhortation, for he is ever wont to draw exhortations from his doctrine. So in another place (Eph. 4. 30), he exhorts us "not to grieve the Spirit of God, by whom we have been sealed to the day of redemption"; he does the same in Gal. 5. 25, "If we live in the Spirit, let us also walk in the Spirit." And this is the case when we renounce carnal lusts so as to devote ourselves, as those who are bound, to the righteousness of God. Thus indeed we ought to reason, not as some blasphemers are wont to do, who talk idly and say that we must do nothing because we have no power. But it is as it were to fight against God when we extinguish the grace offered to us by contempt and negligence.

13. *For if ye will live after the flesh, etc.* He adds a threatening in order more effectually to shake off their torpor; by which also they are fully confuted who boast of justification by faith without the Spirit of Christ, though they are more than sufficiently convicted by their own conscience; for there is no confidence in God where there is no love of righteousness. It is indeed true that we are justified in Christ through the mercy of God alone, but it is equally true and certain that all who are justified are called by the Lord, that they may live worthy of their vocation. Let then the faithful learn to embrace him, not only for justification, but also for sanctification, as he has been given to us for both these purposes, lest they rend him asunder by their mutilated faith.

But if ye by the Spirit, etc. He thus moderates his address that he might not deject the minds of the godly, who are still conscious of much infirmity; for however we may as yet be exposed to sins, he nevertheless promises life to us, provided we strive to mortify the flesh: for he does not strictly require the destruction of the flesh, but only bids us to make every exertion to subdue its lusts.

14. *For whosoever are led by the Spirit of God, etc.* This is a confirmation of what has immediately preceded; for he teaches us that those only are deemed the sons of God who are ruled by his Spirit; for by this mark God acknowledges them as his own people. Thus the empty boasting of hypocrites is taken away, who without any reason assume the title; and the faithful are thus encouraged with unhesitating confidence to expect salvation. The import of the whole is this: "All those are the sons of God who are led by God's Spirit; all the sons of God are heirs of eternal life: then all who are led by God's Spirit ought to feel assured of eternal life." But the middle term or assumption is omitted, for it was indubitable.

But it is right to observe that the working of the Spirit is various: for there is that which is universal, by which all creatures are sustained and preserved; there is that also which is peculiar to men, and varying in its character. But what he means here is sanctification, with which the Lord favors none but his own elect, and by which he separates them for sons to himself.

FROM THE TRACTS

FROM THE TRACTS

THE REPLY TO SADOLET[1]

On the occasion of this pamphlet see Introduction,
pp. xiv-xv.

Calvin begins with expressions of respect for the senior
churchman's learning and good repute. But he indig-
nantly repudiates Sadolet's aspersions on the motives of
the ministers who had served in Geneva, especially Farel,
Viret and himself. He then continues:

I pass in silence over many other invectives which, open
mouthed (as they say), you thunder out against us. You call us
cunning men, enemies of Christian unity and peace, changers
of things ancient and well established, seditious, alike pestilential to souls and both publicly and privately pernicious to
society at large. Had you wished to escape rebuke, you either
ought not, to excite prejudice, to have attributed to us a mag-
niloquent tongue, or you ought to have tempered your own
magniloquence considerably. I am unwilling, however, to dwell
on each of these points. I would only have you consider how
unbecoming, not to say ungenerous, it is thus to vex the innocent in many words which by one word can be instantly refuted, although to inflict injury on man is a small matter, compared with the indignity of that contempt which, when you
come to the point, you offer to Christ and his Word.

When the Genevans, instructed by our preaching, escaped
from the gulf of error in which they were immersed and be-
took themselves to a purer teaching of the gospel, you call it
defection from the truth of God; when they threw off the tyr-

[1] From *Calvin: Theological Treatises,* translated by J. K. S. Reid ("The
Library of Christian Classics," Vol. XXII; Philadelphia: The Westminster
Press, 1954). Used by permission.

anny of the Roman pontiff, in order that they might establish among themselves a better form of Church, you call it desertion from the Church. Come, then, and let us discuss both points in turn.

As to your preface, which, in proclaiming the excellence of eternal blessedness, occupies about a third of your Letter, it cannot be necessary for me to dwell long in reply. For although commendation of the future and eternal life is a theme worthy to be sounded in our ears by day and by night, kept constantly in remembrance, and made the subject of ceaseless meditation, yet I know not for what reason you have so protracted your discourse upon it here, unless it were to commend yourself by some indication of religious feeling. But whether, in order to remove all doubt about yourself, you wished to testify that a life of glory seriously occupies your thoughts, or whether you supposed that those to whom you wrote required to be excited and spurred on by a long commendation of it (for I am unwilling to probe what your intention may have been), it is not very sound theology to confine a man's thoughts so much to himself, and not to set before him as the prime motive of his existence zeal to show forth the glory of God. For we are born first of all for God, and not for ourselves. As all things flowed from him and subsist in him, as Paul says (Rom. 11:36), they ought to be related to him. I acknowledge indeed that the Lord, to recommend the glory of his name to men the better, has tempered zeal for its advance and extension by uniting it indissolubly with our salvation. But since he has taught that this zeal ought to exceed all thought and care for our own good and advantage, and since natural equity also teaches that God does not receive what is his own unless he be preferred to all things, it certainly is the duty of a Christian man to ascend higher than merely to seek and secure the salvation of his own soul. I therefore believe that there is no man imbued with true piety, who will not regard as in poor taste that long and detailed exhortation to a zeal for heavenly life, which occupies a man entirely concerned with himself, and does not, even by one

expression, arouse him to sanctify the name of God. But I
readily agree with you that after this sanctification we ought
to set ourselves no other object in life than to hasten towards
that high calling; for God has set it before us as the constant
aim of all our actions, words and thoughts. Indeed there is
nothing in which man excels the lower animals, unless it be his
spiritual communion with God in the hope of a blessed eternity. In general, all we aim at in our discourses is to arouse
men to meditate upon it and aspire to it.

I have also no difficulty in conceding to you that there is
nothing more perilous to our salvation than a distorted and
perverse worship of God. The primary rudiments by which we
are wont to train to piety those whom we wish to win as disciples to Christ, are these: not to frame any new worship of
God for themselves at random and their own pleasure, but
to know that the only legitimate worship is that which he himself approved from the beginning. For we maintain, what the
sacred oracle declared, that obedience is more excellent than
any sacrifice (I Sam. 15:22). In short, we train them by every
means to keep within the one rule of worship which they have
received from his mouth, and bid farewell to all fictitious
worship.

Therefore, Sadolet, when you uttered this voluntary confession, you laid the foundation of my defence. For if you
admit it to be a fearful destruction to the soul, when by false
opinions divine truth is turned into a lie, it now only remains
for us to enquire which of the two parties retains that worship of God which is alone legitimate. In order that you may
claim it for your side, you assume that the most certain rule
of worship is that which is prescribed by the Church, although,
as if we here opposed you, you bring the matter to consideration in the manner usually observed in doubtful matters. But,
Sadolet, as I see you toiling in vain, I will relieve you from
all trouble at this point. You are mistaken in supposing that
we desire to lead away the people from the method of worshipping God which the Catholic Church always observed.
Either you are deluded about the term Church, or else know-

ingly and willingly you practise deception. I will immediately
show the latter to be the case, though it may also be that you
are somewhat in error. First, in defining the term, you omit
what would have helped you in no small degree to its right
understanding. When you describe it as that which in all past
as well as present time, in all regions of the earth, being united
and of one mind in Christ, has been always and everywhere
directed by the one Spirit of Christ, what becomes of the
Word of the Lord, that clearest of all marks, which the Lord
himself in designating the Church so often commends to us?
For seeing how dangerous it would be to boast of the Spirit
without the Word, he declared that the Church is indeed
governed by the Holy Spirit; but in order that this government might not be vague and unstable, he bound it to the
Word. For this reason Christ exclaims that those who are of
God hear the Word of God, that his sheep are those which
recognize his voice as that of their Shepherd and any other
voice as that of a stranger (John 10:27). For this reason the
Spirit by the mouth of Paul declares (Eph. 2:20) that the
Church is built upon the foundation of the apostles and
prophets; also, that the Church is made holy to the Lord, by
the washing of water in the word of life (Eph. 5:26). The same
thing is declared still more clearly by the mouth of Peter,
when he teaches that people are regenerated to God by that
incorruptible seed (I Peter 1:23). In short, why is the preaching of the gospel so often styled the kingdom of God, but because it is the sceptre by which the heavenly King rules his
people?

Nor will you find this in the apostolic writings only; whenever the prophets foretell the renewal of the Church or its
extension over the whole globe, they always assign the first
place to the Word. For they say that from Jerusalem will issue
forth living waters, which being divided into four rivers will
inundate the whole earth (Zech. 14:8). What these living
waters are, they themselves explain when they say: the law
will come forth from Zion, and the Word of the Lord from
Jerusalem (Isa. 2:3). Chrysostom then rightly admonishes us

to reject all who under the pretence of the Spirit lead us away from the simple doctrine of the gospel; for the Spirit was promised, not to reveal a new doctrine, but to impress the truth of the gospel on our minds. We in fact experience in the present day how necessary the admonition was. We are assailed by two sects, which seem to differ most widely from each other. For what similitude is there in appearance between the pope and the Anabaptists? And yet, that you may see that Satan never transforms himself so cunningly as not in some measure to betray himself, the principal weapon with which they both assail us is the same. For when they boast extravagantly of the Spirit, they inevitably tend to sink and bury the Word of God, and to make room for their own falsehoods. And you, Sadolet, by stumbling on the very threshold, have paid the penalty of the affront you offered the Holy Spirit, when you separated him from the Word. For as if those who seek the way of God stood where two ways meet, destitute of any certain sign, you are forced to present them as hesitating whether it be more expedient to follow the authority of the Church, or to listen to those whom you call the inventors of new dogmas. If you had known or been unwilling to disguise the fact that the Spirit goes before the Church to enlighten her in understanding the Word, while the Word itself is like the Lydian stone by which she tests all doctrines, would you have taken refuge in that most perplexing and thorny question? Learn, then, by your own experience that it is no less unreasonable to boast of the Spirit without the Word, than it would be absurd to bring forward the Word itself without the Spirit. Now if you can bear to receive a truer definition of the Church than your own, say in future that it is the society of all the saints which, spread over the whole world and existing in all ages, yet bound together by the doctrine and the one Spirit of Christ, cultivates and observes unity of faith and brotherly concord. With this Church we deny that we have any disagreement. Rather as we revere her as our mother, so we desire to remain in her bosom.

But here you bring a charge against me. For you teach that

all that has been approved for fifteen hundred years or more by the uniform consent of the faithful, is by our rashness torn up and destroyed. Here I will not require you to deal truly and candidly by us (though this should be spontaneously offered by a philosopher, not to say a Christian). I will only ask you not to stoop to a mean indulgence in calumny, which, even though we be silent, must be extremely injurious to your reputation with serious and honest men. You know, Sadolet, and if you venture to deny it, I shall make it plain to all, that you knew but cunningly and craftily disguised the fact, not only that our agreement with antiquity is far closer than yours, but that all we have attempted has been to renew the ancient form of the Church which, at first distorted and stained by illiterate men of indifferent character, was afterwards criminally mangled and almost destroyed by the Roman pontiff and his faction.

I shall not press you so closely as to call you back to that form which the apostles instituted, though in it we have the only model of a true Church, and whosoever deviates from it in the smallest degree is in error. But to indulge you so far, I ask you to place before your eyes the ancient form of the Church as their writings prove it to have been in the ages of Chrysostom and Basil among the Greeks, and of Cyprian, Ambrose and Augustine among the Latins; and after so doing, to contemplate the ruins of that Church which now survive among yourselves. Assuredly the difference will appear as great as that which the prophets describe between the famous Church which flourished under David and Solomon, and that which under Zedekiah and Jehoiakim had lapsed into every kind of superstition and utterly vitiated the purity of divine worship. Will you here declare one an enemy of antiquity who, zealous for ancient piety and holiness and dissatisfied with the corrupt state of matters existing in a dissolute and depraved Church, attempts to ameliorate its condition and restore it to pristine splendour?

Calvin affirms that the renewal of the Church depends upon the recognition of the authority of the Word of God together with, and never to be separated from, the inspiration of the Holy Spirit. He claims that the scriptural preaching of the reforming ministers has proved a good example to their opponents, and charges that the latter have misrepresented the Reformation doctrine of justification by faith. He then describes the nature of Reformed instruction as follows:

First, we bid a man begin by examining himself, and this not in a superficial and perfunctory manner, but to present his conscience before the tribunal of God and, when sufficiently convinced of his iniquity, to reflect on the strictness of the sentence pronounced upon all sinners. Thus confounded and stricken with misery, he is prostrated and humbled before God; and, throwing away all self-confidence, he groans as though given up to final perdition. Then we show that the only haven of safety is in the mercy of God as manifested in Christ, in whom every part of our salvation is completed. As all mankind are lost sinners in the sight of God, we hold that Christ is their only righteousness, since by his obedience he has done away our transgressions, by his sacrifice appeased the divine anger, by his blood washed away our stains, by his cross borne our curse, and by his death made satisfaction for us. We maintain that in this way man is reconciled in Christ to God the Father, by no merit of his own, by no worthiness of works, but by gratuitous mercy. When we embrace Christ by faith and come, as it were, into communion with him, we term this in the manner of Scripture the righteousness of faith.

What have you here, Sadolet, to bite or grumble at? Is it that we leave no room for works? Assuredly we do deny that for justifying a man they are worth a single straw. For Scripture everywhere cries aloud that all are lost; and every man's own conscience bitterly accuses him. The same Scripture teaches that no hope is left but in the sheer goodness of

God, by which sin is pardoned and righteousness imputed to
us. It declares both to be gratuitous, and finally concludes that
a man is justified without works (Rom. 4:6). But what notion,
you ask, does the very term righteousness suggest to us, if
respect is not paid to good works? I answer: if you would attend to the true meaning of the term *justifying* in Scripture,
you would have no difficulty. For it does not refer to a man's
own righteousness, but to the mercy of God, which, contrary
to the sinner's deserts, accepts a righteousness for him, and
this by not imputing his unrighteousness. Our righteousness,
I say, is that which is described by Paul (II Cor. 5:19), that
God hath reconciled us to himself in Jesus Christ. The means
is afterwards added: by not imputing sin. He demonstrates
that it is by faith only we become partakers of this blessing,
when he says that the ministry of reconciliation is contained
in the gospel. But faith, you say, is a general term, and has a
wider meaning. I answer that Paul, whenever he attributes
to it the power of justifying, at the same time restricts it to
a gratuitous promise of divine favour, and keeps it far removed from all reference to works. Hence his familiar inference: if by faith, then not by works; on the other hand: if by
works, then not by faith.

But, it seems, injury is done to Christ if, under the pretence of his grace, good works are repudiated; for he came to
render a people acceptable to God, zealous of good works. To
the same effect are many similar passages which prove that
Christ came in order that we, doing good works, might through
him be accepted by God. This calumny which our opponents
have perpetually in their mouths, that we take away the desire of well-doing from the Christian life by recommending
gratuitous righteousness, is too frivolous to give us much concern. We deny that good works have any share in justification,
but we claim full authority for them in the lives of the righteous. For if he who has obtained justification possesses Christ,
and at the same time Christ never is where his Spirit is not,
it is obvious that gratuitous righteousness is necessarily connected with regeneration. Therefore, if you would duly un-

derstand how inseparable faith and works are, look to Christ, who, as the apostle teaches (I Cor. 1:30), has been given to us for justification and for sanctification. Wherever, therefore, that righteousness of faith which we maintain to be gratuitous is, there too Christ is; and where Christ is, there too is the Spirit of holiness who regenerates the soul to newness of life. On the contrary, where zeal for integrity and holiness is not in force, there neither the Spirit of Christ nor Christ himself are present. Wherever Christ is not, there is no righteousness, and indeed no faith; for faith cannot lay hold of Christ for righteousness without the Spirit of sanctification.

Since, therefore, according to us Christ regenerates to a blessed life those whom he justifies and, rescuing them from the dominion of sin, hands them over to the dominion of righteousness, transforms them into the image of God, and so trains them by his Spirit into obedience to his will, there is no ground to complain that by our doctrine lust is given free rein. The passages which you adduce have the same meaning. But if you must pervert them to assail gratuitous justification, observe how unskilfully you argue. Paul elsewhere says (Eph. 1:4) that we were chosen in Christ, before the creation of the world, to be holy and unblamable in the sight of God through love. Who will venture thence to infer either that election is not gratuitous, or that our love is its cause? Much rather as the end of gratuitous election is that we may lead pure and unpolluted lives before God, so also is that of gratuitous justification. For the saying of Paul is true (I Thess. 4:7): we have not been called to impurity, but to holiness. This, meanwhile, we constantly maintain, that man is not only justified freely once for all without any merit of works, but that on this gratuitous justification his salvation perpetually depends. Nor is it possible that any work of man can be accepted by God unless it be gratuitously approved. Wherefore I was greatly astonished when I read your assertion that love is the first and chief cause of salvation. O, Sadolet, who could ever have expected such a saying from you? Undoubtedly the blind themselves in their darkness feel the mercy of God too certainly to arrogate to their love the first step in their salvation; but those who have only one spark of divine light feel that their salvation consists in nothing else than in being adopted by God. For eternal salvation is the inheritance of the heavenly Father, and has been prepared solely for his children. Moreover who can assign any other cause of our adoption than that which is uniformly announced in Scripture, that we did not first love him, but were spontaneously received by him into favour and affection?

Your ignorance of this doctrine leads you on to the error of teaching that sins are expiated by penances and satisfactions. Where, then, will be that one expiatory victim from which, if we depart, there remains, as Scripture testifies, no more sacrifice for sin? Search all the divine oracles we possess; if the blood of Christ alone is everywhere set forth as purchasing satisfaction, reconciliation, and cleansing, how dare you presume to transfer so great an honour to your works? Nor have you any ground for ascribing this blasphemy to the Church of God. The ancient Church, I admit, had its satisfactions—not those, however, by which sinners might atone to God and redeem themselves from guilt, but by which they might prove that the repentance they professed was not feigned and might efface the remembrance of the offence which their sin occasioned. For satisfactions were not regularly prescribed to all and sundry, but to those only who had fallen into some grave wickedness.

In the case of the Eucharist, you blame us for attempting to confine the Lord of the universe and his divine and spiritual power (which is perfectly free and infinite) within the corners of a corporeal nature with its circumscribed limits. What end will there be to calumny? We have always distinctly testified that not only the divine power of Christ, but his essence also, is diffused over all and defined by no limits; and yet you do not hesitate to reproach us with confining it within the corners of corporeal nature! How so? Because we are unwilling with you to fasten his body to earthly elements. But if you had any regard for sincerity, you are assuredly not ignorant how great a difference there is between the two things: removing the local presence of Christ's body from bread, and circumscribing his spiritual power within bodily limits. Nor ought you to charge our doctrine with novelty, since it was always held by the Church as a confessed tenet. But as this subject alone would extend to a volume, in order that both of us be spared such toil, it will be better that you read Augustine's *Epistle to Dardanus*, where you will find how one and the same Christ more than fills heaven and earth with the fulness of his divinity, and yet is not everywhere diffused in respect of his humanity.

We emphatically proclaim the communion of flesh and blood which is exhibited to believers in the Supper; and we distinctly show that this flesh is truly meat and this blood truly drink—that the soul, not contented with an imaginary conception, enjoys them in very truth. That presence of Christ, by which we are ingrafted in him, we by no means exclude from the Supper; nor do we obscure it, though we hold that there must be no local limitation, that the glorious body of Christ must not be degraded to earthly elements, and that there must be no fiction of transubstantiating the bread into Christ and then of worshipping it as Christ. We explain the dignity and end of this solemn rite in the most exalted terms we can employ, and then declare how great are the advantages we derive from it. Almost all these things are neglected by you. For, overlooking the divine beneficence which is here bestowed upon us, overlooking the legitimate use of so great a benefit (themes on which it is right especially to dwell), you count it enough that the people gaze stupidly at the visible sign, without any understanding of the spiritual mystery. In condemning your gross dogma of transubstantiation, and declaring that stupid adoration which detains the minds of men among the elements and prevents them rising to Christ to be perverse and impious, we have not acted without the concurrence of the ancient Church, under whose shadow you try in vain to hide the very pernicious superstitions which you here handle.

In auricular confession we have disapproved of the law of Innocent, which enjoins every man once a year to review his sins before his priest. It would be tedious to enumerate all the reasons which induced us to abrogate it. But that the thing was scandalous is apparent if only from this, that pious consciences, which formerly seethed with perpetual anxiety, have been freed from that dire torment, and have begun at last to rest with confidence in the divine favour; to say nothing meanwhile of the many disasters which it brought upon the Church, and which justly rendered it execrable. For the present take this for our answer, that it was neither commanded by Christ, nor practised by the ancient Church. We have forcibly wrested from the hands of the sophists all the passages of Scripture which they had contrived to distort in support of it. The ecclesiastical histories in use show that it had no existence in a purer age. The testimonies of the Fathers agree with this. It is therefore mere deception when you say that the humility therein manifested was enjoined and instituted by Christ and the Church. For though there appears in it a certain show of humility, it is very far from being true that every kind of abasement that assumes the name of humility is commended by God. Accordingly Paul teaches (Col. 2:18), that only that humility is genuine which is framed in conformity to the Word of God.

In asserting the intercession of the saints, if all you mean is that they continually pray for the completion of Christ's kingdom in which the salvation of all the faithful consists, there is none of us who calls it in question. Accordingly, it is labour lost to exert yourself so much over this point; but no doubt you were unwilling to omit the bitter witticism in which you charge us with thinking that the soul perishes with the body. That philosophy we leave to your popes and colleges of cardinals, by whom it was for many years most faithfully cultivated, nor ceases to be cultivated today. To them also your subsequent remark applies: they live luxuriously without any solicitude concerning a future life, and hold us miserable wretches in derision for labouring so anxiously on behalf of the kingdom of Christ. But regarding the intercession of the saints, we insist on a point which it is not strange you should omit. For here innumerable superstitions were to be cut away, which had risen to such a height, that the intercession of Christ was quite erased from men's thoughts; saints were invoked as gods; the offices peculiar to God were distributed among them; nor was there any difference between this worship paid to them and that ancient idolatry which we all rightly execrate.

As to purgatory, we know that ancient churches made some mention of the dead in their prayers; but it was done seldom and soberly, and consisted only of a few words. It was, in short, a mention in which obviously nothing more was meant than to testify in passing to affection for the dead. As yet the architects were unborn, by whom that purgatory of yours was built, and who afterwards enlarged it so greatly and raised it so high that it now forms the strongest pillar of your kingdom. You yourself know what a hydra of errors thence emerged; you know what tricks superstition has spontaneously devised with which to play; you know how many impostures avarice fabricated, in order to bleed men of every class; you know how great detriment it has done to piety. For not to mention how greatly true worship has in consequence decayed, the worst result certainly was that, while without any command from God everyone competed with each other in helping the dead, they utterly neglected the proper offices of charity which are so strongly enjoined.

> There follows a protest against the exclusive use of the word "Church" for the Roman communion, in which are seen many departures from the wholesome practices of the ancient Church. The latter, he claims, "is clearly on our side." He then replies dramatically to the passage in the Cardinal's letter in which a minister of the Reformed Church is represented as appearing in confusion before the throne of divine judgment.

But since towards the end a person has been introduced to plead our cause, and you have cited us as defenders to the tribunal of God, I have no hesitation in calling upon you to meet me there. For such is our consciousness of the truth of our doctrine, that it has no dread of the heavenly Judge, from whom we do not doubt that it proceeded. But it dwells not on those frivolities with which it has pleased you to amuse yourself, but which are certainly very much out of place. For what could be more inopportune than to come into the presence of God, and to set about devising I know not what follies, and framing for us an absurd defence which must immediately fail? In pious minds, whenever that day is suggested, the impression made is too solemn to leave them at leisure so to amuse themselves. Therefore, frivolity set aside, let us think of that day which the minds of men ought always to expect with suspense. And let us remember that, while desirable to the faithful, it may well be alarming to the ungodly and profane and those who despise God. Let us turn our ears to the sound of that trumpet which even the ashes of the dead will hear in their tombs. Let us direct our thoughts and minds to that Judge who, by the mere brightness of his countenance, will disclose whatever lurks in darkness, lay open all the secrets of the human heart, and crush all the wicked by the mere breath of his mouth. Consider now what serious answer you are to make for yourself and your party; our cause, supported as it is by the truth of God, will be at no loss for a complete defence. I speak not of our persons, whose safety will be found not in defence, but in humble confession and suppliant petition; but in so far as our ministry is concerned, there is none of us who will not be able to speak for himself as follows.

"O Lord, I have indeed experienced how difficult and grievous it is to bear the invidious accusations with which I was harassed on the earth; but with the same confidence with which I then appealed to thy tribunal, I now appear before thee, for I know that in thy judgment truth reigns. Supported by confidence in this truth, I first dared to attempt, and assisted by it I was able to accomplish, whatever was achieved by me

in thy Church. They charged me with two of the worst of
crimes, heresy and schism. The heresy was that I dared to protest against dogmas received by them. But what could I have
done? I heard from thy mouth that there was no other light
of truth which could direct our souls into the way of life,
than that which was kindled by thy Word. I heard that whatever human minds of themselves conceive concerning thy
majesty, the worship of thy deity, and the mysteries of thy
religion, was vanity. I heard that their introduction into the
Church of doctrines sprung from the human brain in place of
thy Word was sacrilegious presumption. But when I turned
my eyes towards men, I saw very different principles prevailing. Those who were regarded as the leaders of faith
neither understood thy Word, nor greatly cared for it. They
only drove unhappy people about with strange doctrines, and
deluded them with I know not what follies. Among the people
themselves, the highest veneration paid to thy Word was to
revere it at a distance as something inaccessible, and abstain
from all investigation of it. Owing to the supine dullness of
the pastors and the stupidity of the people, every place was
filled with pernicious errors, falsehoods, and superstition. They
indeed called thee the only God, but they did so while transferring to others the glory which thou hast claimed for thy
majesty. They imagined for themselves and esteemed as many
gods as they had saints to worship. Thy Christ was indeed
worshipped as God and retained the name of Saviour; but
where he ought to have been honoured, he was left almost
destitute of glory. For, spoiled of his own virtue, he passed un-
noticed among the crowd of saints, like one of the meanest
of them. There was no one who duly considered that one sacrifice which he offered on the cross, and by which he reconciled us to thyself; no one who ever dreamed of thinking of
his eternal priesthood, and the intercession depending on it;
no one who trusted in his righteousness only. That confident
hope of salvation, which is both enjoined by thy Word and
founded upon it, had almost vanished. Indeed it was received
as a kind of oracle; it was foolish arrogance, and, as they said,

presumption, for any one to trust in thy goodness and the righteousness of thy Son, and entertain a sure and unfaltering hope of salvation. These were so many profane opinions which, though they were the first principles of that doctrine which thou hast delivered to us in thy Word, they plucked up by the roots. The true meaning of Baptism and the Lord's Supper also was corrupted by numerous falsehoods. And then, when everybody, gravely affronting thy mercy, put confidence in good works, when by good works they strove to merit thy favour, to procure justification, to expiate their sins, and make satisfaction to thee (each of these things obliterating and emptying the virtue of Christ's cross), they were yet quite ignorant in what good works consisted. For just as if they were not at all instructed in righteousness by thy law, they had fabricated for themselves many useless trivialities as a means of procuring thy favour, and on these they so prided themselves, that in comparison with them they almost scorned the standard of true righteousness which thy law commended—to such a degree had human desires usurped the ascendancy and derogated, if not from the belief, at least from the authority, of thy precepts contained in it.

"That I might perceive these things, thou, O Lord, didst shine upon me with the brightness of thy Spirit; that I might comprehend how impious and harmful they were, thou didst bear before me the torch of thy Word; that I might abominate them as they deserved, thou didst disturb my soul. But in rendering an account of my doctrine, thou seest, what my own conscience declares, that it was not my intention to stray beyond those limits which I saw had been fixed for all thy servants. Whatever I did not doubt I had learned from thy mouth, I desired to dispense faithfully to the Church. Assuredly the thing at which I chiefly aimed, and for which I most diligently laboured, was that the glory of thy goodness and justice should disperse the mists by which it was formerly obscured, and might shine forth conspicuously, that the virtue and blessings of thy Christ, all disguises being brushed aside, might be fully displayed. For I thought it impious to leave in obscurity things which we were born to ponder and meditate. Nor did I think that truths, whose magnitude no language can express, were to be maliciously or falsely declared. I hesitated not to dwell at greater length on topics on which the salvation of my hearers depended. For the oracle could never deceive which declares (John 17:3): 'This is eternal life, to know thee the only true God, and Jesus Christ, whom thou hast sent.'

"As to the charge of forsaking the Church, which they are accustomed to bring against me, there is nothing here of which my conscience accuses me, unless indeed he is to be considered a deserter who, seeing the soldiers routed and scattered and abandoning the ranks, raises the leader's standard, and recalls them to their posts. For thus, O Lord, were all thy servants dispersed, so that they could not by any possibility hear the command, but had almost forgotten their leader, their service, and their military vow. To bring them together when thus scattered, I raised, not a foreign standard, but that noble banner of thine which we must follow, if we would be classed among thy people.

"Then I was assailed by those who, when they ought to have kept others in their ranks, had led them astray, and when I would not at all desist they opposed me with violence. On this grievous tumults arose, and the contest flared up into disruption. Who was to blame it is for thee, O Lord, to decide. Always, both by word and deed, have I protested how eager I was for unity. Mine, however, was a unity of the Church which should begin with thee and end in thee. For whenever thou didst recommend to us peace and concord, thou didst at the same time show thyself to be the only bond for perserving it. But if I desired to be at peace with those who boasted of being the heads of the Church and the pillars of faith, I had to purchase it with the denial of thy truth. I thought that anything was to be endured rather than stoop to such an execrable accommodation. For thy Christ himself declared that, though heaven and earth should be confounded, yet thy Word must endure for ever (Matt. 24:35). Nor did I think that I dissented from thy Church, because I was at war with those leaders. For thou didst forewarn us both by thy Son and by the apostles that into that place there would rise persons to whom I ought by no means to consent. Christ predicted not of strangers, but of men who should pass themselves off as pastors, that they would be ravenous wolves and false prophets, and at the same time warned us to beware of them (Matt. 7:15). Where Christ ordered me to beware, was I to lend my aid? And the apostles declared that there would be no enemies of thy Church more pestilential than those from within, who should conceal themselves under the title of pastors (Acts 20:29; II Pet. 2:1; I John 2:18). Why should I have hesitated to separate myself from persons whom they forewarned me to hold as enemies? I had before my eyes the examples of thy prophets who, I saw, had a similar contest with the priests and prophets of their day, though these were undoubtedly the rulers of the Church among the Israelite people. But thy prophets are not regarded as schismatics because, when they wished to revive religion which had fallen into decay, they did not desist although opposed with the utmost violence. They still remained in the unity of the Church, though they were by wicked priests execrated with awful curses, and thought unworthy of a place among men, not to say saints. Confirmed by their example, I too persisted. Though denounced as a deserter of the Church and threatened, I was in no respect deterred or induced to proceed less firmly and boldly in opposing those who, in the character of pastors, wasted thy Church more than any impious tyranny. My conscience told me how strong the zeal was with which I burned for the unity of thy Church, provided thy truth were made the bond of concord. As the tumults which followed were not excited by me, so there is no ground for imputing them to me.

"Thou, O Lord, knowest, and the fact has testified itself to men, that the only thing I asked was that all controversies should be decided by thy Word, that thus both parties might unite with one mind to establish thy kingdom; and I declined not to restore peace to the Church at the expense of my head, if I were found to be the cause of needless disturbance. But what did our opponents do? Did they not forthwith furiously fly to fires, swords, and gibbets? Did they not decide that their only security was in arms and cruelty? Did they not instigate all ranks to the same fury? Did they not spurn all methods of pacification? Thus it happens that a matter, which might at one time have been settled amicably, has blazed up into such a conflict. But although amidst the great confusion the judgments of men were various, I am freed from all fear now that we stand at thy tribunal, where equity combined with truth cannot but decide in favour of innocence."

Following again the pattern of Sadolet's letter, a speech is put in the mouth of a layman imagined to stand in the same situation. Here emphasis is given to the high conception of the Church in which the lay convert has been instructed by his reforming teachers. There is a fresh vehement protest against the imputation of mercenary and schismatic motives to the party of reform, who have desired only the healing of the Church and the establishment of its true unity. Calvin concludes:

The Lord grant, Sadolet, that you and all your party may at length perceive that the only true bond of ecclesiastical unity consists in this, that Christ the Lord, who has reconciled us to God the Father, gather us out of our present dispersion into the fellowship of his body, that so, through his one Word and Spirit, we may join together with one heart and one soul.

BIOGRAPHICAL INDEX

AMBROSE (AMBROSIUS, 340-397) had been a Roman administrator before being made bishop of Milan (374). He was a vigorous defender of church discipline, daring to rebuke the Emperor Theodosius I, and an able contender against the Arian heresy. His writings have importance for discipline as well as doctrine. Calvin has reference in *Inst.* I. 14. 20 to materials in his numerous works on topics of biblical interpretation such as the six days of the Creation (*Hexaemeron*), Paradise, Cain and Abel, and the Hebrew Patriarchs.

ARATUS, a Greek poet and astronomer of Soli in Cilicia, born some years before 300 B.C. and writing about 270. He was widely read, and two centuries later Cicero translated some of his work into Latin. Melanchthon edited with a Latin translation his book *On the Sphere*. He is now best known by St. Paul's quotation of his poem *Phenomena and Signs* 5, as reported in Acts 17. 27-28.

ARISTOTLE (384-322 B.C.), the eminent founder of the Peripatetic School whose philosophy gained complete ascendancy in the medieval universities. His positions were frequently challenged in the 16th century but his works still held a prominent place in Protestant schools, including Geneva. Calvin objects (*Inst.* I. 5. 3) to his argument that the soul cannot function apart from the body or exist without it, but elsewhere refers favorably to Aristotle's opinions (I. 15. 6-7; II. 2. 23).

ARIUS (*c.* 280-337), the most famous of condemned heretics. A presbyter of Alexandria, Arius came to notice in 318 by opposing his bishop, Alexander, who in his doctrine of the Trinity had affirmed the eternity of the Son. Arius asserted that the Father precedes the Son and hence the Son is not eternal: "there was [a time] when he was not." Though this doctrine was condemned in the creed adopted by the Council of Nicaea (325), Arianism in a variety of forms long survived, especially in the Germanic nations (Goths, Vandals, Burgundians, Lombards) who were converted to it from paganism.

AUGUSTINE (AMELIUS AUGUSTINUS, 354-430) was born at Tagaste (Tajelt) in Numidia and studied in Carthage where he adopted but soon repudiated Manichaeism. He taught rhetoric at Rome and later at Milan where he was impressed by the preaching of Ambrose and, reading Christian works with his friends, became devoutly Christian (387). He became a priest at Hippo Regius near Carthage, and in 397 was made bishop. His writings mark him as the greatest of the Fathers of the Church, and include famous classics such as the *Confessions, Enchiridion,* and *City of God.* Calvin cites Augustine far more frequently than any other nonbiblical writer.

BASIL (*c.* 330-379) of Caesarea in Cappadocia, having been educated at Athens, led an ascetic movement and was the author of monastic rules that became authoritative in the Greek and Eastern Churches. In 370 he was made bishop of Caesarea. He wrote extensively and moved in theology from a semi-Arian to an orthodox position. In *Inst.* I. 14. 20 Calvin is thinking of Basil's *Homilies on the Days of Creation* (*Hexaemeron*).

BERNARD, ST. (1091-1153), of Clairveaux, was born in a feudal family at Fontaines near Dijon. He revolted from feudal violence and joined the newly founded community at Cîteaux, but soon (1115) founded a new monastery at Clairveaux. He was often drawn away from this beloved religious home to engage in numerous movements and controversies but did much teaching, preaching, and writing. Calvin seems to have ad-mired Bernard more than any other medieval writer, and many times quotes his *Sermons on the Song of Songs.*

CHRYSOSTOM, JOHN (347-407), called in later times "Chrysostomos," the golden-mouthed, for his distinguished eloquence as a preacher, after a training in rhetoric turned to the study of the Scriptures and became a priest. During twelve years at Antioch his powerful sermons, delivered in series on books of the Bible, made him famous. In 398 he unwillingly became bishop of Constantinople, but, rebuking the empress and the court, he was forced into exile (404). Calvin admired his homilies and makes frequent references to them.

CICERO, MARCUS TULLIUS (106-43 B.C.), was born at Arpinum where he chiefly resided during later life when not in Rome. During some years he pursued literary studies in Athens and Rhodes. He won great distinction both as advocate and as accuser in public trials, and is unequaled as a Latin orator. His philosophical works, especially the *Tusculan Disputations* and *On the Nature of the Gods,* were greatly prized in the Christian schools. Like most Renaissance writers, Calvin held Cicero in great esteem, often referring to his works and sometimes in other contexts reflecting his phraseology.

COCHLAEUS (JOHANN DOBENECK of Wendelstein, 1479-1552) resided in turn at Nuremberg, Mainz, Cologne, Dresden, and Breslau. He was the author of works on the Sacraments and a learned opponent of Luther. Among his very numerous writings are: *A Commentary on the Acts and Writings of Martin Luther, Against the Augsburg Confession and its Author* (Melanchthon), and a large controversial *History of the Hussites*.

CYPRIAN (THASIUS CAECILIUS CYPRIANUS, *c.* 200-258) had been a learned and prosperous pagan rhetorician in Carthage before his conversion to Christianity (246). For ten years, from 248 to his death as a martyr, he was bishop of Carthage and the eminent leader of the North African church. His works *On the Unity of the Church* and *On the Duties of Ministers* give him a notable place among the Latin Church Fathers. Calvin quotes without naming the former work in *Inst.* IV. 1. 1, and refers in IV. 1. 2 to a work erroneously ascribed to Cyprian which is really by Rufinus of Aquileia (370-410). Elsewhere Calvin cites many of Cyprian's letters.

DARDANUS (CLAUDIUS POSTUMUS DARDANUS) was prefect of Gaul, residing at Vienne, under the Emperor Honorius. In 417 Augustine, responding to his request, wrote him a long letter of Christian instruction dealing mainly with the doctrines of the Trinity and the Person of Christ. Calvin quotes this in *Inst.* IV. 17. 24.

EPICURUS (342-270 B.C.) was born in Samos. He studied and taught at Athens, where he gathered a community of disciples. Of his vast production of writings little more than fragments remain. He held that man's chief end is obtained through the highest experience of pleasure, which is not sensual enjoyment but contentment of mind. Calvin sees his teachings through the eyes of Cicero who, in *De finibus* and *De natura deorum*, treats Epicureanism unfavorably. In *Inst.* I. 2. 2 and I. 5. 4, there are condemnatory references to Epicurus' view of the gods as inaccessible and indifferent to man.

ERASMUS, DESIDERIUS (1466-1536), the greatest of Christian humanists, was born at Rotterdam and early placed in a monastery. He became secretary to a bishop (1495) and soon entered the world of scholarly study at Paris. He spent some years in Italy and three periods in England, where he enjoyed the friendship of John Colet and Thomas Moore. It was at Cambridge that his edition of the New Testament in Greek with a Latin translation was prepared, though it was published in Basel (1516). This work was of incalculable importance for the Reformation, from which Erasmus detached himself completely in his controversy with Luther. From 1521 he lived chiefly in Basel, where he died four months after the appearance of Calvin's *Institutes* in that city. Calvin makes many references to his theological opinions and to his interpretations of Bible texts.

FAUSTUS, a bishop and teacher of the Manichaean sect. He came to Carthage (383) and at first attracted Augustine by his "smooth speech" but soon revealed his incapacity to answer searching questions. Augustine tells us of this in *Confessions* (V. 3-7). He attacked the teaching of Faustus in a later work (404) *Against Faustus the Manichaean.*

GALEN (CLAUDIUS GALENUS, *c.* 130-200), one of the most celebrated medical scholars of antiquity, was born in Pergamus and lived at intervals in Rome. He was a voluminous writer in Greek on philosophical as well as medical subjects. In *Inst.* I. 5. 2 Calvin has reference to his meticulous treatises on anatomy, perhaps especially his περὶ χρείας μορίον, on the use of the parts of the body. Other works of Galen are referred to elsewhere by Calvin.

GREGORY THE GREAT (GREGORIUS MAGNUS, 540-604) was the son of a Roman official and became prefect of Rome, but devoted his wealth to monastic foundations and entered a monastery (575). Induced to enter the priesthood, he was papal representative (*apocrisarius*) at Constantinople 579-85 and in 590 was elected pope. He was vigorous in asserting papal claims in relation to the see of Constantinople and to political powers. His writings include *Moralia* (an exposition of Job), the *Pastoral Care,* and the *Dialogue on Miracles.* The last named contains an account of St. Benedict. Calvin usually cites Gregory favorably and chiefly with reference to his letters, which have much to say about the Christian life and church discipline.

IRENAEUS (*c.* 115-190) was born in Asia Minor, probably at Smyrna, and was acquainted with men who had known the apostle John. He taught in Rome and later went to Gaul. After the persecutions at Lyons and Vienne in 177, Irenaeus went on a mission from the surviving Christians there to Rome, and on his return he became bishop of Lyons. He learned the Celtic language of that region in order to preach to the people. He wrote extensively in Greek but most of his writings are lost. His chief extant work is his treatise *Against Heresies,* mainly a refutation of Gnosticism. Calvin comments on passages of this work in *Inst.* II. 6. 4 and elsewhere.

JEROME (EUSEBIUS SOPHRONIUS HIERONYMUS, *c.* 340-420), the most learned of the Latin

Fathers, was born at Stridon in Dalmatia. As a student in Rome he revolted from the licentious society about him and became an intense ascetic, leading many to adopt an ascetic discipline. From 386 he lived in great austerity near Bethlehem, industriously writing on theological issues and pursuing scriptural studies for which he had equipped himself with an excellent knowledge of Hebrew and Greek. At the request of Damasus, bishop of Rome, he undertook the preparation of a Latin version of the Scriptures. This resulted in what is known as the Vulgate Bible.

JUSTIN MARTYR (d. 165) was born at Flavia Neapolis (Nablus) in Palestine of Roman parents. After periods of attachment to each of the chief schools of pagan philosophy he became a Christian under the influence of a Christian hermit. His works are mainly of the class known as "apologetical," i.e., writings in defense of Christian teaching, and are designed to convince both pagans and Jews.

LUCRETIUS (TITUS LUCRETIUS CARUS, c. 99-55 B.C.), the greatest literary representative of Epicureanism, used poetry as a medium for philosophical thought in his long poem *On the Nature of Things*. Calvin is hostile to Lucretius, who advised relaxation from anxious effort to please the gods, and

whose doctrine has been described in the words "salvation through enlightenment."

MANICHAEUS (or MANES, 215-277), founder of Manichaeism, was born near Ctesiphon in Persia. He began in 252 to represent himself as a founder of a new religion on a par with Buddha and Christ, and as the Paraclete mentioned in John 14. 16. After much effort and some success he was crucified. His doctrines reflected the dualism of the ancient Persian religion, man having been created by the good God to combat the ravages of Satan, by whom man is in turn attacked. The new religion spread widely despite persecution, and for centuries affected Christian asceticism and various Christian sects.

OSIANDER, ANDREAS (1498-1552), born in Günzenhausen, spent most of his active life as a priest and (from 1524) Lutheran teacher and pastor in Nuremberg. In 1549 he became a professor at Königsberg. He raised an animated controversy (1550) by his teaching on justification in which he altered the typical Lutheran doctrine of imputed righteousness by his conception of the infusion of Christ's eternal righteousness. Calvin attacks his position with persistence and in detail (*Inst.* I. 15. 3; II. 12. 5-7; III. 11. 5).

PELAGIUS (c. 354-420), a British monk who acquired good learning and wrote at Rome a startling commentary on Romans.

Visiting North Africa (411), he was denounced by Augustine, who wrote a series of treatises to refute his doctrines. His heresy centered in the denial of original sin in man through Adam's fall, and the assertion of the goodness of man's nature. Pelagianism was a persistent heresy, though chiefly in a modified form (semi-Pelagianism). Calvin called the Paris theologians of his time "Pelagians."

PETER LOMBARD (PETRUS LOMBARDUS, *c.* 1105-1160) was born in Lombardy and educated in Bologna and Paris, where he became a famous teacher and writer. His chief work is his *Four Books of Sentences,* a textbook of theology which came to be universally studied in medieval universities. Lombard also wrote commentaries on the Bible. In 1159 he was made bishop of Paris. Calvin regards "the Master of the Sentences" as having departed from true Christian teaching, especially in the doctrine of works.

SABELLIUS (fl. *c.* 250) gave his name to the Sabellian heresy, but very little is known with certainty about his life or his teaching as distinguished from that of others of the "Monarchian" class of heretics. He was associated with the Pentapolis of North Africa and probably taught also in Rome. Like all Monarchians, seeking to guard the unity of the Godhead, he weakened the doctrine of the

Trinity. He is said by some to have interpreted the Trinity in terms of one substantial essence (*hypostasis*) and three manifestations (*prosōpa*). In *Inst.* I. 13. 4 Calvin inadvertently gives him a date later than that of the Arians.

SADOLET (JACOPO SADOLETO, 1477-1547) was born at Modena and studied in Ferrara and Rome. In 1511 he became bishop of Carpentras near Avignon. In 1534 Paul III made him a cardinal, and he was a member of the committee of cardinals that produced the celebrated *Consilium de emendanda ecclesia* (*Advice on reforming the Church,* 1536). His epistle to the magistrates of Geneva is translated, along with Calvin's reply, by H. Beveridge in *Tracts relating to the Reformation* (Edinburgh, 1844), I, 3-71.

SERVETUS (MIGUEL SERVEDO, 1511-1553) was born in Tudela in Spain, studied in Saragossa, Toulouse and Paris, and conferred with Reformed theologians at Basel. In 1531 appeared his startling book *On the Errors of the Trinity.* Other treatises on theology and medicine followed. His *Christianismi Restitutio* (1553) was aimed against Calvin's *Institutio,* and was preceded by a controversial correspondence with Calvin. He was burned in effigy in Vienne after his escape from an Inquisition prison there. Going to Geneva, he was arrested and after a long trial burned at the stake by action of the Council, Calvin having sought the death penalty, but in the "more merciful" form of decapitation.

TERTULLIAN (QUINTUS SEPTIMIUS FLORENS TERTULLIANUS, c. 160-220) was a scholar and advocate of Carthage before his conversion to Christianity (197). He wrote in a vivid style many short treatises, polemical and devotional, but joined the Montanist heretical movement (207). For his *Apology, Testimony of the Soul* and other orthodox works he is regarded as the earliest of the Latin Church Fathers.

VALENTINE (VALENTINUS), to whom Augustine addressed three treatises, including *Of Rebuke and Grace* (Inst. II. 3. 13), was the head of a community of monks in the metropolitan city of Adrumetum (or Hadrumetum), North Africa, on the Mediterranean, southeast of Augustine's see of Hippo.

VIRGIL (PUBLIUS VIRGILIUS [or VERGILIUS] MARO, 70-19 B.C.), the prince of Latin poets, beloved through all centuries of the Christian era, was born near Mantua. As student and writer he lived in Cremona, Milan, Naples, and Rome. Calvin's works contain about a score of references to the *Aeneid,* the *Georgics,* and other poems of Virgil. Cf. *Inst.* I. 5. 5.

The Library of Liberal Arts

AESCHYLUS, *Prometheus Bound*, 143

ANTHOLOGIES ON RELIGION
  Ancient Roman Religion,
    ed. F. C. Grant, 138
  Buddhism, ed. C. H. Hamilton, 133
  Hellenistic Religions,
    ed. F. C. Grant, 134
  Islam, ed. A. Jeffery, 137
  Judaism, ed. S. W. Baron and
    J. L. Blau, 135

ARISTOTLE, *Nicomachean Ethics*, 75
  On Poetry and Music, 6
  On Poetry and Style, 68

ARNAULD, A., *The Port-Royal
  Logic*, 144

ST. AUGUSTINE, *On Christian
  Doctrine*, 80
  On Free Will, 150

MARCUS AURELIUS, *Meditations*, 173

AVERROES, *On the Relation of
  Philosophy and Theology*, 121

BACON, F., *The New Organon*, 97

BAYLE, P., *Dictionary*,
  (Selections), 175

BECCARIA, *On Crimes and
  Punishments*, 107

BERGSON, H., *Introduction to
  Metaphysics*, 10

BERKELEY, G., *Works on Vision*, 83
  *Principles of Human
    Knowledge*, 53
  Three Dialogues, 39

BOCCACCIO, *On Poetry*, 82

BOETHIUS, *The Consolation of
  Philosophy*, 86

ST. BONAVENTURA, *The Mind's Road
  to God*, 32

BOSANQUET, B., *Three Lectures
  on Aesthetic*, 154

BOWMAN, A., *The Absurdity of
  Christianity*, 56

BRADLEY, F. H., *Ethical Studies*, 28

*British Constitutional Law,
  Significant Cases*,
  ed. C. G. Post, 66

BURKE, E., *Appeal from the New
  to the Old Whigs*, 130

BURKE (*cont.*), *On America*, 183
  *Reflections on the Revolution
    in France*, 46

BUTLER, J., *Five Sermons*, 21

CALVIN, J., *On the Christian Faith*, 93
  On God and Political Duty, 23

CATULLUS, *Odi et Amo. Complete
  Poetry*, 114

CICERO, *On the Commonwealth*, 111

Cid, The Epic of the, 77

D'ALEMBERT, J., *Preliminary
  Discourse to Diderot's
  Encyclopedia*, 88

DANTE, *On World-Government*, 15

DESCARTES, R., *Discourse on
  Method*, 19
  Discourse on Method and
    Meditations, 89
  Meditations, 29
  Philosophical Essays, 99
  *Rules for the Direction of
    the Mind*, 129

DEWEY, J., *On Experience, Nature,
  and Freedom*, 41

DOSTOEVSKI, F., *The Grand
  Inquisitor*, 63

DUCASSE, C. J., *Art, the Critics,
  and You*, s1

DUNS SCOTUS, J., *Philosophical
  Writings*, 194

EPICTETUS, *The Enchiridion*, 8

EPICURUS, *The Epicurean Letters*, 141

ERASMUS, D., *Ten Colloquies*, 48

EURIPIDES, *Electra*, 26

FICHTE, J. G., *Vocation of Man*, 50

GOETHE, J. W., *Faust*
  (tr. Morgan), 33
  Faust (tr. Passage), 180

GRIMMELSHAUSEN, H., *Simplicius
  Simplicissimus*, 186

GROTIUS, H., *Prolegomena to The
  Law of War and Peace*, 65

HANSLICK, E., *The Beautiful
  in Music*, 45

HARRINGTON, J., *Political
  Writings*, 38

HEGEL, G. W. F., *Reason in History*, 35

HENDEL, C. W., *Jean-Jacques Rousseau: Moralist*, 96
Studies in the Philosophy of David Hume, 116

HERDER, J. G., *God, Some Conversations*, 140

HESIOD, *Theogony*, 36

HOBBES, T., *Leviathan I and II*, 69

HUME, D., *Dialogues Concerning Natural Religion*, 174
Inquiry Concerning Human Understanding, 49
Political Essays, 34
Principles of Morals, 62

KANT, I., *Analytic of the Beautiful*, 73
Critique of Practical Reason, 52
Foundations of the Metaphysics of Morals, 113
Fundamental Principles of the Metaphysic of Morals, 16
Metaphysical Elements of Justice, Part I of *Metaphysik der Sitten*, 72
Metaphysical Principles of Virtue, Part II of *Metaphysik der Sitten*, 85
On History, 162
Perpetual Peace, 54
Prolegomena to Any Future Metaphysics, 27

KLEIST, *The Prince of Homburg*, 60

LAO TZU, *The Way of Lao Tzu*, 139

Lazarillo de Tormes, The Life of, 37

LESSING, G., *Laocoön*, 78

LOCKE, J., *A Letter Concerning Toleration*, 22
Second Treatise of Government, 31

LONGINUS, *On Great Writing*, 79

LUCIAN, *Selected Satires*, 161

LUCRETIUS, *On the Nature of Things*, 142

MACHIAVELLI, N., *Mandragola*, 58

Masterworks of Prose, ed. T. Parkinson, 168

MEAD, G. H., *Selected Writings*, 177

MILL, J., *An Essay on Government*, 47

MILL, J. S., *Autobiography*, 91
Considerations on Representative Government, 71
On Liberty, 61
Nature and Utility of Religion, 81
Theism, 64
Utilitarianism, 1

MOLIÈRE, *Tartuffe*, 87

MONTESQUIEU, *Persian Letters*, 131

NIETZSCHE, F. W., *Use and Abuse of History*, 11

NOVALIS, *Hymns to the Night*, 115

OCKHAM, WM. OF, *Philosophical Writings*, 193

PAINE, T., *The Age of Reason I*, 5

PALEY, W., *Natural Theology*, 184

PLATO, *Epistles*, 122
Euthyphro, Apology, Crito, 4
Gorgias, 20
Meno, 12
Phaedo, 30
Phaedrus, 40
Protagoras, 59
Statesman, 57
Symposium, 7
Theaetetus (Cornford tr.), 105
Theaetetus (Jowett tr.), 13
Timaeus (Cornford tr.), 106
Timaeus (Jowett tr.), 14

SEVEN COMMENTARIES ON PLATO'S DIALOGUES
BLUCK, R. S., *Plato's Phaedo*, 110
CORNFORD, F. M., *Plato and Parmenides*, 102
Plato's Cosmology, 101
Plato's Theory of Knowledge, 100
HACKFORTH, R., *Plato's Examination of Pleasure*, 118
Plato's Phaedo, 120
Plato's Phaedrus, 119

PLAUTUS, *The Haunted House*, 42
The Menaechmi, 17
The Rope, 43

ROSENMEYER, T., M. OSTWALD, and J. HALPORN, *Meters of Greek and Latin Poetry*, 126

ROUSSEAU, J. J., *Government of Poland*, 165

SCHILLER, J., *Wilhelm Tell*, 181

SCHOPENHAUER, A., *Freedom of the Will*, 70

SELBY-BIGGE, L. A., *British Moralists*, 152

SENECA, *Medea*, 55
Oedipus, 44
Thyestes, 76

SHAFTESBURY, 3RD EARL OF, *Characteristics*, 179

SMITH, A., *The Wealth of Nations*, 125

SOPHOCLES, *Electra*, 25

SPIEGELBERG, H., *The Socratic Enigma*, 192

SPINOZA, B., *Earlier Philosophical Writings*, 163

SPINOZA (cont.), *On the Improvement of the Understanding*, 67

TERENCE, *The Brothers*, 112
The Eunuch, 190
The Mother-in-Law, 123
Phormio, 95
The Self-Tormentor, 149
The Woman of Andros, 18

TOLSTOY, L. N., *What Is Art?* 51

VOLTAIRE, *Philosophical Letters*, 124

WHITEHEAD, A. N., *Interpretation of Science*, 117

WOLFF, C., *Preliminary Discourse on Philosophy*, 167